CW00738644

Awaken
Bible Commentary &

Lessons From Scripture

Volume 1
January - March

Reading Through the Bible in a Year

Discussion
On Selected Verses
From Each Day's Reading

*Is the Bible Relevant
For Today?*

*Can We Apply Old
Testament Lessons to
Our Current Culture?*

*What Should Be Our
Response to This Lost
And Dying World?*

Gary W. Ritter

Reading Through the Bible in a Year

AWAKEN
BIBLE COMMENTARY
AND REFLECTIONS

Volume 1: January – March

Lessons From Scripture

GARY W. RITTER

Version 2021.11.18

Give feedback on the book at my website:
www.GaryRitter.com

ISBN: 9798463819338

SHORT STORY COLLECTIONS
The Panic (Omnibus):
The Panic
Flying Dollars
Spa Treatment

Zapped! (Omnibus):
Zapped!
Wedding Day
You Choose

NON-FICTION
Looking Up – Essays
Awaken Bible Study Notes – Volumes 1-4
Awaken Bible Commentary & Reflections – Volumes 1-4

SCAN FOR GARY RITTER AMAZON AUTHOR PAGE

TABLE OF CONTENTS

Introduction..1

Reading Schedule for January 2

January 1: Genesis 1:6-7 - Waters and Firmament.................................. 3

January 2: Genesis 3 - The Shining Serpent 5

January 3: Genesis 6:1-5 - Sons of God... 7

January 4: Genesis 11 – Babel 9

January 5: Genesis 12:2-3 - God's Promise to Israel 12

January 6: Genesis 15:4-5 - Angel of the Lord.......................................14

January 7: Matthew 6:24 - Believing Loyalty 16

January 8: Matthew 7 - Destruction or Safety.......................................18

January 9: Genesis 24:6,8 - Old Life Before Christ 20

January 10: Genesis 25:20,26 – Waiting..22

January 11: Genesis 28:8-9 - Rebellion's Legacy 24

January 12: Matthew 10:23 - Rejecting Jesus..26

January 13: Matthew 10:28 – Fear..29

January 14: Genesis 35:9-11 & Matthew 11:20-24 - Which God?......31

January 15: Genesis 37:18 & Matthew 12:14 – Conspiracy...............34

January 16: Genesis 39:3 - The Lord's Favor..36

January 17: Matthew 13:12 - Abundance or Not...................................38

January 18: Matthew 13:42-43- Harvest Time 40

January 19: Genesis 44:5 – Divination 43

January 20: Genesis 47:20-21 – Serfdom..45

January 21: Matthew 15:8-9 - Wayward Hearts 48

January 22: Exodus 2:3,10 - What Moses Represents 50

January 23: Matthew 16:18 - The Gates of Hell.....................................53

January 24: Exodus 7:5,16 - The God of the Hebrews 55

January 25: Matthew 18:11 - Missing Verses...58

January 26: Exodus 12:12 - Judgments Upon the gods........................61

January 27: Exodus 13:9 - A Sign on Hand & Forehead......................64

January 28: Matthew 19:28 - Ruling & Judging.....................................67

January 29: Exodus 20:18-21 - Near or Far from God................................70

January 30: Exodus 23:32-33 - The Snare of Other gods 72

January 31: Exodus 25-26 - God's Mercy Seat 75

Reading Schedule for February 77

February 1: Matthew 21:33-46 – Parable of the Tenants........................78

February 2: Matthew 22:1-14 – Parable of the Wedding Feast 80

February 3: Matthew 22:29-30 – The Nature of Angels 83

February 4: Exodus 35:30-31 – God-Given Skills...................................86

February 5: Exodus 38:24 – Plunder & Miracles 89

February 6: Matthew 24:7 – Don't Be Deceived.....................................92

February 7: Matthew 24:44 – The Unexpected Hour 95

February 8: Matthew 25:12,30 – Two More Rapture Warnings...............99

February 9: Matthew 25:40 – As You Did 101

February 10: Matthew 26:8 – They Were Indignant...............................103

February 11: Leviticus 13:2 – A Case of Leprous Disease 106

February 12: Matthew 26:59 – Seeking False Testimony.......................109

February 13: Leviticus 16:8 – For Azazel..111

February 14: Leviticus 18:22 – Abomination...114

February 15: Leviticus 20:26 – Holy To the Lord..................................117

February 16: Mark 1:4 – Baptism of Repentance 119

February 17: Mark 1:34 – Demonic Origins..122

February 18: Leviticus 27:28-29 – Surely Be Put To Death....................125

February 19: Numbers 2:2,17 – At the Center.......................................128

February 20: Numbers 3:12 – Redemption by Levite 130

February 21: Numbers 5:15 – Trial by Ordeal.......................................133

February 22: Mark 4:26-29 – How Grows the Kingdom? 135

February 23: Numbers 9:16 – Supernatural...137

February 24: Numbers 11:4 – Rabble Rousers.......................................140

February 25: Mark 6:22 – Herodias' Daughter.......................................143

February 26: Numbers 16:11 – Presumption 146

February 27: Numbers 18:5 – Wrath No More...149

February 28: Numbers 22:6 – Balaam's Attempted Divination....................151

February 29: Numbers 25:1-3 – Yoked to Baal...153

Reading Schedule for March..155

March 1: Numbers 27:4 – Feminists 156

March 2: Mark 9:2 - Satan On Notice 159

March 3: Numbers 31:49 - Not a Man Missing 162

March 4: Numbers 33:55 - Trouble in the Land..165

March 5: Numbers 35:33 - Blood Pollutes the Land 168

March 6: Deuteronomy 2:34 - No Survivors..171

March 7: Deuteronomy 4:15 - Watch Yourselves...175

March 8: Deuteronomy 7:14 - Blessed Above All Peoples...........................178

March 9: Deuteronomy 9:3 - A Consuming Fire..180

March 10: Deuteronomy 12:23 - Don't Eat the Blood 183

March 11: Mark 13:19 - In Those Days..186

March 12: Deuteronomy 18:20 - The Prophet Who Presumes 189

March 13: Deuteronomy 22:21 - An Outrageous Thing 193

March 14: Mark 14:71 - I Don't Know This Man..196

March 15: Deuteronomy 27:2-3 - Stones on Mount Ebal.............................199

March 16: Deuteronomy 28:15 - All These Curses 201

March 17: Deuteronomy 29:18 - Poisonous & Bitter Fruit...........................204

March 18: Deuteronomy 32:17 - Gods They Had Never Known...................207

March 19: Deuteronomy 34:5-6 - The Holy Stapler 210

March 20: Luke 1:45 - She Who Believed 213

March 21: Joshua 5:15 - Take Off Your Sandals 216

March 22: Joshua 7:11 - Secret Sin 218

March 23: Luke 3:8 - Fruits of Repentance 221

March 24: Luke 4:30 - Through Their Midst 224

March 25: Luke 4:41 - They Knew That He Was the Christ 227

March 26: Joshua 18:3 - Possession of the Land..230

March 27: Luke 5:26 - They Glorified God 233

March 28: Luke 6:25 - Laughing Now 236

March 29: Joshua 24:15 - Choosing Poorly 238

March 30: Judges 2:19 - They Turned Back 241

March 31: Judges 3:1-2 - To Test Israel 244

Introduction

The four volumes that comprise the **Awaken Bible Commentary and Reflections** series have a different focus than the sister compilation of **Awaken Bible Study Notes** that I previously produced. In those prior books my emphasis was to show the prophetic nature of God's Word and to bring out its supernatural aspects. Many liberal theologians over the years have attempted to demythologize Scripture, i.e. to demonstrate that it is more a work of man than of God. I can't even begin to say how wrong-headed that is. One has to have quite a low view of the Lord to go there. That's not my perspective. I have a very high view of God and hope in these pages, just as in the Study Notes volumes, that God gets all the glory, as He should.

Both sets of Awaken books build on the premise of reading through the Bible in a year. The Study Notes are exactly that: in the verse-by-verse reading, they pull from Scripture many of its deeper meanings. The focus of Bible prophecy and the supernatural, I believe, are critical to understanding the larger narrative that God wishes to convey and wants us to understand as we make our way through this world.

In the Commentaries and Reflections presented in this series, again based on a thorough cover-to-cover reading of the Bible, I attempt to relate what the ancient writers conveyed to their audience and show the relevance of those lessons for today, both prophetically and supernaturally. In every era, we have our challenges. Sin is sin and in our world brokenness prevails. People choose to follow God or they reject Him. All this has consequences for better or worse.

The one lesson that shines through from then to now is that God requires us to have *believing loyalty* in Him. This means to love and obey only the God of the Bible and to never worship any other god, whatever its form. If we do this through the saving grace and knowledge of Jesus Christ, the Lord loves that. As a loving parent who wants the best for His children, when we do what He says, He showers us with favor and blessings. Conversely, when we turn from Him in disobedience, we should expect correction, rebuke, and punishment.

The world is rapidly reaching a point of no return. I discuss that in many different ways in these books. Those who don't know Jesus as Lord and Savior face a grim future. Thankfully, we who have given our hearts and lives to Him are assured that He will rescue us from the wrath to come. What encouragement this is in these dark days!

Awaken

Lessons from Scripture

January

Reading Through the Bible in a Year

Old Testament: Genesis 1 - Exodus 26
New Testament: Matthew 1 - Matthew 21:22

Reading Schedule for January

January 1 – January 31			
Jan 1	Gen 1-2, Matt 1	**Jan 17**	Gen 41, Matt 13:1-32
Jan 2	Gen 3-5, Matt 2	**Jan 18**	Gen 42-43, Matt 13:33-58
Jan 3	Gen 6-8, Matt 3	**Jan 19**	Gen 44-45, Matt 14:1-21
Jan 4	Gen 9-11, Matt 4	**Jan 20**	Gen 46-48, Matt 14:22-36
Jan 5	Gen 12-14, Matt 5:1-26	**Jan 21**	Gen 49-50, Matt 15:1-20
Jan 6	Gen 15-17, Matt 5:27-48	**Jan 22**	Ex 1-3, Matt 15:21-39
Jan 7	Gen 18-19, Matt 6	**Jan 23**	Ex 4-6, Matt 16
Jan 8	Gen 20-22, Matt 7	**Jan 24**	Ex 7-8, Matt 17
Jan 9	Gen 23-24, Matt 8	**Jan 25**	Ex 9-10, Matt 18:1-20
Jan 10	Gen 25-26, Matt 9:1-17	**Jan 26**	Ex 11-12, Matt 18:21-35
Jan 11	Gen 27-28, Matt 9:18-38	**Jan 27**	Ex 13-15, Matt 19:1-15
Jan 12	Gen 29-30, Matt 10:1-23	**Jan 28**	Ex 16-18, Matt 19:16-30
Jan 13	Gen 31-32, Matt 10:24-42	**Jan 29**	Ex 19-21, Matt 20:1-16
Jan 14	Gen 33-35, Matt 11	**Jan 30**	Ex 22-24, Matt 20:17-34
Jan 15	Gen 36-37, Matt 12:1-21	**Jan 31**	Ex 25-26, Matt 21:1-22
Jan 16	Gen 38-40, Matt 12:22-50		

January 1: Genesis 1:6-7 - Waters and Firmament

(Genesis 1-2; Matthew 1)

The Word of God is so much deeper than we imagine upon a casual reading. There are often profound meanings that are easy to miss without further study. For instance, in the reading of Genesis 1-2, the verses of Genesis 1:6-7 caught my eye.

Variously in different Bible translations, God says, "*Let there be* [an *expanse* - ESV & NASB] [*a firmament* - KJV] or [*a vault* - NIV]*...*" *that is in the midst of the water or between the waters that are part of the darkness and void* (v2). In the Hebrew, waters can mean exactly what we expect; however, they also have the meaning of danger and violence. In reading the text, don't some questions come to mind? In its initial formation, what were the waters? Where did they come from? Seemingly, they were just there.

But then God divides these waters. In the midst of them, i.e. in between them, He creates an expanse, a firmament, or a vault. In this separated place are the heavens, or the sky as we know it, i.e. the place where the stars reside.

So think about this. There is water below and water above the sky, i.e. the heavens. How does that work? How do the heavens keep these waters apart? Where are the waters above the sky?

Here's a thought. If we think about this in-between space as a vault, maybe we can make sense of another term that we see elsewhere in the Bible. In Jeremiah 10:13 and Jeremiah 51:16 the prophet says that God brings rain from the storehouses, or treasuries of heaven, in a time of war. He unleashes rain and hail to destroy His enemies, bringing them danger and violence. Look at what these two verses in Jeremiah say about this: "*there is a **multitude** of waters in the heavens*" (KJV).

What an interesting statement when we examine this in light of that place between the waters, where one definition is that it's a vault. Perhaps the storehouses of heaven are effectively this vault in the sky where God keeps the waters for His purposes at His chosen times.

There is so much more in God's Word. He gave it to us so that we might understand Him and His ways more. Read His Word daily and use this opportunity to grow closer to Him.

ESV & NASB

*And God said, "Let there be an **expanse** in the midst of the waters, and let it separate the waters from the waters." And God made the expanse and separated the waters that were under the expanse from the waters that were above the expanse. And it was so.*

NIV

*And God said, "Let there be a **vault** between the waters to separate water from water." So God made the vault and separated the water under the vault from the water above it. And it was so.*

KJV

*And God said, Let there be a **firmament** in the midst of the waters, and let it divide the waters from the waters.*

And God made the firmament, and divided the waters which were under the firmament from the waters which were above the firmament: and it was so.

January 2: Genesis 3 - The Shining Serpent

(Genesis 3-5; Matthew 2)

In the account of the serpent tempting Eve in Genesis 3, we tend to pass over the fact that this appears to be a talking serpent, and that Eve apparently had no issues with this. When was the last time you had a conversation with a snake, whether it was a good or an evil one?

The Hebrew word for serpent is *nachash*. As I've noted elsewhere (Awaken Bible Study Notes - Volume 1), the word *nachash* "is typically translated as serpent, which we all know. However, there are variations of the word which give it additional, and very intriguing, meanings. The word can mean the diviner, i.e. one who communicates with the supernatural realm. It can also mean shiny, or shining one, such as a divine being from the heavenlies. Moreover, serpents in the ancient Middle Eastern cultures were divine throne guardians. Perhaps the Biblical writer wanted to convey all these associations to this serpent that tempted Eve?"

What does this mean for our understanding of this incident? First, let's consider what Eden actually was. Eden was the place that God created where heaven and earth met. It was a divine mountain garden. (See Ezekiel 28:13-14: "*You were in Eden, the garden of God...on the holy mountain of God.*") From Genesis 3:8 we know that God spent time there: "*...the sound of God walking in the garden...*" It was a lush and beautiful place; why wouldn't He love being there? But, was God the only other being that frequented it? No; at least one other did, i.e. the serpent. How about others from the heavenly abode?

We know from many places in Scripture that God has a divine family, just as He has a human family. In the Old Testament, members of this family are variously called sons of God (*bene Elohim* - Hebrew), angels, cherubim, seraphim, the heavenly host, etc. Might they likewise have walked in this lovely garden? Is it not perhaps reasonable to consider that their appearance might be exceptionally shiny, even radiant? (They are divine beings, after all!) If that makes sense, then the *nachash* was likely a shining one, just as its name implies. As such, being an intelligent entity, perhaps a cherub (we know from Ezekiel 28:14, if the same being spoken of in this verse as "*an anointed guardian cherub*" is also Satan, whom we associate with the Garden of Eden), then his speaking to Eve would not have been unusual in the least.

Perhaps the *nachash* took on a serpent's appearance, but his presence there was no surprise to Eve, and her having a conversation with him was not out of the ordinary. Adam and Eve before their fall hung out with spiritual beings from what is now to us an unseen realm. But they could see these holy ones and speak with them. Someday, when we as true believers have our glorified bodies, we will once more be united with this other part of God's divine family, as we also will be divine*.

* Just to clarify the word *divine*: we will not be gods. Through our glorified nature, we will be like Jesus (1 John 3:2) and have the characteristics of His body upon His resurrection. Much of what the angels can do, we will probably be able to similarly do, but even more; because in our gloried state, we will even judge angels (1 Corinthians 6:3).

January 3: Genesis 6:1-5 - Sons of God

(Genesis 6-8; Matthew 3)

Genesis 6:1-5 is one of the most fascinating and troubling passages in the entire Bible. Some people want to make what is conveyed here an entirely human scenario, but that completely misses what's really going on, and the larger Biblical narrative.

The text tells us that the sons of God (*bene Elohim* - Hebrew) took human wives. Who were the sons of God? In the Old Testament, it speaks exclusively about them as being members of God's heavenly host; in this case, they were likely high-ranking princes in the spiritual realm and members of what is referred to as God's Divine Council. (Note that in a number of passages in Scripture we see thrones (plural) around God's throne. Who sits on these exalted chairs? Members of Yahweh's spiritual family - members of His Divine Council - who have important positions in His kingdom. An example of this is Daniel 7:9: "*thrones were placed and the Ancient of Days took his seat.*")

The alternative theory to explain what's going on in this scene is what's known as the sons of Seth theory. This theory attempts to explain away the supernatural aspect of these verses. It assumes that Seth's sons were referred to here as God's sons, and that they were somehow more holy than other men alive at the time. Moreover, it also assumes that the daughters of men - all human women - were somehow more wicked than Seth's children. Of course, that makes no sense. In the fall of Adam and Eve, all men and women subsequently inherited a sin nature; none were Godly or more wicked than others in the way this theory wishes to portray.

Just as there was an original rebel (the *nachash* in Genesis 3 that we presume is Satan), there were other rebels. This passage in Genesis 6 tells us that. Confirming verses in the New Testament such as Jude 6-7 and 2 Peter 2:4 speak of the angels "*who did not stay within their positions of authority, but left their proper dwelling.*" As a result, "*God did not spare angels when they sinned.*" What was their sin? They rebelled against God; they disobeyed His command that their place was in the heavenlies and not to dwell among humans.

What did these angels - these sons of God - do? They not only came to live on the earth; they also procreated with human women. From this unholy action, giant beings known as Nephilim came forth. This led to further intermarrying and wickedness throughout the earth so that God finally reached a point that He had to act. He did that by destroying all life on earth through the flood.

What was the problem in all this? Satan's intent has always been to be like God, to replace Him, and to be God. To accomplish this, Satan had to thwart God's plans for humanity. Thus, he introduced rebellion to Adam and Eve, which led to sin. This resulted in God cursing Satan - the serpent - in Genesis 3:15, which effectively informed Satan that he was on a short leash. A time would come when he would be completely defeated by a human descendant of Eve's. From that point, Satan was truly on a mission. He would do everything in his power to keep this human descendant from ever being born, or he would kill Him before God could accomplish His purpose to finally eliminate Satan.

The fall of the sons of God was part of this larger narrative. It is likely that Satan encouraged their disobedience. ("Look at how beautiful those human women are. Wouldn't it be pleasurable to be like men on the earth and to lie with those women?") Regardless how this went down, Satan's intent was to corrupt the gene pool. If man's DNA was corrupted and man's blood no longer purely human, then no human descendant from Eve could be born. Satan could prevent Jesus from ever walking the earth. With this plan, Satan could annul the promises of God and make Him a liar. He could ascend to the throne of God and take over if God lost His divine authority.

Further on in Scripture we'll come across descendants of Nephilim known as Rephaim. Somehow, the progeny of the wicked, disobedient sons of God would continue to be a problem to mankind that God would have to deal with.

January 4: Genesis 11 – Babel

(Genesis 9-11; Matthew 4)

The typical Christian thinking is that sin is the only problem in the world that Jesus came to overcome. In fact, the ancient Jewish concept of what's wrong provides a much bigger picture, and it actually paves the way for all that Jesus has done and will do prophetically so as to redeem the earth.

If we study and understand Scripture in this way, we see that there were three rebellions, not just one. The rebellion we're all familiar with, i.e. Rebellion #1, is the fall of Adam and Eve in the Garden of Eden. Eve was tempted by the serpent, believed its lie rather than God's truth, and thus effectively rebelled against God in her disobedience. This brought sin into the world. But, if we truly look all around us, we see there is much more going on than can simply be attributed to sin.

The book of Genesis is so significant because it provides much of the foundation for the rest of the Bible, both Old and New Testaments. Where does sin lead? If left unchecked, what can result? The answer is depravity. Depravity is sin on steroids. It is moral corruption and wickedness. Was there an event that introduced depravity into the world? Absolutely.

An event took place in Genesis 6:1-5, which is the basis for what God will often refer to as an abomination. Some number of the sons of God left their heavenly abode in rebellion against God and procreated with human women. This was direct disobedience to God's command to them and resulted in Rebellion #2. This "intermarrying" between spiritual beings and human beings brought such depravity among mankind, plus such wholesale corruption of the human bloodline, that God had no choice but to bring the flood and destroy everything on the earth. Had He not done this, it would have been impossible for Him to fulfill His prophetic Word that the Seed of the woman (Eve) would come (fully human) to destroy the serpent and its seed, i.e. anyone who chose to rebel against God.

The account of the Tower of Babel incident in Genesis 11 provides us with the understanding of Rebellion #3. God had told Noah after the flood - just as He had originally told Adam and Eve - to *"be fruitful and multiply"* (Genesis 1:28 and 9:7). Instead, what did mankind do? Led by Nimrod, who had migrated to Babel on the plains of Shinar (in what is today Iraq), men built a *"tower with its top in the heavens"* (Genesis 11:4) so that they could make a name for themselves rather than be *"dispersed over the face of the whole earth."* This tower is what we call a ziggurat. It was meant to make a way to bring God down to man, in order to effectively control Him.

In God's eyes, this was complete disobedience and rebellion against His Word. Of course, it didn't take Him by surprise, but He made an intriguing statement in v7: *"Nothing that they [men] propose to do will now be impossible for them."* To counter this problem, we see in v8-9 that God dispersed men throughout the earth and confused the single language, that had been present since the beginning, into multiple tongues.

Not to make this article too lengthy, but one other factor came into play in this rebellion. In Deuteronomy 32:8 (and you must read the ESV - English Standard Version - translation to see this properly), God set His divine sons over the nations into which He had placed mankind:

> *When the Most High gave to the nations their inheritance,*
> *   when he divided mankind,*
> *he fixed the borders of the peoples*
> *   according to the number of the sons of God.*

These sons of God were obedient at the time God put them over the nations to rule. Their job was to point men back to God while He raised up the nation of Israel to be His special inheritance (Deuteronomy 32:9). Instead, these sons of God rebelled similarly to the fall of their brothers in Genesis 6. In this case, however, they chose to copy Satan's desire to be as God. Rather than direct the peoples of the nations to Yahweh as the One true God, they became the gods over all the nations. It is from this that we subsequently see gods such as Baal, Milcom, Chemosh, and many others throughout Scripture. These gods remain in place to this very day. They become the third reason that Jesus came, i.e. to redeem the nations back to Himself.

In summary, the three rebellions and the way that God is dealing with them through Jesus Christ are as follows:

* Rebellion #1 - sin. Jesus takes away the sin of the world when someone believes in Him and is born again.

* Rebellion #2 - depravity. Jesus sent the Holy Spirit as our Helper to council and guide us in the way of God's righteousness.

* Rebellion #3 - nations following other gods. When Jesus returns in His 2nd coming at the end of the 7-year Tribulation, He will destroy all those who hate God. This will usher in the Millennial Kingdom, when Jesus rules and reigns over the nations of the earth from His throne in Jerusalem. The rebellious sons of God - the gods of the nations - will join Satan in the lowest pit of hell while peace encompasses the earth for 1,000 years.

Isn't God's Word amazing? There is so much more going on than what we might see upon a single reading. God's Word requires a lifetime and more of study for us to understand the bigger picture of His purposes. He wants us to pursue this so that we will know Him more fully.

January 5: Genesis 12:2-3 - God's Promise to Israel

(Genesis 12-14; Matthew 5:1-26)

The prophetic Word that God gives Abram in Genesis 12:2-3 is one of the most significant in the entire Bible:

"And I will make of you a great nation, and I will bless you and make your name great, so that you will be a blessing. I will bless those who bless you, and him who dishonors you I will curse, and in you all the families of the earth shall be blessed."

This Word outlines four major ideas:

1. God will make Israel a great nation
2. Israel will be a blessing to the entire earth
3. God will bless anyone who blesses Israel
4. If anyone curses Israel, God will curse them

This major prophecy is critical for us to understand today. There is a blasphemous teaching that is rampant throughout Christianity today that God is through with Israel because of her disobedience over the years. That couldn't be further from the truth. God has made it very clear in these verses (and in many more subsequent passages in Scripture) that He cherishes Israel, that she has an important role to play in His plans for the world, and that there are consequences for how someone treats Israel - both good and bad. Do not let anyone attempt to convince you that God has no further interest in Israel, and that He has reneged on His promise to His Chosen People. That position is contrary to the Word of God and is in itself a curse upon Israel that will have negative consequences for all who believe it.

Immediately following God's promise to Abram, He demonstrates this principle. Abram will become God's faithful and righteous servant. Although Abram isn't that yet, God brings His promise into action through Abram's foolish lie about his wife Sarai being his sister when they are in Egypt (Genesis 12:13). Pharoah sees the 65-year-old Sarai. Because she is beautiful, he takes her into his household (not knowing that Abram and Sarai are married).

Despite this being an unintentional curse upon Abram through this action, God curses Pharaoh and his house with plagues (Genesis 12:17). This alerts Pharaoh that something is wrong. He confronts Abram, learns the truth, and makes things right with Abram and Yahweh before anything further can go awry.

Watch how people and nations speak about and treat Israel. God is watching. He brings swift justice upon any who transgress His Word.

January 6: Genesis 15:4-5 - Angel of the Lord

(Genesis 15-17; Matthew 5:27-48)

The ancient Israelite understanding of God was different from what it is today. Religious Jews since the time of Jesus have actually rejected what their ancestors believed and knew about Yahweh. Since Jesus came, the Jews have clung to the Shema, Deuteronomy 6:4: *"Hear, O Israel: The Lord our God, the Lord is one"* and insisted (like the Muslims) that God has no Son; He is One, and that's it.

Scripture tells us otherwise right from the beginning. The ancient Israelites knew this and even spoke and wrote of how Yahweh manifested in at least two ways. Consider Genesis 15:4-5 in which God interacts with Abram:

And behold, the word of the Lord came to him: "This man shall not be your heir; your very own son shall be your heir." And he brought him outside and said, "Look toward heaven, and number the stars, if you are able to number them." Then he said to him, "So shall your offspring be."

In these verses we see two interesting aspects of this interaction:

1. The Word of the Lord came to Abram
2. He brought Abram outside and spoke to him

Do you see it? The Word of the Lord is a personal being. "He" brought Abram out to look at the stars. From this and subsequent instances in Scripture we know that the Word of the Lord is not just something spoken. The Word is a physical manifestation of God.

Let's look at what happens when Hagar flees from Sarai after having Abram's child, Ismael, in Genesis 16:7, and what He subsequently spoke to her in verse 10:

The angel of the Lord found her by a spring of water in the wilderness, the spring on the way to Shur… The angel of the Lord also said to her, "I will surely multiply your offspring so that they cannot be numbered for multitude."

Who is the Angel of the Lord? Notice that He said "I" will bring you many offspring. Who but God can make that promise? Only the Lord has that creative ability and the means to make a specific promise of this nature. Thus, it is clear that the Angel of the Lord is Yahweh Himself, and that He appeared to her in person.

From these passages we gain an understanding of God that the Israelites knew: Yahweh had the ability to manifest in person. Later in such verses as Psalm 110:1, it is clear that there are actually two Yahweh's:

> *The Lord says to my Lord:*
> *"Sit at my right hand,*
> *until I make your enemies your footstool."*

How can God speak to God unless there are two persons present?

It is from the Jewish Scriptures, the Tanakh, that the Hebrews developed an understanding of God that they called "The Two Powers in Heaven" or "The Two Yahwehs."

When Jesus came, claimed to be Yahweh, i.e. the Second Power, and actually demonstrated through the miracles He did that He was the Angel of the Lord made flesh, the religious rulers rejected Him and changed their understanding of the Scriptures and what their ancestors had all believed.

A day is coming, however, when *"all Israel will be saved"* (Romans 11:26) and the unbelieving Jews will believe. Just as it says in Psalm 118:26 and Matthew 23:39, on that day the survivors in Israel from the Great Tribulation will say: *"Blessed is He who comes in the name of the Lord."*

January 7: Matthew 6:24 - Believing Loyalty

(Genesis 18-19; Matthew 6)

When Jesus speaks about the problem of serving two masters in Matthew 6:24, His teaching goes to the heart of our relationship with God:

"No one can serve two masters, for either he will hate the one and love the other, or he will be devoted to the one and despise the other. You cannot serve God and money."

Money is only one of many other masters that people can serve. The issue becomes one of serving any other god but Yahweh. When we look at the ancient Israelites, what was it that always got them into trouble? What was the very first of the Ten Commandments that God gave them in Exodus 20:3?

"You shall have no other gods before Me."

Go to the Old Testament and read what God continually warned His people. Pick a prophet and one of the warnings he gave. Here's Jeremiah 25:6 speaking the Word of God to the people of Israel in their captivity and exile in Babylon:

"Do not go after other gods to serve and worship them, or provoke me to anger with the work of your hands. Then I will do you no harm."

Following after other gods was the continual problem Israel faced. Time and again in their history, they came back to Yahweh but fell into apostasy by serving other gods that were such a temptation to them. That resulted in God's anger and judgment. When they turned from Him, He brought them harm. In Deuteronomy 28, God explicitly lays out the blessings He will bestow upon His people for being faithful to Him, but He also describes in great detail the curses they will bring upon themselves for turning to and worshiping other gods in disobedience to Him.

This whole idea about truly and faithfully following Yahweh or turning from Him is why King David was known as *"a man after God's own heart"* (Acts 13:22). We know the sins he committed; he was human - he made bad choices. But the one thing David never did was to waver in his love and dedication to Yahweh. He never followed any other god. There is a term for this: BELIEVING LOYALTY. David's believing loyalty was to Yahweh and Him alone.

There are many gods in this world. They often take different shapes or forms now from what they did in David's day, but in the spiritual realm they are all the same. The gods over the nations in the Old Testament were fallen spiritual entities. They remain to this day. Their purpose is the same now as it was then: they hate God - their creator - and they desire to thwart His plans and purposes for mankind.

The love of money - money as a master - is a god that tears us away from faithfulness and trust in God alone. When Jesus said we cannot serve two masters, He meant that we cannot trust anyone or anything except God alone. Our believing loyalty must be absolute to the God of the Bible.

When we trust God in this way, then it becomes possible for us to do what Jesus commanded in Matthew 6:33:

"Seek first the kingdom of God and His righteousness."

When we do, *"all these things,"* i.e. food, clothing, and peace from the anxiety of tomorrow, will be added to our lives.

January 8: Matthew 7 - Destruction or Safety

(Genesis 20-22; Matthew 7)

The statement by Jesus in Matthew 7:13-14 is one of the hardest in the Bible for people to wrap their minds around. He tells us:

"Enter by the narrow gate. For the gate is wide and the way is easy that leads to destruction, and those who enter by it are many. For the gate is narrow and the way is hard that leads to life, and those who find it are few."

Why is that difficult for many to accept? The argument goes that since God is loving, He would never reject anyone. "My god is a god of love. He would never send anyone to Hell." Notice I don't capitalize god here; that's because people have conjured a god of their own making from their imaginations and desires. They don't worship the God of the Bible.

In fact, God does not reject anyone. People **choose** to reject Him. That choice is what leads to their eternity in Hell. When a person strays from the Word of God and doesn't sit under solid Biblical teaching, he is open to false teaching. G.K. Chesterton said: "When men choose not to believe in God, they do not thereafter believe in nothing, they then become capable of believing in anything."

From that openness to believe in anything comes the false teachers and their diseased doctrine that Jesus speaks of in the next several verses beginning with Matthew 7:15-16:

"Beware of false prophets, who come to you in sheep's clothing but inwardly are ravenous wolves. You will recognize them by their fruits... "

But the question becomes: How will you recognize the false fruit if you don't know what is true and good fruit? Only those of us who read and study God's Word are able to do that. You've likely heard what they say about how IRS Treasury agents are trained to discern counterfeit bills: they study only real ones. That gives them the eye and feel to root out the false money. So it is with us.

This leads to Jesus' Words that follow in Matthew 7:21-23 where He warns:

"Not everyone who says to me, 'Lord, Lord,' will enter the kingdom of heaven, but the one who does the will of my Father who is in heaven. On that day many

will say to me, 'Lord, Lord, did we not prophesy in your name, and cast out demons in your name, and do many mighty works in your name?' And then will I declare to them, 'I never knew you; depart from me, you workers of lawlessness.'"

Many people who walk the wide road toward destruction get on this journey that ends with Jesus telling them how God doesn't know them by their listening to false prophets, believing the lies they tell, and choosing to trust their deceptive words. They have never made the effort to dig into Scripture to truly know who God is and what He wants for each of us.

This is exactly why Jesus follows all this up in Matthew 7:24-27 by urging us to be *"like a wise man who built his house on a rock."* Our rock is Jesus Christ and the Words He gave us to know Him more fully.

If we don't forsake Him and His Word, He will never forsake us.

January 9: Genesis 24:6,8 - Old Life Before Christ

(Genesis 23-24; Matthew 8)

There are many principles that God illustrates to us through the lives and actions of the people who populate the Old Testament. In Genesis 24:6,8 we see one of these principles enacted through Abraham's servant Eliezer when Abraham sent him to the place of his extended family in Ur to seek a wife for his son Isaac:

*"Abraham said to him, "See to it that you **do not take my son back there**...But if the woman is not willing to follow you, then you will be free from this oath of mine; only **you must not take my son back there**.""*

Abraham twice emphasized to Eliezer that under no circumstances should he take Isaac back to the land of Abraham's birth. God had promised Abraham the land of Canaan would be his possession for him and his offspring (Genesis 12:7) and he believed Him. That belief was so deep that even when Sarah died, Abraham would not accept the offer of free land in Canaan near Hebron from the Hittites to bury his wife. Abraham insisted that he pay for that land (Genesis 23:17-18). This initial purchase gave the Israelites everlasting possession of the land, which was to become Israel. (As an aside: This action long ago provided Israel with the legal title to this land. Any claims by any other people group - such as the so-called Palestinians - that they originally had possession of Israel are false. In fact, there are no true Palestinians. That name first came about in 135 BC when the Roman emperor Hadrian renamed Israel to Palestine in order to eradicate any memory of the Jews from the land.)

If God did not want His people to return to the land of their original ancestors and ensured that Abraham understood this, how does this apply to us today?

When we are born again and saved by the blood of Jesus, we become new creatures in Christ. He gives us a new heart. We become aliens and strangers in the world because we have a new home that is promised to us in heaven. Our old home is the world we continue to live in for the time being, but it's a place in which we should no longer ever be comfortable. We should not be like Lot's wife who turned her eyes back toward Sodom because she missed that evil place and her heart wasn't in the escape (Genesis 19:26). For that she paid a great price: the loss of her salvation.

This applies to all Christians, but especially newer and immature followers of Christ: So as to escape the lures and temptations of our old life, there are four things we must avoid:

1. Old people
2. Old places
3. Old patterns
4. Old playgrounds

We must be dead to our life prior to Christ. The only reason for any of us to return to the old things is because God has given us a specific ministry among them. Other than that, we should reject the old life that Satan had ensnared us in through the deceptions of the world.

If we look with longing at our past and think we can dabble in those things that previously kept us from God, we are sadly mistaken. Those old people, places, patterns, and playgrounds will grab hold of us and drag us back away from God's presence. Just ask anyone who has struggled with alcohol, drug, or other dependencies what happened when they compromised to take just one drink, a single toke, or a harmless little snort.

We are to look forward and up toward our Lord and Savior Jesus Christ and His imminent return.

January 10: Genesis 25:20,26 – Waiting

(Genesis 25-26; Matthew 9:1-17)

We live in a "now" world. Because of modern technologies and the conveniences we've become accustomed to in the so-called civilized world, if we're not instantly gratified, that leaves us unhappy and grumbling. Our attention spans have grown increasingly shorter, and our patience wears thin if we have to wait more than a couple minutes for something we want. Have you ever called tech support to fix a problem, waited ten minutes, then took out your frustration on the rep answering your call? Have you ever gone to the McDonald's drive-thru, then fumed at the number of cars ahead of you? Our modern world has spoiled us. Because of that, we often think that God should answer our prayers NOW!

In Genesis 25:20,26 we get an indication that God does things in His own way in His timing:

"And Isaac was forty years old when he took Rebekah...Isaac was sixty years old when she bore them [his twin sons Esau and Jacob]."

For twenty years, Rebekeh was barren *"and Isaac prayed to the Lord for his wife, because she was barren. And the Lord granted his prayer, and Rebekeah his wife conceived (Genesis 25:21)"*

Twenty years! The text doesn't tell us how old Rebekah was when she married Isaac, but given the culture at that time, she was likely quite young, perhaps fifteen or so. In all the intervening years until the Lord granted Isaac's and her petitions for a child, how discouraging that must have been!

Interestingly, Scripture doesn't record Rebekah's death, but Jewish tradition believes she may have been somewhere between 120-130 years old at the time. Apparently, she had no other children besides the twin boys. So, she was maybe thirty-five when she had the two boys and for another possibly ninety years - nothing!

God's answer came and it was limited according to His purposes. Simply having the children they did brought great joy to Isaac and Rebekah, but they had to wonder why it took God so long to answer and why they had no other children.

Aren't we like that? If God doesn't respond instantly to our prayers for healing, deliverance from a difficult situation, or anything else, we wonder what's wrong. If He doesn't answer in the way we envision He should, we're perplexed. Did God not hear me? Have I done something wrong? What's taking Him so long? Why didn't He do it my way?

We're created in God's image, but He is far beyond us in who He is. He is sovereign. He is the Alpha and the Omega. He knows the end from the beginning. Humbling ourselves to this reality and coming before Him on bended knee can be difficult because of our rebellious spirits, but that's exactly what we must do.

Lord, help us come to You with a surrendered and soft heart. You are God and we are not. Have your will and your way, for You are worthy. We give You the glory and praise You deserve. Bless Your Holy Name.

January 11: Genesis 28:8-9 - Rebellion's Legacy

(Genesis 27-28; Matthew 9:18-38)

In today's reading, along with several prior passages, we see the root of the everlasting animosity between the Jews and Arabs. Jacob with the help of his mother Rebekah deceived his father Isaac to receive the first-son blessings in place of his brother Esau (Genesis 27:36). Previously Jacob had negotiated with Esau and stolen his birthright (Genesis 25:33). Now in Genesis 28:8-9, the ultimate basis for Esau losing what his blessings and birthright should have been is repeated from earlier verses:

"So when Esau saw that the Canaanite women did not please his father, Esau went to Ishmael and took as his wife beside the wives he had..."

What wives did Esau have already? He had once before in Genesis 26:34-35 shown his true colors - his rebellious nature - in his choice of mates:

"When Esau was forty years old, he took Judith the daughter of Beeri the Hittite to be his wife, and Basemath the daughter of Elon the Hittite, and they made life bitter for Isaac and Rebekah."

Rather than choosing Israelite women, Esau took Hittites as his wives. In the story of his parents' union, Esau had certainly seen God's intent and learned the lesson: His people were not to intermarry with pagan peoples. Esau disregarded this for his own desires.

This wasn't the first instance of disobedience to the will of Yahweh. After God had told Abraham and Sarah that they would have a child even in their old age (Genesis 15:5), they thought they had to help Him along to fulfill His promise. Sarah gave her servant Hagar to Abraham to be her surrogate in order to bring forth a child (Genesis 16:3). That resulted in the birth of Ishmael.

Ishmael was not the son of the promise, but of the flesh. He was the son that came to Abraham and Sarah when they didn't believe God. He was a son of disobedience.

Ishmael's descendants were numerous. God blessed him with twelve sons, but like their father, whom the Angel of the Lord had decreed to Hagar, their hand would be against everyone and everyone's hand was against them

(Genesis 16:12). In other words, with Ishmael and his descendants, there would always be conflict.

Some years later, Esau came along. What did he do? He joined in the line of Ishmael by marrying his daughter. Disobedience and rebellion multiplied. The loss of favor and blessings from God increased. Seeing how first Isaac then Jacob had God's approval, it's easy to see how hatred grew. Yet this loathing originated because of unbelief, because of disobedience, because of rebellion against God's will.

This hostile attitude of the Arab nations arising from Ishmael and Esau has continued to this day. If you were to ask one of their descendants why they despise Israel, they likely couldn't tell you. It's almost as though it's ingrained in their DNA.

Despite that, God loves the children of Ishmael and Esau who comprise the Arab nations and who are largely Muslim in their beliefs. He has been showing Himself to them in recent years through dreams and visions. He has been drawing them to Himself, even as He wants the direct descendants of Abraham, Isaac, and Jacob to be His true children in Christ.

God is no respecter of persons. He wants none to perish, but all to have eternal life through Jesus Christ (2 Peter 3:9). Some will indeed follow Him; others will not. But a day is coming when everyone will bow before Him and confess that He is Lord (Romans 14:11).

January 12: Matthew 10:23 - Rejecting Jesus

(Genesis 29-30; Matthew 10:1-23)

Upon Jesus calling His disciples, He soon sends them out to the towns and cities of Israel so as to gather her *"lost sheep"* (Matthew 10:6). He instructs the men to proclaim the Good News by telling everyone that "t*he kingdom of heaven is at hand"* (Matthew 10:7). Jesus gives them the power and authority of God in this task, as they are able to demonstrate this truth through healings, casting out evil spirits, and raising of the dead (Matthew 10:8). Yet, Jesus knows there will be many who will not believe despite the evidence of God moving directly in their midst. His prophetic Words bode a dire warning for all who reject Him: *"Truly, I say to you, it will be more bearable on the day of judgment for the land of Sodom and Gomorrah than for that town"* (Matthew 10:15).

That's an awful pronouncement. What do we know about Sodom and Gomorrah? They were such wicked places that not even ten righteous men could be found in them (Genesis 18:32). Abraham had negotiated with the Angel of the Lord all the way down from fifty righteous, but the evil was so pervasive that it had consumed those cities.

In the highways and byways of Israel, the same dynamic of wickedness was present. Jesus knew the hearts of men and their deceitfulness. He knew that in the rejection of His Word, men would come against those who brought it. Man wants what he wants. When something keeps him from his own desires, he will act in his own selfish interests. If the Spirit of the Lord does not convict men's hearts, they will act in their carnal nature. What does that fleshly response produce? In Jesus' Words: *"You will be hated by all for My Name's sake"* (Matthew 10:22). And that hatred toward God brings persecution to His followers.

The majority of the people of Israel were well down that path because of their religious leaders. The Pharisees previously in Matthew 10:34 had accused Jesus of being in league with Satan: *"He casts out demons by the prince of demons."*

Jesus accentuates this warning in Matthew 10:25 in speaking of those who hate God:

"If they have called the master of the house Beelezebul, how much more will they malign those of His household?"

It is this attitude and belief about Jesus that is the grieving of the Holy Spirit. Just two chapters later Jesus declares in Matthew 12:31-32 that:

" *the blasphemy against the Spirit will not be forgiven...Whoever speaks against the Holy Spirit will not be forgiven, either in this age or in the age to come.*"

Hating Jesus is hating God. It is the unforgivable sin. One who hates true followers of Jesus likewise hates God. That has eternal consequences. For the nation of Israel, that heart condition caused the people to continually fall away from Him to worship other gods. God will only completely deal with that apostasy at the end of the Tribulation when 2/3 of Israel perishes and only 1/3 remain alive and are saved (Zechariah 13:8), but it's a difficult outcome.

What lesson can we as Christians draw from this? Jesus never promises us an easy life. In fact, He promises that we will face trials and tribulations because the world hates Him. Thus, it hates us.

In America we have had minimal opposition to the Christian faith since our founding as a nation. That has changed. Even as Jesus prophesied, darkness and lawlessness are coming upon the earth (Matthew 24). It is already upon us, but will grow much worse. Our nation has fallen. It is no longer "one nation under God." What was once a Constitutional Republic has turned into a banana republic. From the 2020 presidential election with its treason and fraud, Christians should no longer expect safety as encapsulated in the First Amendment.

A purge has begun that will expose and weed out all conservatives and Christians. In every other tyrannical nation on earth, their turning to the ways of Satan has always meant persecution for God's people. We simply have to read the Old Testament to see how God's curse upon those who reject Him plays out. The Word of God is clear: judgment comes when people grieve the Holy Spirit.

The Good News for we who believe and don't follow the antichrist spirit of the age is that God will deliver us from the wrath to come. He promised that to the Philadelphia church in Revelation 3:10:

"*Because you have kept my Word about patient endurance, I will keep you from the hour of trial that is coming on the whole world, to try those who dwell on the earth.*"

That is the Word of Promise to the faithful, remnant church. That is the promise of the pre-Tribulation Rapture. Will we be found faithful? Yes, but only if we double down in these perilous times and cling to God, His Word, and His righteousness.

January 13: Matthew 10:28 – Fear

(Genesis 31-32; Matthew 10:24-42)

Jesus knew the price His followers would have to pay in this wicked world. The promise of eternal life in Him comes with a high cost. Yet, Jesus said that it's worth every penny we own and every drop of blood running through our veins. Who we fear and bow down to, even in great peril we might face, is critical to our very lives. He warned us in Matthew 10:28:

"And do not fear those who kill the body but cannot kill the soul. Rather fear him who can destroy both soul and body in hell."

Our eternal destinies are on the line based on who we serve. In the 10/40 Window primarily in the Middle East, our brothers and sisters in Christ confront this issue day in and day out. The majority of Christ-followers in these Muslim, Hindu and Communist countries make a deliberate decision when they ask Jesus to be their Savior and Lord. They know from their surrounding culture that the Name of Jesus is anathema, i.e. a curse, among their people. In a sense, the religions they follow are insecure. The gods of those religions don't seem strong enough to protect their people from the Word of God. They need the adherents of Islam, Hinduism, or Communist atheism to fight for them. The gods of these religions cannot fight for themselves. This causes disciples of these philosophies to come against Christians in defense of their gods. They attack, harm, and kill believers in Christ.

Yet, what did Jesus say? Don't fear them. There is One greater who can do more than destroy the body, which is all these people following false doctrines can do. The God of the Bible can cast the soul into hell. He is the One to fear and revere.

This creates potential conflict for Christians in these hostile nations. Do they acknowledge Christ? Do they approach the Gospel in shame? What are the consequences? Jesus lays it out succinctly in Matthew 10:32-33:

"So everyone who acknowledges me before men, I also will acknowledge before my Father who is in heaven, but whoever denies me before men, I also will deny before my Father who is in heaven."

To a believer these Words should resolve any doubt he may have when opposition comes. Knowing how the Father will view him based on his response in a time of trouble should set his mind and heart straight. Serving

God and Him alone is the only choice. Our brethren overseas have encountered this fact and remained true, even to the death.

And death - even a violent one - may be what one faces in the midst of those who are anti-Christ, and thus, anti-God, i.e. those who hate God. Despite this, Jesus gives this assurance in Matthew 10:39:

"Whoever finds his life will lose it, and whoever loses his life for my sake will find it."

We live in perilous times. Our nation is on a downward course toward insignificance. How do we know this? Because nowhere in the Bible do we find a strong nation such as America. In Ezekiel's War (Ezekiel 38-39), Israel has no allies. Her best friend today is absent. In the Tribulation of the book of Revelation, America doesn't even appear as a powerful nation among the ones described.

The odds are great that we will soon see persecution similar to our brethren in the Middle East. What is currently happening in our nation is right out of the Bible. Lawlessness is rising in ways we never expected. An antichrist spirit is overtaking our land. With these things, fear is rising, and many have no idea where to turn. Even within the church, apostasy is rampant because of Biblical illiteracy and unbelief.

We should embrace the Words of Jesus as He warns of what is to come. We should believe that He is the only answer, whether in a time of prosperity or one of despair.

Let us bolster our faith; let us strengthen it through God's Word. Let's turn to Christ and cling to Him. We have His assurance in Matthew 10:40:

"Whoever receives you receives me, and whoever receives me receives him who sent me."

Let us not fear, whatever the day might bring.

January 14: Genesis 35:9-11 & Matthew 11:20-24 - Which God?

(Genesis 33-35; Matthew 11)

There's a deep connection between Genesis 35:9-11 and Matthew 11:20-24. In Genesis we read:

"God appeared to Jacob again, when he came from Paddan-aram, and blessed him. And God said to him, "Your name is Jacob; no longer shall your name be called Jacob, but Israel shall be your name." So he called his name Israel. And God said to him, "I am God Almighty: be fruitful and multiply. A nation and a company of nations shall come from you, and kings shall come from your own body."

What was it that prompted God to bless Jacob in this manner? Why was it important?

The blessing and favor of God followed the incident at Shechem, in which Jacob's sons took revenge on the Hivites for the defiling of their sister Dinah. Following that, God instructed Jacob to go south from Shechem "up" (into hill country) to Bethel. In his obedience to God, Jacob told those in his household to rid themselves of any of their foreign gods, i.e. the idols that they retained from their homeland. Recall that Rachel had brought Laban's household gods with her when they'd left (Genesis 31:19). Others in Jacob's caravan likely had many more. Everyone did as Jacob commanded, and he left them near Shechem buried under a tree. Following that act, Yahweh appeared to him and blessed him mightily.

What was the reason?

When Jacob left the idols of the other gods behind, that was both a symbolic act and a declaration. In doing this, Jacob turned completely to Yahweh as his God. In initially allowing these idols to remain in his presence and with his retinue, Jacob was effectively telling God that he wasn't sure He was the only One worthy of being worshiped. He was straddling the fence. He was double-minded. However, that had now changed.

Yahweh was now Jacob's God - Him alone - and He knew Jacob's heart in the matter. Jacob had given his believing loyalty completely to God Most High. That enabled Him to bestow this great blessing of fruitfulness upon him.

How does that connect with the passage in Matthew?

"Then he began to denounce the cities where most of his mighty works had been done, because they did not repent. "Woe to you, Chorazin! Woe to you, Bethsaida! For if the mighty works done in you had been done in Tyre and Sidon, they would have repented long ago in sackcloth and ashes. But I tell you, it will be more bearable on the day of judgment for Tyre and Sidon than for you. And you, Capernaum, will you be exalted to heaven? You will be brought down to Hades. For if the mighty works done in you had been done in Sodom, it would have remained until this day. But I tell you that it will be more tolerable on the day of judgment for the land of Sodom than for you.""

Jesus had been going through these cities in Israel proclaiming the Good News of the Kingdom of God. In these cities He had done miracles, signs, and wonders that only God could do. His ability to perform these acts was painfully obvious to anyone with "an eye to see , and an ear to hear." But not to the inhabitants of these cities.

Perhaps it was the religious spirit of the Pharisees that infested them. Perhaps that hardened their hearts. Perhaps they effectively had an antichrist spirit that kept them worshiping gods of their own imaginations. Whatever it was, it was deep and pervasive. Despite what Jesus did, the people of those cities did not respond to Him. Their believing loyalty remained far from Yahweh, and it earned His wrath.

Consider what Jesus said in His "woe" upon them. The anti-God cities of Tyre and Sidon would fare better in the Judgment had they heard His message; the abominable city of Sodom, known for its immorality and wickedness, would would have responded better that Chorizin, Bethsaida, and Capernaum. The fate of Sodom was more favorable than these cities in Israel in which Jesus walked!

The parallel is the heart condition. By turning wholly to Yahweh, Jacob demonstrated himself a man of God. By rejecting Jesus, these cities proved their apostasy to the God of Israel.

God seeks a people who will follow Him obediently. He wants those who love Him and will put aside every other god in their lives. God wants His throne to be in the center of all we do and for us to bring every aspect of our lives before Him, and none other.

Is your believing loyalty to Christ and Him alone? God warns us repeatedly in His Word that this is what He expects. Don't live as an inhabitant of Chorizin, Bethsaida, or Capernaum. Doing so may bring great woe upon you. Alternatively, when you follow Jesus with all your heart, soul, mind, and strength (Mark 12:30), God will bless you mightily.

January 15: Genesis 37:18 & Matthew 12:14 – Conspiracy

(Genesis 36-37; Matthew 12:1-21)

When the prophet tells us in Jeremiah 17:9 that "*the heart is deceitful above all things and beyond cure. Who can understand it?*", the truth he speaks is from of old, arising from the very first sin and the fall of man. Yet, many people don't believe this about the human condition. They choose to believe that man's heart is good and pure, and that it is the circumstances around a person that cause him to react as he does.

In the reading for today we see two incidents that discount this non-Biblical thinking. Joseph, a young man of seventeen, has two dreams that enrage his brothers, who already hate him for the favor he had in their father Jacob's eyes. The dreams are the tipping point for them. Despite their sibling relationship, they despise him even more. In Genesis 37:18 they begin to act on the wickedness in their hearts in a place far from home:

"They saw him from afar, and before he came near to them, they conspired to kill him."

How their hatred must have festered within each one of them for so long to even consider such an extreme action! Only Reuben, the oldest among them, argued to spare his life. He knew the story of his ancestors Cain and Abel, and how even the earth cries out at the shedding of blood and brings a curse upon the murderer (Genesis 4:10-11). He had enough sense not to bring that damnation upon their heads, and, seemingly, the understanding of his responsibility as the oldest for the youngest. However, Reuben is also the son who slept with his father's concubine, Bilhah, the mother of his brother Naphtali (Genesis 35:22), an act which ultimately caused the loss of his firstborn rights .

Following their conspiracy against Joseph, the brothers sold him into slavery. They lied and brought false comfort to their father, who would not be comforted (Genesis 37:35).

Jesus in His ministry regularly confronted the Pharisees for their legalism and lack of mercy. He often went to the synagogues on the Sabbath to test the hearts of these shepherds of Israel. Time after time they failed to show love toward their fellow man. The Law took precedence in their view, and nothing would inhibit their adherence to it.

One day Jesus enters the synagogue and finds a man with a withered hand. The Pharisees, having previously seen Him in action, goad Him by asking, "*Is it lawful to heal on the Sabbath?*" (Matthew 12:10).

As usual, He knows their hearts and lack of compassion, and He heals the man, once more proving His claim to be God is not an empty one. But, the Pharisees are so blinded by the evil within them and the sense of their own righteousness, that they can't see the truth right before their very eyes. The healing incenses them. It results in Matthew 12:14:

"But the Pharisees went out and conspired against Him, how to destroy Him."

Just as with the brothers who schemed to kill Joseph, the Pharisees plotted to likewise eliminate this troublemaker Jesus, who was upsetting the way they thought and viewed the world. The actions of Jesus revealed that which was deep within them. He exposed the nature of their hearts. The bad fruit of their unbelief was brought to light.

There is only one solution to the true nature of man buried deep within us all. That is the answer from the very beginning made known through Jesus Christ. Each one of us must acknowledge our sin and repent of it. We must come to the Father through the Son. As Jesus said in John 14:6, revealing this truth: "*I am the way and the truth and the life. No one comes to the Father except through Me.*"

January 16: Genesis 39:3 - The Lord's Favor

(Genesis 38-40; Matthew 12:22-50)

When bad things happen to us, we cry out with the age-old question, "Why me, Lord?" Perhaps we've served God well and faithfully and haven't deviated from Him. It could even be said that we walked in His righteousness; we've lived and been upright in the Name of Christ. Then the roof caves in over our head, the floor falls out from beneath us, the walls collapse upon the structure of our life. It makes no sense, and the doubts creep in. Wasn't this stuff supposed to happen to people who hate God? How in the world could God let these things happen to me when I've obeyed Him and even produced much good fruit in His Name?

Then we come to the story of Joseph. It says in Genesis 39:3 that:

"His master saw that the Lord was with him and that the Lord caused all that he did to succeed in his hands."

Joseph had been sold into slavery by his jealous brothers. In Egypt he prospered, as did those around him. God blessed him during this time. No doubt, Joseph figured he had it made despite the awful circumstances that had brought him here. In fact Genesis 39:5 telles us:

"From the time that he made him overseer in his house and over all that he had, the Lord blessed the Egyptian's house for Joseph's sake; the blessing of the Lord was on all that he had, in house and field."

But then, Joseph faced a dilemma. His master's wife wanted to seduce him. Instead of giving into the temptation, he refused the lure of the flesh and rebuffed her. He wouldn't give into lust because he knew it wasn't simply an offense against the husband, it was wickedness and sin against God (Genesis 39:9).

The woman accuses him anyway, and he winds up in prison. From great blessing to the lowliest of places; all because he honored God. How could this be? However, once more, he finds favor with those around him. In Genesis 39:21 we see:

"But the Lord was with Joseph and showed him steadfast love and gave him favor in the sight of the keeper of the prison."

And in Genesis 39:23:

"Whatever he did, the Lord made it succeed."

But, he was still in prison.

What happens next shows how everything was orchestrated by God. The king's servants displease him, and they are tossed into prison with Joseph. God graciously enables Joseph to interpret their dreams. The chief baker is executed while the chief cupbearer is restored to his previous position, just as Joseph said.

Yet, once more God seems to forsake Joseph, as the cupbearer forgets him. But timing is everything. Subsequently Joseph will have the opportunity to interpret Pharaoh's dreams. This will cause Pharaoh to exalt him above all others in the Egyptian kingdom. It will enable God to accomplish His purposes through the Exile and the Exodus of the Hebrew people.

That's the point. God has a view that we don't have. He knows the end from the beginning, because He isn't subject to time and space as we are. He knows all that people will do - the various choices they'll make - and He turns their hearts as necessary to achieve His ends.

Joseph had no clue that his life was part of a much larger picture that God was painting. What seemed to be a terrible fate resulted in greater blessings for Joseph. More than that, his circumstances determined the destiny of God's Chosen People and the ultimate creation of the nation of Israel.

All because Joseph was faithful and obedient to Yahweh.

If we are walking that same path of righteousness and bad things happen to us, we should probably take a different perspective than what the world tells us.. Just as God was with Joseph in the midst of difficulties and challenges, and saw him through to even better circumstances than he'd previously enjoyed, so He will do with us.

January 17: Matthew 13:12 - Abundance or Not

(Genesis 41; Matthew 13:1-32)

Jesus began a period of His ministry in which He spoke only in parables. His most famous of these is the Parable of the Sower. Most of us are familiar with this teaching, as we've likely heard it preached on many times. There is one verse that is probably less known in this account. In Matthew 13:12, Jesus makes an incredible statement that has likely confused many people over the years:

"For to the one who has, more will be given, and he will have an abundance, but from the one who has not, even what he has will be taken away."

One way to consider what this means can be in the area of faithful tithing. When we give to God's kingdom by bringing the whole tithe into the storehouse, i.e. by not withholding from God that which is already His, then He blesses us. Luke 6:38 relates this principle like this:

"Give, and it will be given to you. A good measure, pressed down, shaken together and running over, will be poured into your lap. For with the measure you use, it will be measured to you."

In other words, through our obedience in bringing 10% of all that comes into our household, God will return that 10% to us and more. *To the one who has, more will be given.* In contrast, when we keep all 100% of our income and don't give back to the Lord, that entire amount will always be short at the end of the month. *Even what he has will be taken away.*

This is a significant truth about God's kingdom as we make our way through life's journey, but there is a deeper meaning to this parable. It is one of the secrets of the kingdom of heaven that is actually well known because it deals with salvation.

When we are born again through the blood of Christ, we become children of God and heirs to the throne along with our brother Jesus (Romans 8:17). God gives us everything; all that He has is ours in abundance. We have the Spirit of the living God dwelling within us in this life - His presence in the midst of all we face. Better yet, we have eternal life with the amazing promise that we will rule and reign with Jesus (2 Timothy 2:12; Revelation 20:6). In our present physical state, we cannot truly imagine what this will be like - but it will be glorious!

The promise for those who don't know Jesus as Lord and Savior is much darker and foreboding. Someone could have all the riches of this world, but if he doesn't know Christ, he is doomed. He can live in luxury and direct the fate of millions, but without being covered by the blood of the Lamb, he will amount to nothing when he dies. Because he can't take it with him, it will all be lost. *Even what he has will be taken away.*

This is the reason it is so vital that we believe in Jesus and make Him our King. There is life after death, both for believers and unbelievers. For those who follow hard after God, that life is one of abundance, the Lord's favor, His blessings. For the ones who reject Him, i.e. those who choose to go their own way in unbelief, there is nothing but eternal torment.

Why choose disaster when the kindness of God leads us to repentance, and through that the kingdom of heaven?

January 18: Matthew 13:42-43- Harvest Time

(Genesis 42-43; Matthew 13:33-58)

God will prevail upon this earth. Sometimes it's difficult to remember this. We see wickedness all around us, and as times grow dark, we may experience it personally. All too often Christians in America think we'll be shielded from what those in other countries face. But why should we? Are we not all brothers and sisters in Christ? Do we have a birthright that places us above those who suffer for Christ because of where they live? Didn't Jesus say that we will have sorrows in this world (John 16:33)? Was He speaking only to His disciples from His day or only to those in the 10/40 Window? Of course not.

When Jesus began speaking in parables so that only His disciples would understand, and those who didn't know Him wouldn't comprehend, He told the Parable of the Wheat and Tares (Weeds) (also the Parable of the Net - or Dragnet which is a parallel parable). Why would He speak in parables? There is no universal salvation. Jesus made clear that there is a day of judgment. Those who hate God - those who are children of Satan (Matthew 13:38) - are destined to hell because of the choice they've made to reject the One and Only Son of God. Those who choose a path supposedly to heaven other than Jesus as the way, the truth, and the life (John 14:6) are not worthy of God's ultimate mercy. He warned them. They had plenty of notice. But, our choices have consequences.

Who are these people? We see various passages throughout Scripture that define them. Here in Matthew 13:42, they are seen as ones who engage in sin and are law-breakers, the ones who suffer the ultimate punishment. Revelation 21:8 defines them more specifically:

"But as for the cowardly, the faithless, the detestable, as for murderers, the sexually immoral, sorcerers, idolaters, and all liars, their portion will be in the lake that burns with fire and sulfur, which is the second death."

If you examine the Ten Commandments (Exodus 20:1-17), you'll see that these sins correlate with at least five of the commandments. Following the Law doesn't save us, only God's grace and mercy through the shed blood of Christ does. But, once we're born-again, neither can we deliberately commit these offenses against God and expect eternal life. Doing so would mean that we've chosen not to obey God. To this end, 1 John 3:8 says:

"Whoever makes a practice of sinning is of the devil, for the devil has been sinning from the beginning. The reason the Son of God appeared was to destroy the works of the devil."

Is someone truly saved if they make a practice of sinning? No, he is of his father, the devil.

How will this parable play out at the end of the age? What will it look like? Jesus tells us that the angels will reap, gather the weeds, and burn them with fire (Matthew 13:39-40). This will occur at the end of the 7-year Tribulation. The account is expanded upon in Revelation 14:14-20:

"Then I looked, and behold, a white cloud, and seated on the cloud one like a son of man, with a golden crown on his head, and a sharp sickle in his hand. And another angel came out of the temple, calling with a loud voice to him who sat on the cloud, "Put in your sickle, and reap, for the hour to reap has come, for the harvest of the earth is fully ripe." So he who sat on the cloud swung his sickle across the earth, and the earth was reaped.

"Then another angel came out of the temple in heaven, and he too had a sharp sickle. And another angel came out from the altar, the angel who has authority over the fire, and he called with a loud voice to the one who had the sharp sickle, "Put in your sickle and gather the clusters from the vine of the earth, for its grapes are ripe." So the angel swung his sickle across the earth and gathered the grape harvest of the earth and threw it into the great winepress of the wrath of God. And the winepress was trodden outside the city, and blood flowed from the winepress, as high as a horse's bridle, for 1,600 stadia."

This is a description of the slaughter of all the armies of the earth that have gathered on the plains of Armageddon to come against the holy city of Jerusalem; it includes those throughout the earth who have rejected Christ, yet aren't present in Israel. This is the point when Jesus returns in His Second Coming with the armies of heaven, i.e. the glorified believers in the true church - the Bride of Christ. This is expanded on further in Revelation 19:11-21. It's a horrible, bloody scene, yet it's the righteous end of all unbelievers at this coming time in world history.

There's one other point to be made. It comes from our highlighted verse today. Matthew 13:42-43 describes what happens with the tares and the wheat. All the sinners and law-breakers whom the angels have gathered will be thrown...

"...into the fiery furnace. In that place there will be weeping and gnashing of teeth. Then the righteous will shine like the sun in the kingdom of their Father. He who has ears, let him hear."

At the White Throne Judgment depicted in Revelation 20:11-15 the final end of the unbelieving masses will happen. Their names will be shown not to be written in the Lamb's Book of Life, and they will be cast into the Lake of Fire - the fiery furnace. This is a place of eternal torment; truly where they will live forever in a constant state of weeping and gnashing of teeth.

God is love. He is gracious and merciful. He wants none to perish, but all to come to saving faith through His One and Only Son, Jesus Christ. All have that opportunity. Everyone has this choice. Many decide to go their own way.

For those of us who have believing loyalty in Jesus Christ and revere Him as Lord and Savior, our righteousness will indeed shine like the sun. Why would anyone choose anything else?

January 19: Genesis 44:5 – Divination

(Genesis 44-45; Matthew 14:1-21)

God has made it abundantly clear in His revelation that the practice of divination is forbidden, yet in Genesis 44:5 the text tells us this about Joseph:

"Is it not from this that my lord [Joseph] drinks, and by this that he practices divination? You have done evil in doing this."

A few verses later in Genesis 44:15 we learn directly from Joseph:

Joseph said to them, "What deed is this that you have done? Do you not know that a man like me can indeed practice divination?"

It is in Leviticus 19:26,31 where God commands His people:

"You shall not eat any flesh with the blood in it. You shall not interpret omens or tell fortunes."

"Do not turn to mediums or necromancers; do not seek them out, and so make yourselves unclean by them: I am the Lord your God."

So, how and why is that Joseph does divination? It's obvious that Yahweh forbids it.

First, why does God prohibit this practice?

In the ancient cultures surrounding Israel the people worshiped other gods. Because these spiritual beings were not the omniscient, omnipotent, omnipresent Yahweh who was loving, kind, and merciful, who brought rain on the just and the unjust (Matthew 5:45), they wouldn't simply pour out blessings on those they ruled. They had to be appeased. Their wisdom had to be sought in certain ways that were not the ways of Yahweh. In the course of that search, these gods had to teach the nations under their rule that the path to them and to enlightenment they brought was different from the means to attain the favor of God Most High. These gods hated Yahweh, their creator, just as He was the creator of mankind. As such, the people under their rule had to be taught anything but that which would please Yahweh.

Joseph's use of divination was a normal practice in Egypt and elsewhere in the Ancient Near East (ANE). On the surface, in using the cup in question,

Joseph was adhering to the ways of the wise men of that land. In addition, the specific revelation from God shown above in Leviticus had not yet come to the Hebrews. That only occurred 400 years later when Moses delivered God's people from the fiery furnace of Egyptian slavery during the Exodus.

Despite this, I contend that Joseph didn't practice divination as the Egyptians did. Their magicians and sorcerers sought a word from the pagan gods they worshiped. They were far from Yahweh and knowing Him.

Joseph, on the other hand, knew God and worshiped Him alone. In seeking divine guidance, he came before Yahweh and no other god. In fact, later in Scripture we see through the priestly breastplate, and the Urim and Thummim, that God's people actually practiced divination through His approved means to determine His counsel.

Understanding the Biblical text at a deeper level helps us gain insight into seemingly puzzling contradictions of this nature. The more we read God's Word, and through that attain an appreciation for what God desires of us, we can begin to see how some of these situations we read about aren't opposed to Him and what He expects of us after all.

God wants us to know Him more deeply, but that knowing only comes with effort on our part. But, isn't it worth it to seek out the deeper mysteries of God?

January 20: Genesis 47:20-21 – Serfdom

(Genesis 46-48; Matthew 14:22-36)

Lord Acton in the 1800s famously said, "Power tends to corrupt, and absolute power corrupts absolutely." This has always been true since man first sinned, and always will be true until the Lord eradicates sin upon the earth.

In the passage in Genesis 47:13-26 that describes Joseph's work on behalf of Pharaoh in the midst of the 7-year famine, we see this principle at work. After the seven years of plenty that God decreed, Egypt and the entire known world in the Middle East experienced severe famine. Because of God's favor upon Joseph, he earned Pharaoh's trust, and the most powerful man on the earth made Joseph his second in command with power over all people. Joseph's authority was only less than that of Pharaoh himself.

In the course of the famine, acting as Pharaoh's representative and proxy, Joseph distributed the vast food stores that had been accumulated through the years of plenty to those in need. At first the people came to Joseph and bought food with the money they had. But their money ran out.

The people had livestock of many kinds, such as sheep and cattle. When their money was gone, they exchanged these assets for food. The famine continued, and the people were desperate.

They came again to Joseph. Those who were landowners willingly gave that up their land in order to live. Before long they were hungry once more as the famine lingered. They surrendered the very last thing of value they had: their bodies - their very lives. So as to eat, they sold themselves to Pharaoh. From then on, he owned the people. The only ones Joseph did not buy for Pharaoh was the priests - the elite representatives for their pagan gods (which, by the way, seem to have failed the Egyptians). It was only by this very last and hopeless measure that the people found a way to survive. Genesis 47:20-21 tells us:

"So Joseph bought all the land of Egypt for Pharaoh, for all the Egyptians sold their fields, because the famine was severe on them. The land became Pharaoh's. As for the people, he made servants of them from one end of Egypt to the other."

Subsequently, all crops the people grew belonged to Pharaoh, and he required all his subjects to give him 20% of what they grew. To keep them alive in their indentured servitude, he allowed them to retain the other 80% on which to live. The priests weren't subject to this dictate.

All who lived in Egypt had no choice but to live under Pharaoh's dictates in this way. The power he wielded was absolute, even to the possessing of the very lives of those who lived in the land.

What happened in Egypt and to the children of Israel was at the hand of God. He used the absolute and corrupted power of Pharaoh for His own purposes, namely to bring the Hebrew people to a point where they would cry out to Him and He would deliver them. That which was meant for evil, God brought about for good.

Many strongmen over the years have used this template. We've primarily seen it in practice through communist dictatorships. Through a series of maneuvers, the people become serfs, wholly owned and under the control of the dictator in power.

In America, adherents to communism have been working for over 90 years to bring this country under the thumb of this ideology. By infiltrating every area of our society, from schools to seminaries, from media to government, from technology to entertainment, communist ideology has corrupted the minds of all who have been indoctrinated by it.

The Roman Empire died from within through the corruption of its leaders which filtered down to its people. America is on this same course.

Our country was founded as one nation under God, but we have banished God in all strata of our society and culture. A nation that honors and worships God earns His favor and blessings. A nation that turns its back on God earns His wrath and His curses.

The template we see in Genesis with Pharaoh's absolute power - the power of the State - is playing out here in America. The corrupting power of those in charge, using the ideology of communism as their god, is leading America to the place of serfdom. People are being conditioned to rely on the government and what it tells them. In order to stay alive, they will obey unquestioningly.

There is purpose in this in God's greater plans. He is allowing America to come under this servitude in order to fulfill His prophetic Word. The Bible tells us that in the latter days - the end times - lawlessness and deception will rise to levels beyond our imagination. This must happen before our very eyes because a progression of events is working. The stage must be set for the 7-year Tribulation and the strongman of that period: the Antichrist. The world must be ready for him to appear on the scene, essentially snap his fingers, and for the unbelievers remaining on the earth after the Rapture of the true church to do exactly what he commands. The technology and all necessary systems for his rule must be in place at that time.

We shouldn't be surprised that America is going down. This nation doesn't appear in Bible prophecy, other than as a possible side note or two. We cannot be a world power, but simply one of many nations in the global economy as the One World Government takes shape for Antichrist to rule.

The glorious, wondrous Good News is that God has promised His church that we will not experience the worst of this. Revelation 3:10 assures us:

"Because you have kept my word about patient endurance, I will keep you from the hour of trial that is coming on the whole world, to try those who dwell on the earth."

What is this hour of trial? The 7-year Tribulation. God spoke these comforting Words to the church of Philadelphia, the one, true and faithful church. Those of us who are true and faithful to God through Jesus Christ comprise this church today.

This is why we can rejoice, even in the midst of the gathering darkness. As Titus 2:13 says, and which we embrace, we are...

"...waiting for our blessed hope, the appearing of the glory of our great God and Savior Jesus Christ,"

January 21: Matthew 15:8-9 - Wayward Hearts

(Genesis 49-50; Matthew 15:1-20)

The milquetoast Jesus, i.e. the timid and feeble Jesus in the minds of many in the church today, is a figment of their imagination. He is a Jesus they have conjured up out of the depths of their sin because they don't want to hear or know the hard teachings He brought. Better in their estimation is to have a loving, kind, and gentle Jesus, because that person makes them feel better. The problem is that this Jesus they've created to console themselves and purportedly worship is not the Son of God, and certainly not God Himself.

This is not a new phenomenon. The Hebrew people long had problems relating to Yahweh in the way they needed to in order to honor Him for who He was. The Pharisees in Jesus' day were simply an extension of those who made God in their image, and thus got the relationship completely wrong.

Jesus continually clashed with the Pharisees because of this. In the Old Testament we read how God's people constantly disobeyed Him and His laws. Over the 400 years of God's silence from Malachi to Jesus, during what we call the Intertestamental, or 2nd Temple, Period, the Jews determined to correct that situation. The Pharisees arose as a sect that made the Law of Moses preeminent. The Law became everything to them. All their actions revolved around the 613 Mosaic laws articulated in Leviticus plus the Ten Commandments. Their hearts may have been in the right place when the Pharisees first came on the scene, but they didn't stay that way. It was for this reason that Jesus dealt harshly with them.

The Pharisees observed Jesus and had huge issues with Him. He didn't wash His hands according to tradition. The Sabbath to Him was seemingly not a day of rest in observance of the day in the way they defined; rather it was a day that God brought many of His blessings onto people with whom Jesus interacted. Regardless, according to the Pharisees, this simply wasn't right. These and other "transgressions" in the eyes of the Pharisees made them question who Jesus really was and why He thought He could teach the ways of Yahweh. Didn't He know that by breaking the many laws He did that He was in league with the devil?

After one such interchange, Jesus spoke the words of Isaiah to them in Matthew 15:8-9:

"'This people honors me with their lips,

> *but their heart is far from me;*
> *in vain do they worship me,*
> *teaching as doctrines the commandments of men.'"*

In the context of the passage in Isaiah 29, Yahweh had spoken to the priests and prophets. He said that they were asleep to the things of the Lord (Isaiah 29:10), and that any wisdom or discernment they had would perish (Isaiah 29:15). The Lord criticized His people because they turned everything upside down by trying to appropriate the position of God - their Maker - when they should have been listening to Him and been obedient to His commands.

Jesus spoke this truth to the Pharisees. Their legalism had consumed them, causing their entire theology to be flipped around. For them it was what they said and did in observance to the Law that made them holy. But Jesus said those things defiled them (Matthew 15:11).

How dare Jesus say that! Such words offended them!

Then, Jesus laid it down as to what the Pharisees really were. They were blind guides who led their followers into a deep pit (Matthew 15:14)! In other words, the Pharisees were headed straight to hell, and all those who listened to and followed them were destined to join them there.

The point Jesus made was that it's from the heart of man where truth faith arises. People can follow laws and traditions, they can speak pretty words, but unless their hearts have been broken for God, and they've laid down the dos and don'ts of their religious ideals, they will never draw near to Him. The words such people speak ultimately betray them. What they say eventually reveals the true nature of who they are deep inside. Their lips speak of the sinful nature inherent within them.

And there is only one way out of this pit - only one way to escape the fires of hell. That is through a heartfelt love for the Lord, where we lay down our agendas, i.e. the ways of man, for the things of God. Jesus is that way. The Pharisees didn't get it. Neither do many in today's church.

Where is your heart? Are you holding onto this world and all its enticements? Or, have you given up your hold on this life by surrendering all of yourself to Jesus, just like Paul said in Philippians 1:21? The hard truth of truly being His is that:

"To live is Christ; to die is gain."

January 22: Exodus 2:3,10 - What Moses Represents

(Exodus 1-3; Matthew 15:21-39)

Certain incidents in the Bible often foreshadow other events yet to come. This idea comprises the concept of typology. Typology is a symbolic representation, usually showing something in the Old Testament in one manner to portray what will happen in the New Testament.

A familiar example of typology may be the Exodus of the Hebrew people from the fiery furnace of slavery in Egypt. That foreshadows how Christian believers will be delivered from the fires of hell through salvation in Jesus Christ.

In the account of Moses, typology comes into play as a foreshadowing of the pre-Tribulation Rapture. Throughout Scripture, there is abundant evidence of this eschatological (i.e. having to do with end-times) position, which is the Blessed Hope of the church (Titus 2:3).

The Hebrews multiplied greatly under the slavery they were forced into in Egypt following the death of Joseph when another Pharaoh came into power who saw them only as a threat. The description of this phenomenon is captured in Exodus 1:12:

"But the more they were oppressed, the more they multiplied and the more they spread abroad. And the Egyptians were in dread of the people of Israel."

This verse itself contains a typological foreshadowing of the future church. Under oppression and persecution, the church, usually in an underground capacity, typically thrives and grows immensely. We have only to understand what has happened in China for the last half century under Communist persecution to see this. There are believed to be more than 100 million believers in China because of the crackdown on Christianity by the atheist state. The truth about this is attributed to Tertullian in the saying: "The blood of the martyrs is the seed of the church."

Pharaoh decreed that all male Hebrew children should die. The midwives, fearing Yahweh more than man, lied (with God's approval!), and the babies lived. The next decree instructed that all male children should be drowned in the Nile. Opposing Pharaoh's will, one Israelite woman saved her child. Exodus 2:3 says:

"When she could hide him no longer, she took for him a basket made of bulrushes and daubed it with bitumen and pitch. She put the child in it and placed it among the reeds by the river bank."

That child was Moses, and the salvation given to him is similar to that of Noah's. Noah built an ark that he covered "inside and out with pitch" (Genesis 6:14). When God sent the flood to destroy mankind for the wickedness that had come upon the entire earth, the ark became the means of Noah's deliverance. He was kept safe from the wrath of God. In the same manner, Moses in his little ark basket was delivered safely from the hand of Pharaoh.

Moses was named for this incident, as Exodus 2:10 tells us:

"When the child grew older, she [the child's mother] brought him to Pharaoh's daughter, and he became her son. She named him Moses, "Because," she said, "I drew him out of the water.""

His name sounds like the Hebrew word for "draw out." In being drawn out of the waters to safety, Moses was spared from death, just as Noah was. In fact, water in the Bible is typically symbolic of chaos and death.

How does this foreshadow the pre-Tribulation Rapture? The Bible clearly shows that in the latter days lawlessness, deception, and darkness will overtake the earth. It will essentially become an anti-God wilderness; wilderness itself representing a chaotic place lacking God and haunted by demons. (Think Jesus in the wilderness being tempted by Satan in Matthew 4.)

Prior to the 7-year Tribulation, in which God pours out His wrath upon this unbelieving world, He will save His children. Great chaos is coming with death and destruction. God's purpose in the Tribulation is to punish all who have chosen to reject Him, while also making a way for the final salvation of men whose hearts can still be turned toward Him.

There is no place in this horrific event for believers who previously chose to give their allegiance to Jesus Christ. We are the Bride of Christ. Would a loving Bridegroom allow His Bride to experience God's wrath? Of course not!. In fact, as Paul tells us in 1 Thessalonians 1:9-10:

"For they themselves report concerning us the kind of reception we had among you, and how you turned to God from idols to serve the living and true God, and to wait for his Son from heaven, whom he raised from the dead, Jesus who delivers us from the wrath to come."

The key to our deliverance from this wrath is that we have repented from worshiping pagan gods and their idols. Our believing loyalty has turned to God alone. For that reason He mercifully grants us safety when Jesus comes in the clouds for us. He is the ark that keeps us from the waters of the deep and from the anarchy of the wilderness that will consume the world.

The Old Testament has much to teach us. God is the same yesterday, today, and forever (Hebrews 13:8). He shows us what has been and what is to come. His Word informs us and brings us comfort. He pours out His mercy toward those who honor and revere Him.

What a loving and mighty God He is! Thank you, Lord, for this great salvation.

January 23: Matthew 16:18 - The Gates of Hell

(Exodus 4-6; Matthew 16)

One of the most misunderstood verses in the Bible is Matthew 16:18 where Jesus, speaking to Peter and His disciples, says:

"And I tell you, you are Peter, and on this rock I will build my church, and the gates of hell shall not prevail against it."

Most of us are aware that the Catholic church has appropriated Jesus' Words to Peter. They have misinterpreted them and determined that the rock is Peter himself. In this delusion, they say that the church was built on and around him as the first pope and Christ's legitimate representative of God on earth. Catholicism has built a line of succession on this falsehood in which each new pope is the vicar of Christ, i.e. the earthly representation of Christ on earth. Thus, the Vatican argues that only the Catholic church is the one true church. All other churches are corrupted. Catholic encyclicals, i.e. doctrinal decrees, even curse those (as "anathema") who do not hold to the teachings of the Vatican. Thus, the Protestant Reformation begun by Martin Luther is considered in Catholicism as an aberration. Those who adhere to any Protestant denomination are wayward, and they must be brought back into the fold by renouncing the "lies" they've believed. This is the basis for the ecumenical movement that has been gathering momentum ever since the 1960s with the First and Second Vatican Councils.

What does this verse really mean?

The area of Caesarea Philippi is in the northeast part of Israel. The most prominent landmark of the region is Mount Hermon, which towers above everything else with its majestic snow capped peaks.

This is where correctly interpreting Scripture becomes very important. Mount Hermon is where it is believed that the rebellious sons of God (*bene Elohim*) descended from heaven to earth to procreate with human women as recounted in Genesis 6:1-4. Without that proper background, our understanding of Jesus's statement to Peter becomes flawed.

The foothills of Mount Hermon, in what was previously known as Bashan, were honored by the ancients because of the presence of the gods, i.e. God's sons who chose to disobey Him and decided to set themselves up as gods in His place. This was the original sin of Satan. It was subsequently repeated by other disobedient *bene Elohim* over the years.

The ruins of a temple to one of these gods is in this place. It is the temple of Banias, who we know better from Greek mythology as Pan. This was literally the entrance to the underworld; Hades in the New Testament, Sheol in the Old Testament - hell as we know it. Jesus stood at this place - on the rocks that comprise this temple. This was ground zero - the entrance to the demonic headquarters - the gates of hell.

In standing at this very place and making this declaration, Jesus was putting Satan and the entire demonic realm on notice. God was here on earth. He intended to take the fight against all evil and destroy it. The church as the aggressor would be God's instrument to wage war. Hell would not prevail. Through this proclamation, Jesus was telling all the forces of wickedness that their time was short.

One of the reasons Jesus came was to reclaim the nations. This was the beginning. The final battle - which won't actually be a battle at all - will be at the end of the 7-year Tribulation when Jesus returns in glory. At that time, He will subdue the nations and all demonic entities. He will destroy all unbelieving mankind with the sharp sword that comes from His mouth - the Word of God - and rule over the nations with a rod of iron (Revelation 19:15).

All may seem to be lost as we observe the world around us today. Do not fear. God is sovereign. He has everything under control. Jesus will return at just the right time. Our job - as the church - is to occupy until He comes. Let us strengthen our faith with the Word of God so that we can be salt and light to this lost and dying world.

January 24: Exodus 7:5,16 - The God of the Hebrews

(Exodus 7-8; Matthew 17)

The peoples of the earth served gods that were not the Lord God, Yahweh, the great I AM. Rather, their allegiance was to the sons of God (*bene Elohim*) who were over the nations. Following the Tower of Babel incident in Genesis 11, in which man was disobedient to God and did not go out into the world to be fruitful and multiply as He had instructed Noah and his descendants (Genesis 9:1,7), Yahweh came down in displeasure to scatter mankind throughout the earth and confuse his language. From this event God had finally tired of making himself known to all peoples and determined to raise up a single nation to be His own. To accomplish this, He did two things which are captured in Deuteronomy 32:8-9.

Note: to understand the Biblical narrative correctly, it's vital to read these verses in a translation that is true to the original text. Only the English Standard Version - ESV - uses the Dead Sea Scrolls for this passage - the gold standard for translation - and gives us the true meaning.

> *"When the Most High gave to the nations their inheritance,*
> *when he divided mankind,*
> *he fixed the borders of the peoples*
> *according to the number of the sons of God.*
> *But the Lord's portion is his people,*
> *Jacob his allotted heritage."*

In any other Bible except the ESV, the translators make *"sons of God"* into *"sons of Israel"* - NIV - or *"children of Israel"* - KJV. Reading these verses in this way causes the entire meaning to be lost and brings an incorrect understanding to the overall Biblical narrative.

What are these verses saying? When God scattered mankind, He placed people into various nations. At that time, He appointed His divine sons - the sons of God - *bene Elohim* - to superintend these nations for the purpose of their pointing the hearts of men toward Himself. Following this, He raised up Israel to be His people, i.e. His allotted heritage. (This occurs immediately after Babel in Genesis 12 when God calls Abram out of Ur.)

Why is a translation that says the sons or children of Israel were placed over the nations incorrect? Because God never placed Israel in that position to rule over nations! They had enough trouble ruling themselves according to

God's commands, let alone direct the course of other countries. God raised up Israel to be a blessing to nations, not to rule over them (Genesis 12:3; 28:14).

This rebellion among men brought another rebellion among God's heavenly host. Psalm 82 shows us God in His Divine Council - among the sons of God - angrily denouncing them for their disobedience. The sons He had placed over the nations had fallen and rebelled like their divine brothers had earlier in Genesis 6. In their disobedience, they set themselves up as gods in place of Yahweh. They received the worship of the nations when they should have deflected it toward God Most High. (For confirmation of this understanding, we have only to reflect on Daniel 10:13,20 in which the Prince of Persia and the Prince of Greece contend with the angel Gabriel as he tries to come to Daniel, but is delayed 21 days because of these evil spiritual rulers.)

All this is background for Moses' encounter with Pharaoh in Egypt. The primary wicked spiritual prince over a nation appoints a hierarchy in the divine realm to rule under him (think Ephesians 6:12). These demonic entities appear as many different gods. In Egypt there was the river god (of the Nile), a frog god, and a god of every other creature one can imagine. It was in this environment that the children of Israel had been steeped for 400 years. Pharaoh was the representative of the gods on earth in Egyptian thinking. It was against this understanding that Moses was contending. He had to convince Pharaoh that there was a God above all their other gods, the great I AM who was more powerful than any of the Egyptian deities.

Thus, we see in Exodus 7:5,16 the following:

"The Egyptians shall know that I am the Lord, when I stretch out my hand against Egypt and bring out the people of Israel from among them."

"And you shall say to him, 'The Lord, the God of the Hebrews, sent me to you, saying, "Let my people go, that they may serve me in the wilderness." But so far, you have not obeyed.'"

When God turned the Nile River into blood, caused the plagues of frogs, gnats, flies, etc., this action was a polemic, i.e. a hostile attack, on these false, pagan gods. Yahweh showed Himself as superior to them, and He wanted both the Egyptians and the children of Israel to know that there was no other God like Him.

Pharaoh and Egypt end up learning this the hard way. God's Chosen People have struggled with this concept for all of their existence. Today most people in the world choose any god but Jesus Christ. This choice has consequences. For Pharaoh, it meant his destruction. For Israel, it has meant millennia of alternating blessings and curses. For people today it means the difference between heaven and hell.

When we believe God's Word and trust in Jesus, our eternity is secure. Let us not follow any other god. Let us give our hearts to the Lord, the One true God!

January 25: Matthew 18:11 - Missing Verses

(Exodus 9-10; Matthew 18:1-20)

Depending on your Bible translation, you may have noticed that periodically throughout the New Testament there are seemingly missing verses. If you look more closely, you'll typically see that a footnote on the page says something like "some manuscripts add verse" so and so, and the verse is shown. This has caused a number of people through the years to view this situation with suspicion, even going so far as to accuse that these Bible translations without the verses as part of the main text are corrupted.

Is that the case? Is any translation that doesn't contain every verse that others have somehow tainted by a grand plot to deceive? The Gospel of Matthew has three such incidences of missing verses. Wikipedia lists sixteen such missing verses altogether in the New Testament plus a number of other partial subtractions.

The absent Matthew verses are:

Matthew 17:21
Matthew 18:11
Matthew 23:14

For today, let's just briefly discuss Matthew 18:11. Without that verse, the text in context of the ESV translation in Matthew 10-12 reads:

10 *"See that you do not despise one of these little ones. For I tell you that in heaven their angels always see the face of my Father who is in heaven.* **12** *What do you think? If a man has a hundred sheep, and one of them has gone astray, does he not leave the ninety-nine on the mountains and go in search of the one that went astray?"*

Conversely, the KJV shows:
10 *"Take heed that ye despise not one of these little ones; for I say unto you, That in heaven their angels do always behold the face of my Father which is in heaven.*
11 *"For the Son of man is come to save that which was lost.*
12 *"How think ye? if a man have an hundred sheep, and one of them be gone astray, doth he not leave the ninety and nine, and goeth into the mountains, and seeketh that which is gone astray?"*

The most infamous of the missing verses occurs in John 7:53-8:11. The note in many Bibles says "The earliest manuscripts do not include" these verses. What were some translation teams trying to hide?

Well...nothing.

The Bible is the most well documented of any ancient writing. There are thousands and thousands of complete or partial Scriptural manuscripts. In the early days, since the printing press wasn't invented until 1436, the Word of God spread by the laborious effort of scribes hand copying each and every word of all the books of the Bible. The New Testament gospels and epistles began in or were sent to one church where they were copied and sent on to another. The astounding fact of the matter is their consistency, which gives us the assurance that God's Word is true. There are minor copy errors, but nothing doctrinal that gives us pause. However, some of the scribes in the process viewed some passages and believed further explanation was necessary.

In the course of their copying effort, if a scribe wanted to add a little context to a passage, he would often add a margin note. Thus, for example in Matthew 18, because the scribe was apparently unsatisfied with how the text read, he would have written in the margin the additional words: *"For the Son of man is come to save that which was lost."*

Imagine how the copying process occurred. Let's say five scribes in different cities each received the same gospel. Their job was to copy it one or more times to send it on to the next city and perhaps another set of scribes. If one of the scribes looked at what became Matthew 18 and wanted further explanation in that one little section to pass on, he would have added off to the side in the margin those extra words that made him feel better.

The next or the next scribe down the line would have seen those words. At some point, one of the scribes would have decided to add them as an integral part of the text. From that addition, in this instance, verse 11 became the authorized and subsequent manuscript version in this particular copying stream. That's likely how the King James ended up with this verse, whereas other manuscripts didn't.

It can be useful to read different Bible translations. Some make certain passages easier to understand or, as we've been discussing, may add minor context. There's nothing sinister about this. For my part, I take the perspective that God allowed these differences to perpetuate. As long as a particular Bible translation isn't knowingly corrupted as some cults have done with their versions, I have no problem with or without the additions.

The important thing is that we actually read our Bible. God gave us His Word for a purpose, and that wasn't to sit on a shelf gathering dust. The Word of God - all of it, Old and New Testaments - gives us everything we need to live for and to serve the One who loves us beyond all measure and has given Himself for our redemption. Let us honor God by reading and studying His Word.

January 26: Exodus 12:12 - Judgments Upon the gods

(Exodus 11-12; Matthew 18:21-35)

In delivering His children from the fiery furnace of slavery in Egypt, God had very specific objectives to accomplish through the Exodus. The Egyptians served other gods. They did not know or worship Yahweh. The Hebrew people had lived in that environment for 430 years. In their verbal history, they knew of Yahweh, but had no personal revelation of Him. There are varying ideas as to how the 430 years is calculated and how many generations were involved in this timeframe, but the point is that God - the Great I AM - was likely not uppermost in their thoughts.

(Note: If you wish to investigate an interesting rabbit trail, the timeframe of the Exile and the number of generations is explored in these two links from Answers in Genesis and may surprise you - it certainly surprised me:

https://answersingenesis.org/bible-timeline/genealogy/the-amram-question/

https://answersingenesis.org/bible-questions/how-long-were-the-israelites-in-egypt/)

As a result of how the gods of Egypt were perceived by both the Egyptians and the Hebrew people, Yahweh needed to take drastic action to get their attention. The Egyptians placed their faith and trust in their many gods and had no idea there was One greater. The Hebrews probably didn't care much because of the burdens of slavery, having likely lost all hope in their heritage.

When Moses showed up proclaiming that Yahweh was greater, and demonstrating that fact, God indeed made these two groups realize that the Egyptian gods were worthless and without power or authority. Exodus 11:3 tells us:

"Moreover, the man Moses was very great in the land of Egypt, in the sight of Pharaoh's servants and in the sight of the people."

Of course, Moses' greatness was because of the God he represented.

But God had another purpose in mind in bringing the plagues and freeing His people. In the course of the Passover narrative, the Lord declares in Exodus 12:12:

"For I will pass through the land of Egypt that night, and I will strike all the firstborn in the land of Egypt, both man and beast; and on all the gods of Egypt I will execute judgments: I am the Lord."

God's intent was to execute judgments on all the gods of Egypt, showing definitively that He was Lord over them all. That had become very clear with every plague He sent that literally belittled the Egyptian gods. They could do nothing against the Lord, their creator. God glorified His Name. The pagan people of Egypt saw that as did the children of Israel.

Despite this, Pharaoh retained a hard and unrepentant heart. Because he wouldn't give glory to God, he and his nation suffered the consequences.

In this context, let's briefly explore Revelation 9:20, which occurs in the midst of the second set of God's plagues on earth during the Tribulation - the devastating Trumpet Judgments

"The rest of mankind, who were not killed by these plagues, did not repent of the works of their hands nor give up worshiping demons and idols of gold and silver and bronze and stone and wood, which cannot see or hear or walk..."

Notice the similarity with the outcome of the plagues in Egypt. God does everything He can to awaken mankind to the error of following other gods that have been spawned from the demonic realm. We know that during the Tribulation, many who did not believe in Jesus prior to its advent, and thus missed the Rapture, come to faith in Him during these awful seven years. But the cost is high. The vast majority of these newly minted Christians will lose their lives for their faith.

Because of their hard hearts and the cost of discipleship, most inhabitants of the earth will refuse God's merciful offer of eternal life with Him in favor of a brief reprieve from despair or death that the world seems to offer. People will continue following the gods of their imaginations, if not the gods that manifest during this time. Yet, none of these gods can save. Regardless, no one will repent. Their pagan ways will seem the more attractive choice. But, it will be to their eternal regret.

God makes a way for all people to know and follow Him. He does it through different means depending on our personal circumstances. If it was up to Him, He would not allow a single lost sheep to die in the wilderness. The sad truth is that it's up to each of us, and many people choose to reject God's merciful offer of redemption. For that choice, there are consequences.

As people of God, we know that because of the narrow gate, very few will enter into God's Kingdom. Yet, we are to do our part by telling others the Good News. Let us make sure we obey Jesus by following His command in Matthew 28:19-20:

"Go therefore and make disciples of all nations, baptizing them in the name of the Father and of the Son and of the Holy Spirit, teaching them to observe all that I have commanded you. And behold, I am with you always, to the end of the age."

When we do this, we can be assured that God will bless us just as the master did with his faithful servant in Matthew 25:23:

"His master said to him, 'Well done, good and faithful servant. You have been faithful over a little; I will set you over much. Enter into the joy of your master.'"

January 27: Exodus 13:9 - A Sign on Hand & Forehead

(Exodus 13-15; Matthew 19:1-15)

As Moses led the children of Israel out of Egypt, God communicated several key points He wanted them to recognize. They were to remember this day through the eating of unleavened bread and the consecration of their firstborn. God wanted them to know that He was bringing them into a land of His choosing through this Exodus, and during the journey they would face various foes. The promise, however, was their destination as a land of milk and honey, and of freedom. It would be good, but it would also be necessary in the future to tell their children so that they understood their heritage and destiny.

For their remembrance, God indicated that the Hebrews should do something as a physical sign. He told them in Exodus 13:9:

"And it shall be to you as a sign on your hand and as a memorial between your eyes, that the law of the Lord may be in your mouth. For with a strong hand the Lord has brought you out of Egypt."

He repeated that admonition in Exodus 13:16:

"It shall be as a mark on your hand or frontlets between your eyes, for by a strong hand the Lord brought us out of Egypt."

What was the point?

We see His purpose in the second half of each verse. The Israelites were to know that Yahweh delivered them. It was by His hand that they gained their freedom. None of the gods they had known in Egypt did this; the people hadn't done it under their own power. God wanted them to realize they were His, and His alone. Yahweh was the author of their freedom. Through this physical remembrance, they were to get their hearts right now and into the future, and in so doing, they were to worship and glorify the Lord of their salvation.

In the time of Jesus we see this practice having evolved into a religious, legal obligation among the observant Jews. In their times of prayer, they strapped phylacteries onto their foreheads and arms with portions of the Torah inside these little boxes as a reminder to keep the Law. Religious Jews have continued this custom to this day.

This sign on a Jew's hand or forehead tells him that he belongs to Yahweh. It reminds him of his redemption and who is his God.

In the Tribulation, Satan will use a similar device. The devil isn't particularly innovative. He likes to copy what God has previously done and twist its purposes. At the midpoint of the Tribulation, the false prophet will introduce the Mark of the Beast as a means to control the populace by causing people to worship the Antichrist. The Mark will be something that goes on the back of the hand or on the forehead. By taking the Mark, Antichrist will accomplish two objectives:

1. It will be a test of loyalty. Anyone who takes the Mark chooses Antichrist over Jesus Christ. Anyone who rejects Jesus and takes the Mark has declared that he follows Satan and worships only him.
2. By taking the Mark, the recipient gains access to the commercial system of buying and selling. Without the Mark, he is prevented from engaging in commerce of any sort. For anyone who has not determined to follow only Jesus, the temptation to take the Mark will be immense. Only by this sign will he be able to work, to feed his family, or to do anything in the society and culture of that day.

During this final period of human history, all mankind will have the opportunity to make a final, irrevocable choice. Will a person choose the temporary benefit by taking the Mark, thus enslaving himself to Satan then and forever? Or will he count the extreme cost of discipleship by refusing the Mark, and in so doing, rely only upon God and His mercy? More than that, a person doing this will be singled out, persecuted, and likely die.

God in His mercy will deliver all current true believers from this coming wrath through the Rapture of the church. Those who become followers of Christ during the Tribulation will find God's mercy and deliverance by demonstrating their believing loyalty to Him in saying no to Satan's enticing offer of the temporary pleasures of this world. By standing for God, these new believers will find eternal life.

How much easier we have it today! We must not let the cares of this world weigh us down. One of the joys we have is how easy it is for us to follow the Lord. In tomorrow's world of the 7-year Tribulation, it will be much more difficult.

We should tell everyone we meet how good God is. By their choosing His love and mercy today, He will keep them (and us!) from the hour of trial that is coming upon the whole earth.

January 28: Matthew 19:28 - Ruling & Judging

(Exodus 16-18; Matthew 19:16-30)

A time is coming when Jesus will sit on His throne in Jerusalem. The nations of the earth will no longer go their own way to follow any god but Him; the peoples throughout the world will bow down and worship the King of kings. Jesus will rule and reign, and He will bring peace. It will be a glorious time - one hard for us to imagine given the discord and chaos that surrounds everyday life of today. But, during the Millennial Kingdom, the 1,000 years when Christ is present here among us - truly Emmanuel, God with us - life will be much different.

The logistics of who rules over what is an interesting study. Where does Israel fit into this picture? How about Christ-followers? The Bible actually outlines all this for us.

In Matthew 19:28, we partly see how Israel will work. Jesus is speaking to His disciples about the Kingdom of Heaven:

"Jesus said to them, "Truly, I say to you, in the new world, when the Son of Man will sit on his glorious throne, you who have followed me will also sit on twelve thrones, judging the twelve tribes of Israel.""

First, we need to understand that aside from the 7-year Tribulation, believers from any era will not be spending much time in what we typically think of as heaven, i.e. a spiritual realm in the sky. The Millennial reign of Christ takes place on earth. For that period, we will not spend our time sitting on clouds, strumming our harps, and eating heavenly bon-bons. God will put us to useful, meaningful work!

Following the Millennium, God makes a new heaven and new earth, purging the old with fire to purify all that was. But, guess what? He makes a new earth for a purpose. Once all the old has passed away, we will inherit this new earth! We still won't be occupying "heaven" as passive beings. God has glorious plans for us during that future time and forever, and it will also involve purposeful work.

However, let's get back to the time Jesus sits on His throne in Jerusalem. In the above verse, Jesus told His disciples - whom He was with personally - that they will rule with Him in Israel. Not only that, but David will have a major role in ruling, just as Ezekiel 37:24 says:

"My servant David shall be king over them, and they shall all have one shepherd. They shall walk in my rules and be careful to obey my statutes."

How this will likely work is hierarchical rulership. Jesus reigns at the top of the hierarchy. He will rule the entire world. Psalm 2:6-8 speaks of this:

""As for me, I have set my King
  on Zion, my holy hill."
I will tell of the decree:
The Lord said to me, "You are my Son;
  today I have begotten you.
Ask of me, and I will make the nations your heritage,
  and the ends of the earth your possession."

Under Jesus, David will be king over Israel. Under David, Jesus' disciples from His incarnation on earth will administrate from their positions. It is also probable that the twelve patriarchs - the sons of Israel - will have ruling authority within this scheme.

This blueprint addresses Israel. What about the rest of the world?

Paul in 1 Corinthians 6:2-3 lays this out:

"Or do you not know that the saints will judge the world? And if the world is to be judged by you, are you incompetent to try trivial cases? Do you not know that we are to judge angels? How much more, then, matters pertaining to this life!"

Revelation 2:26-27 provides another look at this:

"The one who conquers and who keeps my works until the end, to him I will give authority over the nations, and he will rule them with a rod of iron, as when earthen pots are broken in pieces, even as I myself have received authority from my Father."

From these passages we understand that Gentile believers - those who have received their glorified bodies - will administer the affairs of the nations outside of Israel. No doubt we will be organized hierarchically for this according to our abilities.

We get one more glimpse of this from the time when Jethro, Moses' father-in-law visited him. Jethro saw how much work was necessary for Moses to judge the affairs of the Israelites. Prior to that, Jethro, a pagan Midian priest, had become a follower of Yahweh (Exodus 18:11-12). Perhaps God gave him a measure of wisdom for his conversion. He advises Moses on a better way to handle the issues of the people in Exodus 18:21-22:

"Moreover, look for able men from all the people, men who fear God, who are trustworthy and hate a bribe, and place such men over the people as chiefs of thousands, of hundreds, of fifties, and of tens. And let them judge the people at all times. Every great matter they shall bring to you, but any small matter they shall decide themselves. So it will be easier for you, and they will bear the burden with you."

This is likely a foreshadowing of the hierarchical arrangement for ruling in the future for both Israel and for us as we superintend the nations under Jesus' guidance.

God has much in store for those who love Him. He created us for a reason. If you think heaven will be boring; think again! A time of immense joy, peace, and purpose is coming. And we have the great privilege of participating alongside Jesus! Can you imagine?

January 29: Exodus 20:18-21 - Near or Far from God

(Exodus 19-21; Matthew 20:1-16)

As God was introducing Himself to the Israelites during the Exile through various encounters, in which Moses was the intermediary, an interesting dynamic comes into focus. The passage in Exodus 20:18-21 gives us an indication of this interplay:

"Now when all the people saw the thunder and the flashes of lightning and the sound of the trumpet and the mountain smoking, the people were afraid and trembled, and they stood far off and said to Moses, "You speak to us, and we will listen; but do not let God speak to us, lest we die." Moses said to the people, "Do not fear, for God has come to test you, that the fear of him may be before you, that you may not sin." The people stood far off, while Moses drew near to the thick darkness where God was."

The narrative likely isn't chronological. The events of this passage probably occurred prior to Moses going up on the mountain and receiving the Ten Commandments. God wanted the people to know of His might and power, and to impress upon them that He was God above every other god they knew. This display of thunder, lightning, and the shaking of the mountain would certainly have gotten their attention.

Moses warned them not to approach the mountain of God lest they die. These natural phenomena reinforced that command.

There are a couple of things happening here. God told the people not to approach Him because they would die. Why? Because they remained in a sinful condition. How could this be? They had washed their garments as an act of consecration (Exodus 19:10). Despite this, there appears to be an issue. God told Moses not to let the people break through to look at Him (Exodus 19:21). It's as though they'll try to get close so as to gawk at Him like He's an object of curiosity. If that's the case, they were treating Yahweh as any other god; they had no reverence or honor of Him.

With that mindset, their hearts weren't right. In that condition, the impure must be burned up by the pure. By coming into God's presence in the continuing filthy rags of their sin, it was an impossibility that they could live.

By controlling nature and displaying the physical effects that God did, it reminded the people of how small they were before Him, and it caused them to want nothing to do with His presence. They backed away and were more than happy to let Moses encounter God.

Thus, Moses went up onto the mountain. He remained forty days and was given the Ten Commandments. During this time, he surely enjoyed the presence of the Living God. However, the people, relieved at not having to face God, quickly forgot about Him. Off the hook, they will quickly revert to the pagan ways they learned in Egypt.

The moral of the story with the children of God is that when they were near to Him, they trembled. They were fearful because they surely knew they would die in their sin. As they drew away and God became distant, so did any faith they had. The farther from God they were, the easier it was for them to forget and direct their attention onto themselves and the things of the world.

Isn't this the same with Christians today? When we maintain a reverent fear of God by honoring Him through reading the Word daily, praying without ceasing, coming into His presence clothed in the righteousness of Christ, and by living in obedience to His commands, we have no need to be concerned. He assures us of His love through the favor of His blessings.

However, a Christian who ignores the things of God soon falls away. What is it that keeps him close? If Christ isn't at the center of his life, He's somewhere off to the side and certainly not near. When that happens, it's easy to slip into a life of sin, because justifying ungodly actions becomes easier. For this person, the voice of the Holy Spirit's counsel and guidance can no longer be heard; his own thoughts dominate, perhaps aided by the whisperings of Satan.

It's not easy to maintain the discipline necessary for our personal relationship with God to flourish. Yet, we must. Is Jesus simply another shiny object in our lives that grows dull? Or is He the reason we live?

January 30: Exodus 23:32-33 - The Snare of Other gods

(Exodus 22-24; Matthew 20:17-34)

From the very first when God called His children out of Egypt, the most important commandment He gave was that they should follow no other gods but Him. This was so important that Yahweh enshrined this ordinance as the first two of the Ten Commandments in Exodus 20:3-4:

"You shall have no other gods before me.

"You shall not make for yourself a carved image, or any likeness of anything that is in heaven above, or that is in the earth beneath, or that is in the water under the earth. You shall not bow down to them or serve them, for I the Lord your God am a jealous God, visiting the iniquity of the fathers on the children to the third and the fourth generation of those who hate me, but showing steadfast love to thousands of those who love me and keep my commandments."

In Egypt, the Israelites had lived for 430 years in the presence of a pagan people who worshiped the gods of creation but not the Creator God. Other than through verbal history, the Hebrews had no true understanding of who I AM was. As a result, the desire to worship these other gods was deeply ingrained in them. This is one reason Yahweh had to constantly remind them not to turn from Him.

Several verses in today's reading in a single chapter stress this very fact:

Exodus 23:13
"Pay attention to all that I have said to you, and make no mention of the names of other gods, nor let it be heard on your lips."

Exodus 23:23
"You shall not bow down to their gods nor serve them, nor do as they do, but you shall utterly overthrow them and break their pillars in pieces."

Exodus 23:32-33
"You shall make no covenant with them and their gods. They shall not dwell in your land, lest they make you sin against me; for if you serve their gods, it will surely be a snare to you."

We've spoken before as to who and what these pagan gods were and are, even today. They are the rebellious, fallen sons of God; highly placed spiritual beings in God's kingdom who became disobedient to Yahweh. Rather than direct humanity toward God as He had instructed them to do, they made the choice to reject Him and become gods in their own right in order to accept worship and gain authority over their own worldly territories. Just like Satan, they are divine entities with much power and influence. Is it any wonder that Yahweh commanded His people not to follow them?

Just from these above verses we can see some of what they entice men to do:

- Cause their names to be on men's lips
- Cause men to bow down to them
- Cause men to serve them
- Cause men to do as they do
- Cause men to sin against God
- Cause men to be entrapped in the snares they set

These gods cause men to turn from the Living God. This is an abomination to the Lord. When men follow these gods, Yahweh does everything possible in His great love to turn their hearts, because He knows the consequences to mankind for this false worship. God has made it very clear that He wants none to perish, but all to have eternal life with Him (2 Peter 3:9). Sadly, just as the spiritual sons of God had the free will choice to do as God said, so do all human beings. And many choose to follow any god but the One true God. This appears to be as deeply ingrained in us as it was for the Israelites.

The gods of yesteryear took the form of the day that was familiar to the people then. They took on the persona of the sun, moon, waters, frogs, snakes, you name it. These same gods today continue to use many of the same deceptions of the past, and more. As a result, we have Gaia and the worship of Mother Earth. The god of social justice is quite prominent. The god of so-called racial equity dominates. Of course, the same gods of the past of money, greed, power, and control, are ubiquitous. In the church, along with the social gospel, the god that advocates for ecumenism, i.e. unity among all religions, is highly popular. Legalism's god is always a favorite. In recent decades the gods of false doctrines, such that there is a new breed of apostles and prophets, has deceived many. These examples are just a few of the many gods rampant throughout culture, society, and in religious circles. If nothing else, the gods of the world are prolific and have seemingly endless ways to turn men's hearts toward evil.

Jesus came to set this right. He came to redeem sin, eliminate depravity, and reclaim the nations of the earth. The pagan gods are His target, and He will vanquish them.

In the meantime, the people of God - true Christ-followers - must refuse to be enticed by these impostors. We cannot be double-minded and think we can follow any of the world's gods along with God Most High. We cannot combine our worship by creating a syncretistic blend of Christ and other gods. Interfaith dialogue and similar efforts within the church are a snare.

God is jealous of us because He is for us. Only He can and will deliver us. Lord, help us to follow only You.

January 31: Exodus 25-26 - God's Mercy Seat

(Exodus 25-26; Matthew 21:1-22)

In reading detailed descriptions in the Bible, lists of laws, or genealogies, it's easy to be overwhelmed by the text. Often, people attempting to read their entire Bible get bogged down in these portions of Scripture and lose their resolve to remain faithful to God's Word. What I typically recommend for these passages initially is to quickly skim them and move on. Don't feel guilty; simply continue the next day: persevere. Through repeated readings of these parts of the Bible, there will come a time when God will reveal a deeper meaning when it's useful for you to know it.

The descriptions in the passages of today's reading can certainly cause one to question their intent in this noble effort of consuming all of God's Word. But, let's take a moment and see something more that we might have missed.

The description of the constructing of the Ark of the Covenant has much symbolism, which can help us to better understand God's character. The very name, the Ark of the Covenant is important. A covenant is a promise; in this case it is the testimony of God to His people. What is that testimony? It's shown in the context of the passage.

Inside the ark, the two tablets of the Law of Moses are placed. The Law is the testimony of God revealing His will to mankind as to right behavior before Him. It is His promise that if man follows God's Law, he will be in right relationship with Him.

Notice where the Mercy Seat is placed. It is placed above the Law. This is symbolic that God's mercy trumps the Law. Look at what it says in Micah 6:8:

> *"He has shown you, O man, what is good.*
>   *And what does the Lord require of you?*
> *To act justly and to love mercy*
>   *and to walk humbly with your God."*

John 15:12-13 puts this into concrete terms for us:

"This is my commandment, that you love one another as I have loved you. Greater love has no one than this, that someone lay down his life for his friends."

God's commandment - His Law - is actually one of love and mercy.

It is on the Mercy Seat that God Himself sits. At this seat of Mercy is where God meets us.

The cherubim are throne guardians. They likewise are a symbol of God's mercy. When Adam and Eve sinned, and God required them to leave the Garden of Eden, He placed cherubim before the entrance to keep them from returning. In their human, sinful condition, they could no longer come into God's presence without immediately dying. The cherubim mercifully kept them from making such a drastic error.

The gold that overlays everything represents God's purity and glory. It is symbolic of His refining fire. By going through that fire, man can be purified of his sin and once more come before God.

Note that the Ark resides in the Most Holy Place. It is only there that God resides. For us to meet Him there, we must be redeemed of our sinful nature and become holy ourselves.

How do we do this? How do we meet these criteria of following the Law and receiving His mercy?

For the ancient Israelites, it meant sacrificing animals and shedding their blood so that it might cover their iniquities. Hebrews 9:22 instructs us that:

"Indeed, under the law almost everything is purified with blood, and without the shedding of blood there is no forgiveness of sins."

Over the years, the Hebrew people killed a lot of animals to get temporarily right with God! But, then came Jesus.

Jesus became the sacrificial lamb who died once for all that our sins could be permanently removed. They weren't simply covered by His blood, through Jesus. When we believe in and trust Him, God removes and forgets our sins as far as the east is from the west (Psalm 103:12).

What a glorious, loving, and merciful God we serve!

Awaken

Lessons from Scripture

February

Reading Through the Bible in a Year

Old Testament: Exodus 27 - Numbers 25
New Testament: Matthew 21:23 - Mark 8:21

Reading Schedule for February

February 1 – February 29			
Feb 1	Ex 27-28, Matt 21:23-46	**Feb 16**	Lev 22-23, Mark 1:1-22
Feb 2	Ex 29-30, Matt 22:1-22	**Feb 17**	Lev 24-25, Mark 1:23-45
Feb 3	Ex 31-33, Matt 22:23-46	**Feb 18**	Lev 26-27, Mark 2
Feb 4	Ex 34-36, Matt 23:1-22	**Feb 19**	Num 1-2, Mark 3:1-21
Feb 5	Ex 37-38, Matt 23:23-39	**Feb 20**	Num 3-4, Mark 3:22-35
Feb 6	Ex 39-40, Matt 24:1-22	**Feb 21**	Num 5-6, Mark 4:1-20
Feb 7	Lev 1-3, Matt 24:23-51	**Feb 22**	Num 7, Mark 4:21-41
Feb 8	Lev 4-6, Matt 25:1-30	**Feb 23**	Num 8-10, Mark 5:1-20
Feb 9	Lev 7-9, Matt 25:31-46	**Feb 24**	Num 11-13, Mark 5:21-43
Feb 10	Lev 10-12, Matt 26:1-19	**Feb 25**	Num 14-15, Mark 6:1-32
Feb 11	Lev 13, Matt 26:20-54	**Feb 26**	Num 16-17, Mark 6:33-56
Feb 12	Lev 14, Matt 26:55-75	**Feb 27**	Num 18-20, Mark 7:1-13
Feb 13	Lev 15-17, Matt 27:1-31	**Feb 28**	Num 21-22, Mark 7:14-37
Feb 14	Lev 18-19, Matt 27:32-66	**Feb 29**	Num 23-25, Mark 8:1-21
Feb 15	Lev 20-21, Matt 28:1-20		

February 1: Matthew 21:33-46 – Parable of the Tenants

(Exodus 27-28; Matthew 21:33-46)

This parable is the story of Israel. God chose Israel to be His special inheritance (Deuteronomy 32:9). When mankind rebelled at the Tower of Babel and Yahweh scattered them into nations, He effectively divorced the majority of men for the time being in order to raise a nation loyal to Him. From that time, Israel was to be God's Chosen People; a light and blessing to the nations. They were to be the nation that lived for God and drew others back to Him.

As in the parable, the Lord – the master – built that vineyard of Israel. Throughout the years the Lord sent His servants for the harvest. As in the vineyard, the tenants – the people of Israel – killed and beat those servants, i.e. the many prophets that came in the Name of the Lord. Time and again the prophets came to warn, to bring correction, and to harvest Israel that she might receive the blessings of God. But, in the hardness of their hearts, the tenants – the people of Israel – determined that they knew a better way to their inheritance. Finally, when the master sent his son – when Yahweh sent Jesus – the tenants who the master had hoped to favor, i.e. the Jews and their religious leaders, killed the master's son. Israel rejected the Son of God and killed Him. That resulted in God's curse upon them.

When Jesus asked the chief priests and elders what the master of the vineyard would do in this situation, they answered correctly in Matthew 21:41:

They said to him, "He will put those wretches to a miserable death and let out the vineyard to other tenants who will give him the fruits in their seasons."

The wretches in this case were those very priests and elders. They pointed their index fingers at the faithless tenants, while at the same time their other three fingers were pointing back toward themselves.

Because of their cluelessness, Jesus had to make this clear to them. He did so in Matthew 21:43-44:

"Therefore I tell you, the kingdom of God will be taken away from you and given to a people producing its fruits. And the one who falls on this stone will be broken to pieces; and when it falls on anyone, it will crush him."

The prophecy proved true. Just as the Word of God the prophets had spoken to Israel time and again to warn them of their sins, yet proclaim the blessings that would someday come, so it was with Jesus' Words.

The people that produced the fruit in God's Kingdom were the Gentiles in the form of the church. During the Church Age from the time of Pentecost to now, Israel was literally destroyed as a nation. Yet because God is faithful, He is in the process of restoring her. That process of restoration began when Israel miraculously became a nation again on May 14, 1948. That also set the final days time clock ticking with its hands nearing midnight.

God has much to do to redeem the hearts of His people Israel. They are largely secular today, but that will change during the 7-year Tribulation. At the end of that period, they will finally turn to the One they pierced and proclaim Yeshua Jesus as Messiah Lord and Savior.

The Church Age is almost at its end. The church did as the Lord instructed in bringing many among the nations back to Him. Yet, the church itself has fallen into much apostasy in these end times. As has happened throughout Biblical history, there remains only a remnant of true believers.

Soon, God will turn His attention back to Israel. In so doing, He will remove those who currently love and follow Him. God's judgment is about to fall upon the earth to accomplish all that He has purposed for so long.

Thankfully, because of His great love, He will keep those who retain their believing loyalty in Him from the coming wrath as we learn in 1 Thessalonians 1:10:

*. . . and to wait for his Son from heaven, whom he raised from the dead, Jesus who delivers us from **the wrath to come**.*

Let us be sure that we are faithful to the very end.

February 2: Matthew 22:1-14 – Parable of the Wedding Feast

(Exodus 29-30; Matthew 22:1-22)

As was usually the case, when Jesus spoke to the crowds, the religious rulers were right there, listening, critically examining, and scheming how to use His Words against Him. The Pharisees and chief priests may not have understood all that Jesus implied in His parables, but they did get the point that He was often speaking about them in their relationship with God, and it was never good.

This parable describes the circumstances surrounding the Son of God during His marriage feast after consummation with His Bride – the church. Jesus came to the nation of Israel that Yahweh had chosen as His very own of all nations on the earth. The inhabitants of Israel were God's Chosen People, special and blessed, because of their unique status. But, as in the parable, when the feast was prepared and the guests invited, most ignored or rejected the invitation. The nation of Israel was largely indifferent to Jesus when He came to walk among them, and the primary offenders were the overtly religious. When Jesus pointed this out, the Pharisees realized they were the target, but in their hardened hearts, they couldn't find room for the truth of God.

Because of what Israel as a whole did to Jesus, the Father in His anger – just as the parable's king – destroyed those who didn't honor Him. In preparation for the feast, God sent His prophets and heralds, but few listened. As a result, He brought great destruction upon the land and punished His people for their blasphemous response to His righteous offer of goodness for them.

To compensate for the lack of guests that should have come from those who already lived in the kingdom, the king invited anyone and everyone who would come to the feast. Gentiles throughout the world were invited to join the kingdom in the form of those who would believe in Christ and be part of His church. They were given wedding garments, linen robes of righteousness, and welcomed as only a king could who graciously treated his honored guests.

Revelation 19:6-10 describes this amazing fulfillment of Jesus' parable:

Then I heard what seemed to be the voice of a great multitude, like the roar of many waters and like the sound of mighty peals of thunder, crying out,

"Hallelujah!
For the Lord our God
    the Almighty reigns.
Let us rejoice and exult
    and give him the glory,
for the marriage of the Lamb has come,
    and his Bride has made herself ready;
it was granted her to clothe herself
    with fine linen, bright and pure"—
for the fine linen is the righteous deeds of the saints.

And the angel said to me, "Write this: Blessed are those who are invited to the marriage supper of the Lamb." And he said to me, "These are the true words of God." Then I fell down at his feet to worship him, but he said to me, "You must not do that! I am a fellow servant with you and your brothers who hold to the testimony of Jesus. Worship God." For the testimony of Jesus is the spirit of prophecy.

This occurs at the very end of the Tribulation. The glorified saints who were Raptured and spent the last seven years in heaven in consummation of the marriage now accompany the bridegroom to the marriage feast arrayed in their fine linen, i.e. their wedding garments (Revelation 19:14). Jesus comes in His glory in the 2nd Coming with His Bride right behind Him. He wages war on those gathered on the plains of Armageddon who plan to destroy the holy city of Jerusalem. With simply a Word He destroys all who have opposed Him during this period.

Shortly after this, the great wedding feast will be given. To emphasize that this celebration is only for those who have believed in, trusted, and followed Jesus, i.e. those who have been washed in the Blood of the Lamb, the parable gives us one more detail. In Matthew 22:11-14, we see the following interchange and consequence:

"But when the king came in to look at the guests, he saw there a man who had no wedding garment. And he said to him, 'Friend, how did you get in here without a wedding garment?' And he was speechless. Then the king said to the attendants, 'Bind him hand and foot and cast him into the outer darkness. In that place there will be weeping and gnashing of teeth.' For many are called, but few are chosen."

All who will enter the kingdom of heaven must have a wedding garment. All must have come to Jesus, believing in Him as the way, truth, and life. None will sneak into the kingdom in their own righteousness; all must enter clothed in the garments of fine linen, i.e. the purity found only through the forgiveness of sins that Jesus alone provides.

The consequence for rejecting the kingdom that God offers everyone is the outer darkness described in the parable. It is a horrible place where all who reside will experience great remorse forever. When Satan is seized and bound for a thousand years in the deep pit (Revelation 20:2-3), the souls of the many unbelievers who died likewise inhabit this place for that entire time.

When Satan is released at the end of the Millennium to wage and lose his final war against God, all who have opposed Him will be resurrected to stand before the Lord at the Great White Throne Judgment (Revelation 20:11-15). Books are opened and deeds double-checked. All are judged and punished for their choice in life to reject the One who could have redeemed them. At that point, Satan and all sinful humanity are cast into the Lake of Fire for their fearful end.

Aren't you glad you've surrendered your life to Jesus?

February 3: Matthew 22:29-30 – The Nature of Angels

(Exodus 31-33; Matthew 22:23-46)

So, what is it? Do angels marry or not? In the verses we're discussing today, it would seem that they don't.

The Sadducees have confronted Jesus about the issue of marriage and divorce. These are the seemingly secular religious rulers, if we can call them that. They were part of the Jewish Sanhedrin along with the Pharisees, but they had a completely different orientation. The Pharisees were extremely religious and showed that through their adherence to the Law of Moses, such that they became extremely legalistic; they developed extensive rules and regulations to interpret what God had set forth for them. In contrast, the Sadducees took a more literal view of the Law and Scripture. If they didn't see something in God's Word, they didn't extrapolate a better understanding. For them, it was either there or it wasn't. The major area of disagreement between the Pharisees and Sadducees that the Gospels depict revolves around the afterlife. The Pharisees believed in the resurrection of the dead, whereas the Sadducees did not.

Jesus had to correct the Sadducees' misunderstanding of what happens after death. In fact, in Matthew 22:29-30, He accused them of not having any real grasp of the One they purported to follow:

But Jesus answered them, "You are wrong, because you know neither the Scriptures nor the power of God. For in the resurrection they neither marry nor are given in marriage, but are like angels in heaven."

Jesus was speaking about men and women who died knowing God, i.e. believers in Yahweh. Jesus declares that God is greater than they imagine, and the Sadducees haven't really studied the Scriptures as deeply as they say. Then, Jesus says that humans, who have been resurrected from the dead, will have the same characteristic as angels – **in heaven**. They won't marry: **in the spiritual realm**.

Why is this important? First, we need to clarify some terminology between the Old and New Testaments. OT Scripture shows us that there are numerous celestial beings called by various names. Among them are sons of God (*bene Elohim*), host of heaven, stars, cherubim, seraphim, and angels. In the NT, the term sons of God is applied exclusively to believers in Jesus Christ. Other than that, the primary spiritual entities discussed are angels. (Paul, in Ephesians

6:12, also references the demonic spiritual hierarchy we face.) It's not that the other inhabitants of heaven have gone away, it's almost as if the Gospel writers wanted to simplify their references. In addition, the concept of sons of God becomes critical in the NT, but that's a discussion for another day.

This issue of angels marrying is seemingly contradictory to what we previously saw in Genesis 6:1-4:

*When man began to multiply on the face of the land and daughters were born to them, the sons of God saw that the daughters of man were attractive. And they took as their wives any they chose. Then the Lord said, "My Spirit shall not abide in man forever, for he is flesh: his days shall be 120 years." The Nephilim were on the earth in those days, and also afterward, when the **sons of God** came in to the daughters of man and they bore children to them. These were the mighty men who were of old, the men of renown.*

Some Biblical scholars dispute that the sons of God in this passage are actually spiritual beings. They hold that this term applies to a Godly line of men marrying an ungodly line of women. That's not what the text says, and it's a badly mangled interpretation. The *bene Elohim* in these verses are indeed spiritual sons of God.

And that's the problem for some people. Didn't Jesus subsequently say: "*they [resurrected mankind] neither marry nor are given in marriage, but are like angels in heaven"?* Doesn't that definitively prove that spiritual beings can't procreate?

Well, no. The Genesis account says the sons of God, i.e. angels in NT terminology, took human wives who bore them children.

So, what is it? Can divine beings become like men and have sexual relations with women? That's where it becomes important to parse the text more closely. Jesus referred to the angels when they were **in heaven**, i.e. in the unseen realm. He said nothing about when they step away from their true home.

Look at Jude 6:

*And **the angels who did not stay within their own position of authority,** but **left their proper dwelling,** he has kept in eternal chains under gloomy darkness until the judgment of the great day—*

And 2 Peter 2:4:

For if God did not spare angels when they sinned, but cast them into hell and committed them to chains of gloomy darkness to be kept until the judgment;

The angels in this case were the *bene Elohim – the sons of God.* What did they do? They strayed from the spiritual realm and sinned. Sinned how? Read the rest of 2 Peter 2 and you'll see that their sin was of an abominable sexual nature. In fact, that sin was so great in God's eyes that He relegated these angels, i.e. His divine sons, to the lowest level of hell called Tartarus, until the final judgment.

Can there really be any other explanation for this punishment other than these spiritual beings had sexual relations with human women completely against God's command?

The nature of angels is that God has given them great powers and capabilities, yet they have boundaries beyond which they are not to transgress. Despite God's command in this regard, the Genesis account shows they rebelled against His explicit order. That sin resulted in such wickedness throughout the earth that God had no choice but to destroy all life on it except for the one righteous man Moses and his family.

As we draw near to the Tribulation, lawlessness is again rising mightily. Soon, a day will come when God pours out His wrath upon this rebellious unbelieving planet, once more destroying all who choose to follow their own ways rather than those of God. Disobedient sons of God – allies of Satan – will perform their evil deeds in greater measure to bring mankind with them into hell.

However, before this darkness descends completely, God will rescue those who trust and believe in His Son. Jesus will come for us in the clouds and take us to our true home – our heavenly home.

February 4: Exodus 35:30-31 – God-Given Skills

(Exodus 34-36; Matthew 23:1-22)

God gives to His people all that they need to serve Him well. In the account of the building of the tabernacle and its many accouterments, Yahweh singles out two men whom He has appointed to lead this effort. Earlier in Exodus 31:1-11 God first calls Bezelel and Oholiah. When He provides more details as to what He wants, God renews this call in Exodus 35:30-31:

Then Moses said to the people of Israel, "See, the Lord has called by name Bezalel the son of Uri, son of Hur, of the tribe of Judah; and he has filled him with the Spirit of God, with skill, with intelligence, with knowledge, and with all craftsmanship,

A couple verses later God also calls Oholiab by name.

Look at what the Lord has filled these men with in all the associated verses:

- The Spirit of the Lord
- Skill
- Intelligence
- Knowledge
- All craftsmanship
- Ability to devise artistic designs
- Ability to work in gold, silver, and bronze
- Ability to cut stones
- Ability to carve wood
- Ability to work in every skilled craft
- Ability to teach
- Ability to work as engraver, designer, and embroiderer
- Ability to do any work in construction of the sanctuary

These men knew all these trades because of what God gave them to serve in His Name. And these capabilities weren't given only to Bezelel and Oholiab. In their leading and teaching role, many other men contributed to the overall effort as we see in Exodus 35:10:

"Let every skillful craftsman among you come and make all that the Lord has commanded:

More than that, the women added much as Exodus 35:25-26 details:

And every skillful woman spun with her hands, and they all brought what they had spun in blue and purple and scarlet yarns and fine twined linen. All the women whose hearts stirred them to use their skill spun the goats' hair.

This was truly a team effort because everyone had something he or she could bring to the table in service to Yahweh.

Note that the Israelites could build and construct the tabernacle and all these items because of what they'd gotten coming out of Egypt. God had told them they would plunder the Egyptians (Exodus 3:22), and they did. Think about this. They were slaves and literally had nothing but the meager clothes on their backs. Look at all they are able to contribute to this building project. Exodus 36:6 tells us they brought so many contributions that they had to be told to stop because the craftsmen had too much!

So Moses gave command, and word was proclaimed throughout the camp, "Let no man or woman do anything more for the contribution for the sanctuary." So the people were restrained from bringing,

This gives us the principle that God supplies everything in this world. He owns the cattle on a thousand hills (Psalm 50:10). All that the Israelites had was given by the hand of God. So it is with us.

And so it is with our skills, craftsmanship, wisdom, knowledge, and understanding. All the abilities we have come from God. When our egos rise up, and we become arrogant in our ways because of what we think *we* have done, it's good to remember that we are not our own creator.

In addition, this example provides us background for what Paul detailed about the church as the Body of Christ in 1 Corinthians 12, specifically verse 14:

For the body does not consist of one member but of many.

That's the point about how God brings together those who serve Him into a functioning whole. The Israelites became such a body in their service to God, and so do we. That's why we can echo Paul's words in Romans 8:28 with confidence:

And we know that for those who love God all things work together for good, for those who are called according to his purpose.

February 5: Exodus 38:24 – Plunder & Miracles

(Exodus 37-38; Matthew 23:23-38)

Have you ever considered how much plunder the Israelites actually took from the Egyptians in their Exodus, and the implications of that?

God told Moses that the people would plunder their former captors, and they did so as we learn in Exodus 12:35-36:

The people of Israel had also done as Moses told them, for they had asked the Egyptians for silver and gold jewelry and for clothing. And the Lord had given the people favor in the sight of the Egyptians, so that they let them have what they asked. Thus they plundered the Egyptians.

In the next verse (Exodus 12:37), we're told the number of men who left Egypt was about 600,000. We're then given a more specific number in the text of 603,550 men in Exodus 38:26 and elsewhere. It has been said by many Bible scholars that this number likely equated to around 2 million people when wives and children were considered.

The building of the tabernacle, the ark, and all the other associated items took a lot of materials. In constructing the sanctuary alone, Exodus 38:24 says:

All the gold that was used for the work, in all the construction of the sanctuary, the gold from the offering, was twenty-nine talents and 730 shekels, by the shekel of the sanctuary.

A talent was about 75 pounds. Twenty-nine talents at 75 pounds is 2,175 pounds, or just over a ton of gold.

The amount of silver was greater at 100 talents (7,500 pounds, or over 3.5 tons), while bronze in this particular passage was 70 talents (5,250 pounds, a little over 2.5 tons).

These metals alone for this particular project weighed about 7 tons. Don't forget also the amount of other materials like fabrics, etc. that were needed.

The Israelites had a lot of stuff! They were greatly weighted down and had to transport it all. They did so in carts with oxen, slow-moving beasts at best. Their massive caravan would have been lucky to make 10 miles in a day.

In taking account of the huge number of people and the great quantities of plunder they brought with them, what did that really mean?

Let's think about it from the perspective of the Egyptian pursuit once Pharaoh came to his hard-hearted senses and decided to chase them down to destroy them. They had chariots and horses, which could move swiftly. We aren't told in the text how much of a headstart the Israelites had, but the implication is that it wasn't all that long. In addition, God had the Israelites go roundabout the long way before they reached the Red Sea (Exodus 13:17-18). In the natural, it seems reasonable to believe that the Egyptians could have and should have come upon them much sooner, perhaps somewhere in the wilderness.

But God...

Consider what God in Exodus 19:4 says:

You yourselves have seen what I did to the Egyptians, and how I bore you on eagles' wings and brought you to myself.

He bore them on eagles' wings.

Might this mean their Exodus was aided by a supernatural event even before the parting of the Red Sea?

During the Tribulation we see similar language. At the midpoint of the seven years, the Antichrist desecrates the temple. Israelites who have somehow heard the Words of Jesus in Matthew 24:18, "*then let those who are in Judea flee to the mountains,*" and heeded them, do so. Revelation 12:14 describes this:

But the woman was given the two wings of the great eagle so that she might fly from the serpent into the wilderness, to the place where she is to be nourished for a time, and times, and half a time.

The woman is Israel – the people who believe Jesus' warning. They flee from Jerusalem to, in all likelihood, the mountains of Petra in Jordan, a distance of about 100 miles. We don't know the numbers, but we do know that Antichrist wants them dead. He isn't going to let grass grow under his feet in pursuing them. Some of the women might be pregnant, winter might be upon them with impassable roads, it could be the Sabbath when all transportation is shut down in Israel.

Once again, in the natural, there may be great odds against the people making this journey safely.

But God...

What does the above verse say? The people in flight were given *"two wings of a great eagle."* Just like in the original Exodus, Israel was born away on eagles' wings. Is this also a supernatural event? Does God miraculously transport them to Petra as He possibly did for their journey to the Red Sea?

To use New Testament language, were the Israelites *translated* from one place to another in the past as they may likewise be in the future? Were they *Raptured* similar to how Philip was after encountering the Ethiopian eunuch (Acts 8:39-40)?

There are many supernatural aspects in Scripture that we pass by because we're not necessarily taught in church to think about the Bible in this way. However, when we begin to understand that God is actively at work on this earth among His people, we realize that He is in our midst; He surrounds and protects us with His presence.

February 6: Matthew 24:7 – Don't Be Deceived

(Exodus 39-40; Matthew 24:1-22)

The end of the age is coming. Jesus warned His disciples that this world as we know it has a finite life span. Unfortunately, through the years, Jesus' Words have been twisted and misunderstood. Among other disputes within the church that have arisen from this teaching is the timing of how all this will occur.

A large part of this problem of interpretation is sequencing. Bible prophecy often has a telescoping aspect. The far away seems near. Prophets saw the future as God intended, but they couldn't necessarily distinguish between what would happen sooner versus later. This resulted in dual fulfillment of some prophecies, and the mashing together of many events so that they all seemed to happen at the same time. This is the issue associated with Jesus' prophecies in Matthew 24.

How do we know this? First, in Matthew 24:4 (ESV), Jesus warns His disciples about one major principle after they've asked Him what the end will look like:

And Jesus answered them, "See that no one leads you astray."

The NIV and KJV translations use the word "deceive." Make sure you aren't deceived. That's the principle command beginning this passage of end-times events. If you're Jesus' disciple, you need to rightly divide the Word of God to get this right.

Jesus says that over the years false prophets will arise; wars; rumors of wars; nations fighting other nations; internal conflict within nations as factions, i.e. kingdoms, contest with one another, and a multitude of natural catastrophic events such as famines and earthquakes. These will all increase dramatically in latter days, but as with the labor of a woman soon to give birth, they are simply the signs of this impending event (Matthew 24:5-8).

We have seen all these signs ramp up since the beginning of the 20th Century. World War I followed by WWII, followed by the birth of Israel as a nation as a major milestone that initiated the Middle East conflicts; increasing civil unrest within nations, including America, beginning with the radical 1960s until today with such animosity between people of differing political, racial, and social beliefs that civil war seems imminent; multiplied natural disasters of unprecedented scope and of such intensity as has never before been experienced on earth. All these are but birth pains.

The next Word that Jesus says is critical: "Then." Matthew 24:8 records this:

"Then they will deliver you up to tribulation and put you to death, and you will be hated by all nations for my name's sake."

Websters Dictionary 1828 gives this second definition of the word "then": *Afterward; soon afterward or immediately.*

Thus, the various birth pains happen, and only then does the next event occur. Speaking of the church, Jesus tells us that "they" will deliver us up to tribulation and all nations will hate us because of the Name of Jesus. Who are "they"? Unbelievers to whom Christianity is a threat. What do true Christians do? They discern and perceive the truth. In this, they are not deceived as is the rest of the world. "They" cannot abide by this because it doesn't allow them to control Christ-followers as they can everyone else. This tribulation has been happening in the 10/40 Window for many years. I believe it must come to America for fulfillment of the prophecy.

Following this – let's call it for what it is – persecution, Jesus tells us the next sequence of events in Matthew 24:10-12:

"And then many will fall away and betray one another and hate one another. And many false prophets will arise and lead many astray. And because lawlessness will be increased, the love of many will grow cold."

"And then" indicates this comes after, or perhaps in the midst of, the tribulation of persecution. Who will fall away? One must be part of something to fall away from it. In this case, again, the church is the object from which people will turn away. Within the church, betrayals will occur. More and more false doctrines will be taught as so-called prophets tickle the ears of many.

We've already seen a great increase in lawlessness in just the last couple years. It is caused by those with hard hearts whose conscience has been seared and the truth is foreign to them. This results in growing coldness, indifference, and the lack of any kind of love for others. What has been visibly progressing to this point will grow more pronounced.

Have we seen the indicators of these things? Absolutely. Consider how churches have abandoned the Bible as the inerrant, infallible Word of God. The people in these churches believe anything because they've discarded the truth. All who embrace the falsehoods will turn against those who hold to true Biblical values. The wolves in sheep's clothing will act on behalf of the world – because they are of the world – and only a remnant of the true church will remain.

All this will continue up until the Rapture when Jesus snatches this remnant – His true Bride – away to deliver the unbelieving world up to God's wrath. During the Tribulation, a revival of belief in Christ will cause many to follow Him, contrary to all the suffering they will endure from those who hate Christ. This brings us to Matthew 24:13-14 in the timing sequence:

"But the one who endures to the end will be saved. And this gospel of the kingdom will be proclaimed throughout the whole world as a testimony to all nations, and then the end will come."

Those who come to faith during this awful period must endure. As they do, their perseverance of belief in Jesus will save them. As to the Gospel being preached throughout the world, God has it covered with the witnesses He brings forth, and even an angel proclaiming the Good News. All these things happen according to God's sequential timing; then the end comes with the return of Jesus in His Second Coming.

After warning of all these things that the His church will experience, Jesus turns His attention back to Israel and the events that will happen beginning at the midpoint of the Tribulation. Antichrist will desecrate the newly built temple, and those who have heard and believed Jesus' Words will flee to the stronghold of Petra, as the Great Tribulation of the second half of the 7-year horrors continue to befall the earth.

The chaos and violence are so immense during this time that humanity would completely destroy itself and the physical world without God's intervention. However, He brings an end and does so because of those who have come to faith in Him, and in order to save them for His future purposes.

It all makes sense when we get the timing right. Everything will occur in its proper order. Thank God He has given us this glimpse of things to come so that we can prepare; that we can brace ourselves in order to be a light to the world as we occupy until Jesus returns.

February 7: Matthew 24:44 – The Unexpected Hour

(Leviticus 1-3; Matthew 24:23-51)

One of the passages in Matthew 24 that has caused a differing of opinions revolves around what is headed in the ESV *"No One Knows That Day and Hour."* This section is where Jesus speaks about His return, but which return is it? There are those in the Bible prophecy community who believe that Jesus is referring to His 2nd Coming. Others – myself included – believe this pertains to the Rapture. Let's examine this a little more.

In our highlighted verse of Matthew 24:44, Jesus says the following:

"Therefore you also must be ready, for the Son of Man is coming at an hour you do not expect."

This statement is one of the keys to the timing, and we'll tackle it right away. We know the Tribulation is a 7-year period; some try to make it half that, but given the overwhelming textual evidence, that perspective doesn't hold up. The midpoint of the Tribulation at 1,260 days, or 42 months, is also well known. It is then that Antichrist desecrates the temple, marking the beginning of the Great Tribulation, which the world certainly experiences, but is aimed at Israel as God moves to bring His people to the realization that Jesus is their Messiah. Most everyone agrees that Jesus returns at the end of the Tribulation in glory to destroy the unbelieving hordes of nations that have gathered on the plains of Armageddon to attack Jerusalem, God's holy city. This is the point at which Jesus' Bride accompanies Him to earth to watch His astounding victory over all who hate Him.

My rhetorical question is: Does Jesus come on the concluding day of the Tribulation at an unknown time?

Sure, one could argue that no one knows the time of day, i.e. the exact hour, at which Jesus will appear, but will His return really be a surprise? Is it possible that some astute person, who has become a Christ-follower during these awful days of God's wrath, could calculate exactly the day Jesus returns? If I know the exact beginning of the Tribulation, i.e. at the signing of the Antichrist covenant, and I know the exact day in relation to that initial event at which Antichrist commits the abomination of desolation, could I not with great accuracy determine the date Jesus swoops down out of heaven causing all peoples on earth to mourn (Matthew 24:30)? If that's the case, how could Jesus in Matthew 24:36-51 be speaking of His final return?

On the other hand, why does it make perfect sense that Jesus' discussion revolves around the Rapture? Three brief points:

- Days of Noah
- Thief in the night
- Wicked servant

Days of Noah

It's true that the Tribulation will be a time of unprecedented wickedness beyond anything we can possibly imagine. The days of Noah were filled with depravity unlike anything the world had ever known. But, what about the timing? Those days were before God dealt with the pervasive evil that had consumed the earth. It was that very wickedness that caused God to act and bring the flood.

Those days before that catastrophic event were normal for the inhabitants of the world at that time. The people were doing everything that people do living their normal lives. In spite of Noah's preaching and warning that the end was nigh, the people in their self-centered absorption were oblivious. As far as they were concerned, nothing was drastically different from earlier times.

For those of you who watched the movie, *The Hunger Games,* think of life in the capitol. These were the elites who were pleased with what they had; they flaunted it and cared nothing for anyone else. Many have pointed out the comparison with the 2021 inauguration of Joe Biden in Washington, DC. Lady Gaga, who sang the National Anthem, perhaps quite purposefully with the outfit she wore, would have fit right into the crowd of elites in Panem, the capital of that fictional, dystopian nation portrayed in the movie.

We live in the days of Noah. God has to deal with the utter depravity in this world just as He did in the Genesis 6 account.

Thief in the Night

A thief comes when no one expects him. He'll typically come in the dead of night when everyone slumbers in deep sleep. If the homeowner – the master of the house – knows the thief is coming at a certain hour, would he not remain vigilant to deal with the intruder? If the time when Jesus comes in the power of heaven is easy to figure, how does that comport with the description of an unexpected intruder? Obviously, it doesn't.

As part of this description, Jesus talks about what happens with the people at the time He comes back. It's an unexpected event. Suddenly, one person disappears; another vanishes. Some Bible teachers have likened this to the harvest at the end of the age when the angels first reap the tares. Again, that makes no sense because of the unexpected nature of this situation. What occurs here is not known like the timing at the final reaping.

The Rapture is an imminent event. It will take the world by surprise. True Christians who are looking for it know that the timing is near, just as Jesus speaks earlier referring to the leaves of the fig tree (Matthew 24:32-33). When those leaves appear, summer is near. When all the events of which Jesus speaks occur, His return isn't far away.

Wicked servant

The faithful servant watches and waits for the return of his master when he's gone The wicked servant takes advantage of the master's absence to enjoy the privileges of his master's house. The faithful servant is the one the master will reward because he was diligent to obey all that he'd been commanded. The wicked servant, who, by the way, is a member of the master's household, is condemned for his waywardness.

What is the parallel to the church of being in the master's household? Faithful Christ-followers will do as Jesus commanded, i.e. to watch and be alert for His return. Believers who willfully ignore the warning to be ready at any time for Jesus' coming are actually characterized as wicked in this parable. Why? Because they've chosen to reject what Jesus commanded them to do.

The end result is shocking. When the master returns, the wicked servant is cast into a place of torment. What does this mean for a presumed Christian – a member of the master's household – who doesn't obey Jesus concerning His return? Perhaps it doesn't mean eternal damnation; perhaps as someone has suggested, it means he must endure some of the Tribulation. This is a controversial idea, but how else to explain the punishment the master metes out upon the wicked, unfaithful servant? This will be between that person and God to sort out.

In summary, this passage in Matthew cannot apply to anything but the Rapture. In examining the events portrayed in detail, it's plain to see that the timing simply doesn't work for it to be about Jesus' final 2nd Coming return.

Let us as faithful servants keep a sharp lookout; let us know the times by watching for the tender fig leaves, and our master – Jesus – will reward us.

February 8: Matthew 25:12,30 – Two More Rapture Warnings

(Leviticus 4-6; Matthew 25:1-30)

How anyone can read the New Testament and come away not seeing the many instances where the pre-Tribulation Rapture is discussed, nor the warnings associated with it, is beyond me. Today, I want to briefly illustrate two more instances that point to this blessed event, yet the dire outcome for those who don't believe in it.

In Matthew 25 Jesus brings us the Parable of the Ten Virgins and the Parable of the Talents. In these parables the pre-Trib Rapture is clearly in view.

The Parable of the Virgins has five foolish and five wise virgins. These are illustrative of ten people in the church, i.e. of Christianity as a whole. The five wise virgins have the oil of the Spirit, i.e. they are born again. The five foolish virgins are in the church but not saved. Anyone who professes to be a Christ-follower must receive the gift of the oil of the Holy Spirit living inside him to truly be a member of the Body of Christ, and one who will become a Bride of Christ.

When the bridegroom returned unexpectedly for his bride as the ancient Galilean custom required, his virgin fiancée had to be ready whenever he came. That time was determined by the bridegroom's father, so whenever he believed it was appropriate is when it happened. The Father will determine when Jesus returns. Remember, He said while on earth that He didn't know when that would be (Mark 13:32). For this imminent, unknown time, the Bride, the true church of Jesus Christ, must be ready. She must be alert and watchful.

A believer must be filled with the Holy Spirit, i.e. a real believer and not just a church attender. Jesus will return for those who are ready. For those foolish ones who have never come to know Jesus in Spirit and in truth, they will be shut out from the wedding. Jesus doesn't know them.

The warning to the church is that she must be occupying as Jesus has instructed, or she will lose the privilege of Him snatching His Bride up to heaven. As Jesus says in Matthew 25:13:

"Watch therefore, for you know neither the day or the hour."

The Parable of the Talents gives a similar admonition but puts it in more dire language. The master goes away and gives valuable items to his servants, i.e. members of his household. The two who have invested wisely are rewarded; the one with a warped understanding of his master, who squanders what he's been given, is punished.

When Jesus returns for His church, He will judge all who profess His Name. Some are truly His because they bear fruit, and through that, effectively prove they are saved. Others in the church will bear no fruit. They demonstrate their lack of salvation by the absence of fruit in their lives. They become poster children for James' discourse and as he concludes in James 2:26:

For as the body apart from the spirit is dead, so also faith apart from works is dead.

Dead faith is no faith at all. Jesus is certainly speaking in this parable about the Church Age – not the Tribulation. Thus, He's referring to our current times and the state of the church. There will be no church, per se, during the Tribulation. This is a pre-Tribulation Rapture discussion.

Anyone in the church who says he's a Christian, yet isn't actually born again – the proof of which is his absence of fruit – will have taken from him what little he has. He will not be Raptured despite his having been a church member. Attendance isn't enough. That doesn't prove saving faith. For that person who has chosen not to seek out the Lord in all His fullness, he will receive his just reward. The Master will return in Matthew 25:30:

"And cast the worthless servant into outer darkness. In that place there will weeping and gnashing of teeth."

Such is the fate of those who refuse the love of Christ and don't embrace all that He has for us. We, as true believers, have the task within the church to judge others (1 Corinthians 5:12). If they are found wanting, we must bring them correction through the truth. Perhaps some will be saved.

February 9: Matthew 25:40 – As You Did

(Leviticus 7-9; Matthew 25:31-46)

We know that from the time of Jesus, the only way to eternal life is through Him (John 3:16). Believers who have died and risen, and those alive and translated in the Rapture, will all be justified by grace through Jesus for their works in Christ at His mercy seat (Hebrews 9:5; Romans 3:24-25). Their sins have been covered; His righteousness has clothed them. They will not appear naked and without defense. Their Advocate on high will represent them and keep them from the judgment they deserve. It's an amazing promise that God has given us; it is our hope and confidence.

It's easy enough to conclude the fate of unbelievers from the time of Jesus onward. That's fairly simple. They either know Jesus as Savior and Lord or they don't. If not, their destiny is written: they will be cast into the Lake of Fire. But what about all the rest of the people in the world who died prior to Jesus' coming?

There is another judgment at the end of the age. Following the 1,000 years that Jesus reigns on the earth in the Millennial Kingdom, when that period comes to an end and Satan is thrown into that fiery lake for all eternity to join his henchmen – Antichrist and the False Prophet, whom God sent there after the Tribulation – the Great White Throne Judgment will determine who goes where forever and ever.

Jesus speaks of this when He describes the gathering of nations before Him once He has appeared in His 2nd Coming. All people great and small are resurrected to stand before Him. This is the point in time that every knee bows and every tongue confesses that Jesus is Lord (Philippians 2:10-11; Romans 14:11). In this assembly, He places the sheep on His right and the goats on His left (Matthew 25:33). The goats are surely those throughout the ages who have rejected God to one degree or another; perhaps through apathy, perhaps willfully and violently. But who are the sheep?

Revelation 20:10-12 describes this dreadful time:

Then I saw a great white throne and him who was seated on it. From his presence earth and sky fled away, and no place was found for them. And I saw the dead, great and small, standing before the throne, and books were opened. Then another book was opened, which is the book of life. And the dead were judged by what was written in the books, according to what they had done.

The books contain the life history of every individual from the very beginning. They describe every thought made and act done by those gathered before this throne of righteousness and purity. Among the books opened is the Book of Life. This is the book in which all being judged hope at that very instant that their names are written.

What is the criteria for this? Jesus spells them out by describing acts of kindness: giving food, drink, and clothing; by welcoming a stranger or visiting someone in prison. In this evaluation, there are those who did these things and may not have even recognized the righteousness of the act: "*Lord, when did we...?*" (Matthew 25:37) Jesus will say these Words of comfort and hope as Matthew 25:40 shows:

And the King will answer them, 'Truly, I say to you, as you did it to one of the least of these my brothers, you did it to me.'

It is to these that Jesus gives life.

In contrast will be those who had no part in the righteous acts described in these passages, and who will tremble at what is coming. Through hatred of God or purely self-interest, these lived in such a way that they rejected the One who created them and gave them blessings in their existence. They rejected God by refusing to seek Him out or even do acts of kindness. They were so self-absorbed, perhaps they didn't have a clue. To their question in this regard, Jesus gives them the death sentence in Matthew 25:45-46:

Then he will answer them, saying, 'Truly, I say to you, as you did not do it to one of the least of these, you did not do it to me.' And these will go away into eternal punishment, but the righteous into eternal life."

What is this death sentence? Revelation 20:15 makes the decree:

And if anyone's name was not found written in the book of life, he was thrown into the lake of fire.

That day is coming. Thankfully, God has made a way that we who believe in His Son will not face it. It's not clear where glorified believers are at that time – perhaps we'll be onlookers in the divine courtroom. What we do know for certain is that through the blood of the Lamb we have been redeemed and are saved from the fate of the wicked.

February 10: Matthew 26:8 – They Were Indignant

(Leviticus 10-12; Matthew 26:1-19)

On first reading, in suggesting the connection I propose in this commentary, you may say, "What?" But, hear me out. What if the original fall of the sons of God (*bene Elohim*) foreshadowed the indignation of the disciples when the woman anointed Jesus with oil, and the subsequent action by Judas?

The first rebel was Satan. Rebellion began in his heart sometime prior to when he tempted Adam and Eve in the Garden. First, why did he fall?

God created the heavenly host before the creation of the earth and all that is in it. How do we know? Consider Job 38:4-7 where the Lord questioned Job and his audacity in questioning Him:

> *"Where were you when I laid the foundation of the earth?*
> *Tell me, if you have understanding.*
> *Who determined its measurements—surely you know!*
> *Or who stretched the line upon it?*
> *On what were its bases sunk,*
> *or who laid its cornerstone,*
> *when the morning stars sang together*
> *and all the sons of God shouted for joy?"*

From this passage we see that God obviously created the divine beings in the heavens before the earth. Otherwise, how could they celebrate?

When God brought everything into existence on each day of creation, He said the result was good. However, in bringing forth man and all He invested into him, God said the outcome was very good (Genesis 1:31). For Satan to subsequently question God and His sovereignty in His decisions and attempt to undermine this, there was something about mankind that stuck in his craw.

We know later that Paul says in 1 Corinthians 6:3 that Christians in the eternal state will judge angels. This implies mankind in our glorified condition is above angels. This is likely the problem that Satan had. God had given him the knowledge that men would eventually have a higher ranking in the heavenlies than the various spiritual entities. No doubt it was this that rankled and caused Satan a bitterness of heart that morphed into the raging jealousy that caused him to act as he did.

Satan didn't stop with Adam and Eve. When that plan resulted in God's curse upon him in Genesis 3:15, he knew that one of their descendants was prophesied to destroy him. In his mind, the battle was engaged; the war begun.

There has to be an originating cause for the episode recounted in Genesis 6:1-4 when the sons of God came to earth, trespassing from their heavenly abode (Jude 6), to procreate with human women. The purpose was to pollute the human bloodline, i.e. to corrupt human DNA to such an extent that the Seed of the woman in Genesis 3:15 could not be born. In all likelihood, Satan stirred up the sons of God with his whisperings and gossip: "Do you see how beautiful those human women are? Why are men on earth the only ones to take pleasure in them? Yahweh has given us the means in our spiritual bodies to transform into human likeness; why not take advantage of it?"

Do you see it? Satan's indignation, and that which he stirred up in his divine brothers, was the basis for this attack on humanity, which has carried through to this day and will continue until the very end of Jesus' Millennial reign on earth.

Now, let's briefly consider the oil-anointing incident with Jesus. The Passover was at hand. Jesus and His disciples gathered at the house of Mary, Martha, and Lazarus in Bethany. The woman was Mary who poured the alabaster flask of very expensive perfume upon Jesus' head, as confirmed in John 12:3. And what was the response of the disciples? Here it is in Matthew 26:8:

And when the disciples saw it, they were indignant, saying, "Why this waste?

Who was the one disciple consumed with money? Judas, of course. Elsewhere, in John 12:6, the narrative tells us that Judas didn't really care about the poor because he stole their money for himself. Is it out of the realm of possibility that he often complained about this to the other disciples? Upon Mary showing her reverence for Jesus through this act with the oil, that was certainly too much for Judas. His greed and his murmurings were the originating cause of all the disciples being indignant at this "waste."

The value of Jesus and His being the Son of God was lost on Judas. His greed caused his indignation to overflow to those around him. Surely Jesus wasn't worth the amount lost by the squandering of the anointing oil! Just like men didn't have the value that God placed on them to make them above Satan and all others in heaven.

Judas was a product of Satan. It was Satan's character that he infused into Judas. Greed, jealousy, indignation: these all came together when Mary used the oil as she did. These deep-seated sinful elements that Satan had surely fostered in Judas for many years came together in such a way that he then betrayed Jesus. Just as Satan and the sons of God betrayed Yahweh.

Judas didn't guard his heart, nor were the disciples at that moment guarding theirs. Satan used their fleshly nature to further his agenda; that same flesh which will someday be transformed into a new and glorious body enabling us to be above the angels such that we will judge them.

Satan couldn't countenance that; yet it is his fate. What he attempted to thwart will come back upon him. What Satan has sown; he will reap.

February 11: Leviticus 13:2 – A Case of Leprous Disease

(Leviticus 13; Matthew 26:20-54)

From our western cultural perspective, it's difficult to read many passages in Leviticus and come away with much understanding. They apply to a time and place that is foreign to us. So, our eyes glaze over and we skim our daily reading, hoping the next day's chapter will pertain to us. Leprosy? Who gets that disease anymore? What is a leukoderma (Leviticus 13:39 – ESV)? What in the world is warp and woof?

If you're not a scholar and this isn't your field of specialization, it's probably not necessary to know the ins and outs of the various things we read in Leviticus. However, what may be useful is finding parallels in the descriptions of ancient customs to what we know today.

One such example – perhaps an imperfect one – is seeing what happened with someone who contracted, in the example of our text today, *a case of leprous disease* (Leviticus 13:2).

Some disease would afflict an Israelite, and he would go to the priest for diagnosis. The priest would examine his patient, since he was acting effectively as doctor in this instance, and pronounce his verdict and treatment. In Leviticus 13:4-6, we've got just such a description:

*"But if the spot is white in the skin of his body and appears no deeper than the skin, and the hair in it has not turned white, **the priest shall shut up the diseased person for seven days**. And the priest shall examine him on the seventh day, and if in his eyes the disease is checked and the disease has not spread in the skin, **then the priest shall shut him up for another seven days**. And the priest shall examine him again on the seventh day, and if the diseased area has faded and the disease has not spread in the skin, then the priest shall pronounce him clean; it is only an eruption. And he shall wash his clothes and be clean."*

Another subsequent situation occurs in Leviticus 13:45-46:

*"The leprous person who has the disease shall wear torn clothes and let the hair of his head hang loose, and he shall cover his upper lip and cry out, 'Unclean, unclean.' He shall remain unclean as long as he has the disease. He is unclean. **He shall live alone. His dwelling shall be outside the camp**."*

From these two sets of verses, let's strip away some of the specifics to look at the generality of what occurs. A person contracts an illness – an affliction – and he goes to the doctor. The physician examines him and concludes that his disease is infectious. Because of that, the patient should be isolated from others so as not to spread what he has. After seven days, the doctor looks at him again. Things are progressing, but in the interest of public safety, the patient remains away from others. However, the person with something more serious has to be removed from the general populace for an extended period. This results in him being quarantined.

You may be thinking, "This is all well and good, but so what?" How about if we change the time period and the affliction? Why not consider this from our perspective today with the very infectious Wuhan virus?

If our society had a normal approach to this, similar to what occurred with the ancient Israelites, or even up to the year 2019, the treatment for the virus would have been very different from what it's been. Think back to the old days when the flu was a thing. How would that be treated? The person would stay home, suffer his ordained number of days, and emerge back into society after that period.

And what about everyone else in this person's sphere or the region in which he lived? They would be unaffected; they would continue to live their lives.

But where are we today post 2019? Because of the fear, uncertainty, and doubt that has been generated by the political class, egged on by the politicized medical community, our approach to the Wuhan virus has been turned completely on its head.

Instead of the sick, or the potentially diseased, person staying home, or wearing a face mask if he must go out in public, it's all people who are told they must wear face coverings and/or be locked down!

I think a pretty good rule of thumb is that if a practice worked well Biblically, it'll probably work today. If what is mandated today is drastically different from what God previously directed, then the likelihood is that it's problematic. We surely see that today.

But, we know that times aren't normal. We are on a progression course heading toward the Tribulation. Because of that we've reached the stage where Isaiah 5:20 reflects everyday life:

Woe to those who call evil good
    and good evil,
who put darkness for light
    and light for darkness,
who put bitter for sweet
    and sweet for bitter!

Oh, yes, what about that leukoderma? Strong's Concordance says it's an eczema or a harmless eruption of the skin. As for warp and woof, that pertains to woven material and that which affects it on the inside or outside of a garment.

See, Leviticus is applicable for today

.

February 12: Matthew 26:59 – Seeking False Testimony

(Leviticus 14; Matthew 26:55-75)

Can you imagine the animosity the religious leaders had against Jesus? One could definitively say that His Words certainly didn't tickle their itching ears. Quite the opposite. Every Word Jesus uttered must have grated on them and aroused their sensibilities against Him. To relate these hateful thoughts and feelings to current events, think about how the Left reacted to Donald Trump. Not even getting political, consider Trump Derangement Syndrome (TDS). Every person, Left and supposedly Right, who opposed him, seemingly went over the edge to such an extent that literally everything that happened in America and around the world was Trump's fault. The hatred was so deep it was truly irrational. To that end, the life's purpose of these people was to criticize, judge, and punish Trump and his supporters – to destroy them completely.

Now take this image and apply it to how the Pharisees, chief priests, scribes, and elders plotted and schemed to do away with Jesus. Their existence was consumed with planning how to destroy Him. How many times do we read in the Gospels where Jesus speaks and acts, and these religious leaders go away seeking to arrest Him (e.g. Matthew 21:46)? How consumed with their anti-God fervor they must have been! Their hard hearts were like that of Pharaoh with the Israelites. Each instance of God's hand moving brought greater hardening.

After the Passover meal and Judas' betrayal, Jesus was brought before Caiaphas the high priest as Peter watched. Now think about this. Jesus is standing before the Sanhedrin, the religious council comprised of Pharisees and Sadducees. These men studied the Law. They knew the Law of Moses inside and out. Of course, this was also the same group against which Jesus had pronounced the seven woes, calling them hypocrites, blind guides, whitewashed tombs, and a brood of vipers (Matthew 23). Maybe they weren't so Godly after all.

To that end, consider what they did as Jesus stood in their midst, as reported in Matthew 26:59:

Now the chief priests and the whole council were seeking false testimony against Jesus that they might put him to death,

In contrast, what did the ninth of the Ten Commandments say (Exodus 20:16), the Law they said they followed above all else?

You shall not bear false witness against your neighbor.

No wonder Jesus called them hypocrites. These men encouraged others to bring lying testimony against Jesus.

Such actions have consequences. Jesus concluded the woes He spoke over the religious leaders in Matthew 23:35 with these Words: *"... so that on you may come all the righteous blood shed on earth..."*

All people who have ever lived and those still to come have this death sentence upon them. We may think the Pharisees and their ilk, or the haters today with TDS, are the worst people in the world. Unfortunately, it is ALL who reject the Word of God and choose to deny Jesus Christ as Lord and Savior. The blood shed upon the ground of this earth cries out for vengeance. Thankfully, there is mercy. But it is only found in the Person of Jesus.

February 13: Leviticus 16:8 – For Azazel

(Leviticus 15-17; Matthew 27:1-31)

For those of you who read Leviticus closely, you may have wondered about the passage we'll discuss today. Leviticus 16:8 (ESV) reports the Lord commanding Moses:

And Aaron shall cast lots over the two goats, one lot for the Lord and the other lot for Azazel.

"But wait," you say, "my Bible (i.e. NIV, KJV, etc.) says the other lot is for the **scapegoat**. What's this Azazel?" This is exactly the problem. As I've indicated elsewhere, some Bible translations unfortunately obscure a deeper meaning in the original Hebrew text.

When we look at Merriam-Webster's Dictionary, these two definitions are given for scapegoat:

. . . a male goat upon whose head are symbolically placed the sins of the people after which he is sent into the wilderness in the biblical ceremony for Yom Kippur . . . one that bears the blame for others

This provides some reasoning behind the ceremony, but not enough. This goat is sent to the desert bearing the sins of Israel. The Strong's Concordance for scapegoat (#5799) leads us to the Brown-Driver-Briggs Lexicon (a.k.a. BDB, which is a standard reference for Biblical Hebrew and Aramaic). Looking deeply into the word scapegoat in this manner, we see that BDB gives us these interesting tidbits:

- "proper name of spirit haunting desert"
- "a fallen angel"

Here's where it gets quite interesting. Leviticus 16:20-22 and Leviticus 16:26 give us this description:

"And when he has made an end of atoning for the Holy Place and the tent of meeting and the altar, he shall present the live goat. And Aaron shall lay both his hands on the head of the live goat, and confess over it all the iniquities of the people of Israel, and all their transgressions, all their sins. And he shall put them on the head of the goat and send it away into the wilderness by the hand of a man who is in readiness. The goat shall bear all their iniquities on itself to a remote

*area, and he shall let the goat go free in the wilderness... And he who lets the goat go to **Azazel** shall wash his clothes and bathe his body in water, and afterward he may come into the camp."*

Again, we see, this animal is for a scapegoat, i.e. for Azazel, in order to remove the sins of the people.

The ancient Israelite understanding brings this into focus. The goat is given over to Azazel; it is banished to the realm outside of Israel. Azazel is actually a proper name. He is a demonic entity who inhabits the wilderness to which the goat is sent. The context for this is one of realm distinction, i.e. cosmic geography. The wilderness is a place of chaos; it is an anti-God realm outside of where Yahweh dwells. It is the territory of demons; more specifically, it's where Azazel lives. He controls that which occurs there.

What is the nature of the wilderness and this place that Azazel inhabits? Sin. Anyone or anything that opposes God has a sin nature. Where does sin belong? Away from those who believe in and trust the God of the Bible. Thus, sin belongs outside the camp. As such, sin must be relegated to the territory of the demonic realm. It must be sent to where it belongs. Sin's owner is Azazel. He is the scapegoat; it is to him that the sins of the people – that have been placed on the head of the goat by the priest – are given.

It's important to note that these sins and this goat are not given to Azazel as an offering of worship. They are banished away from God's people. One of the great misunderstandings of the Israelites in exiting Egypt was of the gods of that land versus the One true God. The Israelites had spent 400 years steeped in a pagan multi-god culture. They had participated in various rites of sacrifice to these gods that Yahweh had to correct (see Leviticus 17:5). Thus God told them definitively in Leviticus 17:7:

"So they shall no more sacrifice their sacrifices to goat demons, after whom they whore. This shall be a statute forever for them throughout their generations."

So it is with us today. We may not necessarily pursue goat demons, but any god that isn't God Most High, Jesus Christ, is on a par with them. The gods of money, sex, power, or any other are simply today's manifestations of goat demons and thousands of other gods. We are to worship and bring our sacrifices to the Creator of all, not to anything that He has made. What are these sacrifices? Paul in Romans 12:1 lays it out:

I appeal to you therefore, brothers, by the mercies of God, to present your bodies as a living sacrifice, holy and acceptable to God, which is your spiritual worship.

We are the sacrifices. It was for us that Jesus became the scapegoat. Our sins no longer must be sent outside the camp in a yearly ritual. Jesus took all our sins upon Himself once for all. We are to honor and revere Him in our bodies and through everything we do.

He is worth it.

February 14: Leviticus 18:22 – Abomination

(Leviticus 18-19; Matthew 27:32-86)

In this day and age, this essay cannot be written and the words spoken, otherwise, the wrath of the woke crowd is aroused. Too bad. Let's talk about what the Bible says about depravity.

Leviticus 18 is a forbidden chapter by anyone who desires to live according to the gospel of self and not the Word of God. The practices spoken of here are either perverted or ignored. After all, according to the cognoscenti of today, i.e. those who are the smartest and most informed people on the planet, the Bible is either a dead letter that has no relevance to our enlightened times, or like the Constitution, a living document that must be adapted to the cultural mores of our society. I'm not sure how they can have it both ways, but pretzels probably aren't aware of how they're twisted into shape either.

This chapter outlines God's prohibitions against sexual practices that rise as such a stench in His nostrils that they literally make Him sick. Depravity seems like too tame a word. Here is what Websters says as a definition of depravity: "the quality or state of being corrupt, evil, or perverted." It pertains to all that and more in the eyes of God.

We'll take a moment and point out some verses in which God declared such perversions should not be done.

Leviticus 18:21
"You shall not give any of your children to offer them to Molech, and so profane the name of your God: I am the Lord."

The sacrifice of children to pagan gods debased the value of life that God created. Any people in ancient days, whether in pagan lands or Israelite, who committed such an act aroused God's great wrath. This sacrifice to Molech has carried forward to today through the abortion of unwanted children. These children are mercilessly killed on the altar of self – "my body, my choice." No, it's not your body. It belongs to God, as does that life within your womb. America has sacrificed over 60 million children to this god of convenience. We have shed the blood of the innocent, and it cries out for vengeance.

Leviticus 18:22
"You shall not lie with a male as with a woman; it is an abomination."

God does not change. He is the same yesterday, today, and forever. There are civil laws that pertained only to Israel in the Old Testament, but God's moral laws were not only for then. They remain in effect. Let's be clear: God considers homosexuality an abomination. There are no loopholes, and no homosexuality advocates who can alter that despite their warped logic. America has bowed its knee to the LGBT god; we worship this foreign entity with pomp and fervor, even having gone so far during the Obama Administration as to light up the White House in rainbow colors, mocking God in the process of celebrating homosexuality as the law of the land. The powers that be at the highest levels of government have made the definitive statement that we are no longer a Christian nation. God will not allow this to stand.

Leviticus 18:23
"And you shall not lie with any animal and so make yourself unclean with it, neither shall any woman give herself to an animal to lie with it: it is perversion."

Bestiality has always been an underground practice, but make no mistake, it has been present since the beginning and will gain favor as we near the Tribulation. It is the height of perversion, which makes it all the more attractive to those who hate God. Sex is their god. Any way they can attain it, either with another human or via intercourse with an animal, they will do so, and in the process spit in God's eye. As this practice increases in popularity, and probably becomes legal, it simply adds to the iniquities that God is surely recording as the final justification to punish America in its wickedness.

And how will God deal with this evil? As He did with every other nation on earth and the people of Israel. He spells it out in Leviticus 18:24-25:

"Do not make yourselves unclean by any of these things, for by all these the nations I am driving out before you have become unclean, and the land became unclean, so that I punished its iniquity, and the land vomited out its inhabitants."

America is already under this curse. We have transgressed the boundaries of decent conduct that God expects for humanity. Depravity has overtaken the moral fiber of the inhabitants of this country. We have become degraded in our thinking, and the hearts of the populace are exceedingly evil – led into this state by the very people who should have guided this nation in a Godly manner. These individuals – the highest officials in government, even many religious leaders – have taken us to the very edge of the cliff. One little push, and America, which has already embraced every sin and depraved act possible, will fall to its death. Whatever this looks like in America, God will vomit us out of the land.

The only way for anyone to escape the destruction that comes with God's wrath poured out upon an unbelieving, trespassing people, is belief and trust in Jesus Christ. He is the way, the truth, and the life. Every other path, including and especially committing these perverted sexual practices, leads to death.

February 15: Leviticus 20:26 – Holy To the Lord

(Leviticus 20-21; Matthew 28)

One of the commands that God has consistently given to His people, whether Israelites or Christ-followers, is for us to remain apart from those who are unbelievers. This command is captured in Leviticus 20:26 where Yahweh instructs:

"You shall be holy to me, for I the Lord am holy and have separated you from the peoples, that you should be mine."

What's the big deal with this? Why is it so important?

This separation is known as consecration, or the act of making something sacred. How is it sacred that we stay apart from others?

What we must understand is the nature of those who don't follow the Lord. You've likely heard it said that there are two types of people in the world: 1) those who believe in God, and who because of their faith in Christ, will spend eternity with Him, and 2) those who don't believe in or who reject God through His Son, and who will spend eternity in hell in torment. That's a huge distinction!

Why will people in the second category face such a fate? It really goes back to mankind's choice over many years, in more situations than can be recounted, to worship any god but the One true God. Adam and Eve's original rejection of God's sovereignty was the beginning. It continued through the Genesis 6 rebellion of God's divine sons and their procreation with human women, whereby all humanity became so wicked – so anti-God – that Yahweh literally had no option but to destroy all flesh. This mutiny against God and His decrees exploded worldwide following the Tower of Babel incident. God placed His faithful sons from the spiritual realm over the nations to superintend them and point men back to Him while He raised up Israel to be a light to those nations (Deuteronomy 32:8-9 – ESV; note: you won't understand this if you read these verses in any other Bible translation because they get it wrong). Astoundingly, somehow, for some reason, ALL these princes – these holy sons of God – turned from Him. They appropriated that which wasn't theirs, i.e. the worship of the people of the nations, and corrupted mankind. We see this clearly in Psalm 82, where God in His Divine Council, i.e. the assembly of all His children in the heavenlies, excoriates these rebellious sons and sentences them to death like any mere human. For any being, spiritual or human, to receive praise, glory, and worship that belongs to Yahweh alone, is an abomination and worthy of their divine demise.

The issue here is that the peoples in these nations, ruled by these so-called gods, have learned and taken to heart the lessons from these rebellious entities. They have mastered the false concept that Yahweh is not God Most High (e.g. in Israel), or that He is only one of many gods (e.g. in Hinduism), or that He is the insubordinate one who opposed the enlightenment that Lucifer brought (e.g. in Gnosticism), or that creation rules since all beings are god (e.g. in Gaia worship). In all these religious expressions, men lift up the god in which they believe and perform rites and sacrifices to it for a variety of reasons.

What's even worse is that these exercises of false worship are contagious. They suck others in who then turn away from the truth. Through these various religions, the God of the Bible is spurned and mocked. The ancient Israelites and Christians over the years have been deceived by these gods, with many becoming double-minded and/or syncretistic in their beliefs. Being in the presence of these false gods and their followers for any length of time has been a deadly disease for all but those with the most stout-hearted faith in Christ and the believing loyalty to Him that cannot be swayed. Unfortunately, people like this are all too few.

Thus, God says to remain apart from these who dishonor Him. Holiness in His Name can only be achieved in an environment that doesn't influence and attempt to make believers in Yahweh followers in anything but Him.

Our hearts must be for Jesus and Him alone. He alone is holy. The way, truth, and life that come from Jesus show up all pretenders to His throne as worthless. Tragically, there's something about the glittery baubles associated with false gods and those who worship them that mesmerizes and attracts.

Let us reject all that attempts to draw our hearts away from our Savior and Lord. In order to achieve that, we must be consecrated and set apart, holy only unto God.

February 16: Mark 1:4 – Baptism of Repentance

(Leviticus 22-23; Mark 1:1-22)

Do you know what has largely been lost in these ending days of the Church Age? Do you understand why so many are falling away and churches becoming apostate? There's a very simple answer.

One message was preached from the beginning of the Gospels that was a necessary requirement for entering the Kingdom of Heaven. John the Baptist spoke it first as we see in the very opening verses of our reading today in Mark 1:4:

John appeared, baptizing in the wilderness and proclaiming a baptism of repentance for the forgiveness of sins.

John proclaimed *a baptism of repentance.* Why would he do that? As the rest of the verse says: *for the forgiveness of sins.*

Why is forgiveness of sins important?

God in His mercy has granted to those with eyes to see and ears to hear the keys to His kingdom. Can anyone who is prideful or arrogant enter its gates? No. All who come to Him must be as little children.

Assuming a child has not been corrupted by those around him – unfortunately, a very real possibility these days – that child isn't full of self. He isn't prideful. He may be willful, e.g. "That toy is mine!" but he isn't demanding because his ego is puffed up. He may have a sense of entitlement and attachment to something, but his character is sufficiently soft and malleable, and his heart not hard, so that he's open to correction and instruction, i.e. he's teachable.

This is what Jesus said that all who come to Him must be like. There is a humility in the innocence of children. That is our template. We must be humble.

In our humility, we can more easily recognize our sinful nature. As we realize this, we see that we can do nothing about it. Our sins are beyond our own capabilities of redeeming. With that understanding we can humbly come to our Savior in our sinful condition and ask for Him to forgive us. And the amazing thing is that He loves us so much that He willingly grants us forgiveness and opens the gates of heaven when we place our faith and trust in Jesus.

John the Baptist wasn't the only one bringing this message. It is consistent throughout the New Testament. We see several verses later in Mark 1:14-15 the very first message that Jesus preached:

Now after John was arrested, Jesus came into Galilee, proclaiming the gospel of God, and saying, "The time is fulfilled, and the kingdom of God is at hand; repent and believe in the gospel."

Jesus told those listening that they must repent in order to enter God's kingdom. Repentance was message number one.

The apostles also made repentance a priority. Here is Paul in Acts 17:30-31 speaking to the men of Greece on Mars Hill:

"The times of ignorance God overlooked, but now he commands all people everywhere to repent, because he has fixed a day on which he will judge the world in righteousness by a man whom he has appointed; and of this he has given assurance to all by raising him from the dead."

When the apostles gathered in Jerusalem for Pentecost and the Holy Spirit came upon them, Peter stood up before the crowd and preached the message that God gave him. Acts 2: 38 records his words to those who would become the planters of churches throughout the region:

And Peter said to them, "Repent and be baptized every one of you in the name of Jesus Christ for the forgiveness of your sins, and you will receive the gift of the Holy Spirit."

It's well known that when something is repeated in Scripture, its emphasis is to highlight an important concept. Repentance in this case is that vital ingredient to our relationship with God that is a bottom line necessity. Without repentance there is no forgiveness of sins. The Bible is replete with passages showing us this critical aspect for Jesus to accept us as His own.

This is the problem among so-called believers today. They claim the Name of Christ because they've prayed the salvation prayer, but they've never repented. They've come to the foot of the cross thinking they can continue living life on their terms. God says otherwise. His requirement is first and foremost that all who come to Him repent. Only then can He complete the work of salvation in them.

How do these people approach Christ in this unrepentant condition and believe all is good between them and God? The church first and foremost must preach the truth of the need for repentance. If it doesn't, it will be filled with those who think they're saved but are actually still unbelievers.

Sadly, this is what we see. Every gospel but the true one is preached, from social justice to hyper-grace to even one that emphasizes distinction between races. How can this be? Repentance is a forgotten word. Sin is a foreign concept. Pagans fill the pews.

Jesus said this would happen in the last days. We are surely there. For those of us who truly love the Lord, let us remain humble and repentant in our relationship with Him. That is the way to everlasting life.

February 17: Mark 1:34 – Demonic Origins

(Leviticus 24-25; Mark 1:23-45)

The question arises, "Where did demons come from?" In reading the Bible, there seems to be no origin for these nasty beings; all of a sudden they appear to do Satan's bidding and torment mankind. The reality is that there is a clear and rational explanation, but it all has to do with interpreting Scripture correctly.

The Gospel of Mark shows events moving swiftly, with one thing happening after another at an almost lightning pace. As Jesus goes from place to place and the narrative evolves, we quickly reach a point where He is healing and casting out demons. After restoring Peter's mother-in-law from her fever, word of this spreads in the entire village, and many people gather at her door. In Mark 1:34 the author recounts:

And he healed many who were sick with various diseases, and cast out many demons. And he would not permit the demons to speak, because they knew him.

Here we see two pertinent facts for our discussion today:

1. There were many demons
2. They knew Jesus

Back to our earlier question: Where did they come from? Let's also add: How did they know Jesus?

Scripture doesn't directly provide the answer for either question, but the most logical means of answering goes back to Genesis 6. Nothing else in the Scriptures makes sense. More than that, if we interpret it wrongly, it distorts the entire Biblical narrative.

Genesis 6:1-5 says:

When man began to multiply on the face of the land and daughters were born to them, the sons of God saw that the daughters of man were attractive. And they took as their wives any they chose. Then the Lord said, "My Spirit shall not abide in man forever, for he is flesh: his days shall be 120 years." The Nephilim were on the earth in those days, and also afterward, when the sons of God came in to the daughters of man and they bore children to them. These were the mighty men who were of old, the men of renown.

The Lord saw that the wickedness of man was great in the earth, and that every intention of the thoughts of his heart was only evil continually.

If one goes down the rabbit trail of the sons of Seth explanation for this passage, he'll never arrive at a correct interpretation. The only sensible account is one that takes the text literally for just what it says. The sons of God, i.e. the *bene Elohim*, stepped out of their heavenly abode and had sexual relations with human women. That mating produced the hybrid offspring known as Nephilim. This corruption of the human bloodline resulted in further debasement of humanity. The plague of DNA alteration spread quickly and thoroughly until everyone but Noah and his sons was infected. The wickedness that came about was an abomination to God and, if left unchecked, would have thwarted His plans for the redemption of man by the ultimate Seed of the woman, Jesus Christ (Genesis 3:15).

God had to destroy the monstrosity of interbreeding. He literally had no choice. Thus God brought the worldwide flood to annihilate every living creature except for the ones who escaped on the ark. This included the Nephilim population of these half-human, half-spiritual entities.

The flood did its work. Everything perished throughout the planet. The Nephilim died – kind of. Their human aspect – their bodies – drowned, but unlike the souls of humans when they died at that time that went to Sheol, the souls of the Nephilim remained. The divine part of their being was released – they became bodiless entities. (Is this one reason Satan is called the prince of the power of the air, i.e. because he controls them in that condition of their existence? - Ephesians 2:2) In this state they inhabited dry and arid wastelands; they were tormented and restless. As such, they roamed the earth seeking a body to re-inhabit, i.e. to possess. A human that had rejected God was best because it was an empty vessel devoid of His Spirit, but they would enter animals if necessary (Matthew 8:31).

These are what we know as demons. They are lesser beings at the beck and call of Satan and his more powerful brothers who have likewise rebelled against God.

As to how they knew Jesus: it was from of old. He is the 2nd Person of the Trinity; He is God. It was He who brought the flood and the demise of the Nephilim. Jesus is the One responsible for the tormented existence of these spiritual creatures. Is it any wonder they know, hate, and fear Him?

As the God of all creation, Jesus has complete dominion. He has already defeated every demonic entity, whether a ruler, authority, cosmic power, or spiritual force. It is why 1 John 4:4 gives us this assurance:

Little children, you are from God and have overcome them, for he who is in you is greater than he who is in the world.

Demons must yield to the Name of Jesus. His Name is above every other name. Every creature great and small will bow and confess Him as Lord. We can rejoice because we who know and love Him have already done so. What a great comfort that is!

February 18: Leviticus 27:28-29 – Surely Be Put To Death

(Leviticus 26-27; Mark 2)

Leviticus brings us God's holy laws for the Israelites. When they obeyed His laws and walked in the ways that He commanded, He promised His people great blessings. If they turned from God to follow other gods and chose to live as they wanted, God made it abundantly clear that He would punish them with drastic measures (Leviticus 26). One of the most important laws that God decreed was that which dealt with something being devoted to destruction. Here is what Yahweh told the Israelites in Leviticus 27:28-29 about this concept:

"But no devoted thing that a man devotes to the Lord, of anything that he has, whether man or beast, or of his inherited field, shall be sold or redeemed; every devoted thing is most holy to the Lord. No one devoted, who is to be devoted for destruction from mankind, shall be ransomed; he shall surely be put to death."

To be devoted to destruction is to be given totally to the Lord. This is a death sentence. Whoever or whatever is devoted to destruction must be put to death for the law to be fulfilled. Note that the verse says "no one" who is given over and so devoted to God from "mankind." It applies personally to an individual or group of people. We see the effect and impact of this throughout the Old Testament, but for now let's consider the case of Jephthah and his daughter in Judges 11.

Although the son of a prostitute and shunned by the rest of his family, God chose Jephthah to be a judge over Israel to bring her redemption during a period of oppression by the Ammonites. While leading his men in the Spirit of the Lord to where they would engage the enemy, Jephthah made a drastic vow (Judges 11:29). As recounted in Judges 11:30-31, this is what happened:

And Jephthah made a vow to the Lord and said, "If you will give the Ammonites into my hand, then whatever comes out from the doors of my house to meet me when I return in peace from the Ammonites shall be the Lord's, and I will offer it up for a burnt offering."

Let's pause to see what a burnt offering entailed. The very first chapter of Leviticus addresses this. Everything stated there deals with male animals. In every case, however, the animal is killed so that its blood can be thrown upon the altar, e.g. Leviticus 1:5. A burnt offering, just as with something devoted to destruction, is a death sentence for whatever is being offered to the Lord.

The incident with Jephthah is one that Bible students have long debated because of what happened when he returned home in victory. Judges 11:34-35 details this poignant situation:

Then Jephthah came to his home at Mizpah. And behold, his daughter came out to meet him with tambourines and with dances. She was his only child; besides her he had neither son nor daughter. And as soon as he saw her, he tore his clothes and said, "Alas, my daughter! You have brought me very low, and you have become the cause of great trouble to me. For I have opened my mouth to the Lord, and I cannot take back my vow."

Jephthah's rash vow meant that his own daughter must be the offering that he would make to the Lord for his success in battle.

The point of contention is: Does the text mean what it says? Did Jephthah devote his daughter to destruction by actually giving her as the burnt offering to fulfill his vow?

His daughter knew that she had been given as a sacrificial lamb for the redemption of Israel. She asked for a two-month reprieve to enjoy the remnant of her short life. Judges 11:39-40 then says:

And at the end of two months, she returned to her father, who did with her according to his vow that he had made. She had never known a man, and it became a custom in Israel that the daughters of Israel went year by year to lament the daughter of Jephthah the Gileadite four days in the year.

Was she sacrificed? It certainly appears so. Subsequently in Israel, the females in the land remembered her and lamented over her. Why would they lament if she hadn't been devoted to destruction – killed – and made a burnt offering to complete Jephthah's vow?

Could Jesus have been thinking of Jephthah in His declaration during the Sermon on the Mount in Matthew 5:37?

"Let what you say be simply 'Yes' or 'No'; anything more than this comes from evil."

In other words, don't make vows – especially rash ones! Let your word be what it is lest something you say comes back to bite you. This is indeed what happened with Jephthah and his daughter. It's a tragic incident that need not have occurred, but Jephthah, being under the Law, believed he had to honor his vow. We can learn from this by heeding the Words of Jesus.

February 19: Numbers 2:2,17 – At the Center

(Numbers 1-2; Mark 3:1-21)

We first encounter the term "tent of meeting" in Exodus 33:7-11 as the tent that Moses pitched outside the camp, where he would seek the Lord and speak with Him face to face. This tent was the temporary tabernacle of God that was a place of worship and where He dwelt. When Moses entered the tent, the pillar of cloud would descend upon this physical structure indicating God's presence. This is what we refer to as the Shekinah glory of God, actually a term not used in the Bible, but clearly evident in numerous instances of Yahweh's manifestation on earth., e.g. during Israel's flight from Pharaoh in Egypt.

When the Lord instructed Moses how they were to camp during the Exodus, He had them erect the tent of meeting at the center of all they did. He said in Numbers 2:2:

"The people of Israel shall camp each by his own standard, with the banners of their fathers' houses. They shall camp facing the tent of meeting on every side."

Likewise, in Numbers 2:17, Yahweh told them how they were to march:

"Then the tent of meeting shall set out, with the camp of the Levites in the midst of the camps; as they camp, so shall they set out, each in position, standard by standard."

In all they did, whether at rest or on the move, the tent of meeting was to be the focus of their lives. The Israelite tribes arrayed around it were to protect this dwelling place of God, while the Levites were to transport and maintain it (Numbers 1:53).

God's purpose in this physical positioning was to keep His people's eyes on Him, so that they would remember He was the One who delivered and sustained them. He was God; there was none like Him; they were to worship none besides Him.

Some years ago Campus Crusade for Christ (now renamed CRU) developed the Four Spiritual Laws. (See info at: https://www.gotquestions.org/four-spiritual-laws.html.) Along with these "laws" they also created images showing how they worked in a person's life. Someone can have either a Self-Directed Life or a Christ-Directed Life.

The image showing a Self-Directed Life depicts a circle with a chair (throne) at its center. Self has the primary focus in this type of life, as it sits on that throne. Within the circle are various dots representing the various interests and activities a person has. Outside the circle is the cross of Christ. The Self-Directed Life has these three characteristics:

- Self is on the throne
- Interests are directed by self, resulting in discord and frustration
- Christ is outside the life

In contrast is a Christ-Directed Life. The image for this shows a circle with a chair (throne at its center) and on that chair is the cross of Christ. All other interests and activities in a person's life are also within that circle, but they are in orderly submission to Jesus Christ. The Christ-Directed Life has these three characteristics:

- Christ is on the throne
- Self is yielding to Christ
- Interests are directed by Christ, resulting in harmony with God's plan

This is the image God portrayed in His arrangement of the tribes of Jesus around the tabernacle. We today, like those ancient tribes, are to keep our focus on Christ. This results in all aspects of our lives being in harmony with God. It means we live in obedience to Him and walk in righteousness because of Him. We yield to Him in all things and give Him all glory for everything in our lives.

When the Israelites kept this picture at the forefront, God highly favored them with immense blessings. All too often over the centuries, they forgot who gave them life and all they had. They put self on the throne and suffered the consequences.

The same is true with us. Christ must be our all in all. In our making Him the reason for our existence and acting accordingly, we please Him, and His Shekinah glory even overshadows us. What a blessing it is to live for Jesus!

February 20: Numbers 3:12 – Redemption by Levite

(Numbers 3-4; Mark 3:22-35)

When the Lord redeemed the children of Israel from the fiery furnace of slavery in Egypt, because of the blood He shed of the Egyptian firstborn, the Israelites incurred a debt that had to be paid. Yahweh informed Moses of this in Exodus 13:1-2

The Lord said to Moses, "Consecrate to me all the firstborn. Whatever is the first to open the womb among the people of Israel, both of man and of beast, is mine."

From that point forward, from every tribe of Israel, the firstborn were to be consecrated, i.e. set apart, for the Lord. During the Exodus, however, a dramatic event changed this dynamic.

Moses had gone up on Mount Sinai where he remained 40 days and nights in the presence of Yahweh. During that time, He gave Moses the Ten Commandments. At the end of that period, God told Moses that the *"people whom you brought up out of the land of Egypt have corrupted themselves."* (Exodus 32:7)

Because of their 400+ years in captivity in Egypt, the Israelites had been thoroughly indoctrinated in the ways of the Egyptians with their pagan deities. With Moses gone, they reverted to what they knew. They demanded that Aaron fashion an idol for them that they could see in their worship, and to which they would give thanks for their escape from captivity. Aaron crafted the golden calf, which just happened to pop out of the fire (Exodus 32:24), and the people broke loose in celebration. What this meant was that they engaged in pagan revelry, which included a sexual orgy.

Moses knew the extent of this great sin as soon as he saw it in the camp, and that Yahweh would punish the Israelites. His response was hard and swift. Exodus 32:26 tells us:

. . . then Moses stood in the gate of the camp and said, "Who is on the Lord's side? Come to me." And all the sons of Levi gathered around him.

When they stood with him, Moses ordered the Levites to kill every participant in these festivities, even family members if they were guilty. And they did, as recounted in Exodus 32:28-29:

And the sons of Levi did according to the word of Moses. And that day about three thousand men of the people fell. And Moses said, "Today you have been ordained for the service of the Lord, each one at the cost of his son and of his brother, so that he might bestow a blessing upon you this day."

Their obedience to Moses and to the Lord set the Levites apart that day. Because they faithfully served Yahweh, He ordained them for His service. This took shape with the dedication of the tabernacle. And how they would serve Yahweh going forward.

Recall that in the Exodus all firstborn among the Israelites were to be consecrated. Now God changed this. He said in Numbers 3:12-13:

"Behold, I have taken the Levites from among the people of Israel instead of every firstborn who opens the womb among the people of Israel. The Levites shall be mine, for all the firstborn are mine. On the day that I struck down all the firstborn in the land of Egypt, I consecrated for my own all the firstborn in Israel, both of man and of beast. They shall be mine: I am the Lord."

Rather than the firstborn from every tribe, the tribe of Levi took their place. When the census of the Levites was taken, their numbers came to 22,000. However, in the count of all firstborn males, the total came to 22,273 (Numbers 3:39,43). From this difference of 273 firstborn that the Levites could not redeem, the people had to pay a redemption price. Everything had to be done in order and with the legal precision that God set forth.

The setting apart of the sons of Levi carries forward to this day. The Orthodox Jews in Israel have been planning for years to build a third temple on the Temple Mount. Of course, this is currently thwarted because it is currently under control of Muslims, and the Dome of the Rock and the Al Aqsa Mosque sit on the spot where they desire to build the temple.

The temple will be built. Somehow the Jews will move forward with it, perhaps because the two Muslim structures will be destroyed during the Psalm 83 War or Ezekiel's War, or arising from the negotiations that Antichrist concludes in confirming the peace treaty that begins the 7-year Tribulation.

In this preparation for what they don't understand, i.e. that this Tribulation Temple is not the temple of God, but of man, and will eventually be desecrated by Antichrist, the Temple Institute in Israel has been busy. From the Israel Telegraphic Agency came this news release on August 2, 2016:

The Temple Institute, dedicated to reestablishing the Holy Temple in Jerusalem, announced it is opening a school for training Levitical priests for their eventual service in a new temple.

The institute ran several pilot programs in recent years and now "is embarking on a mission to teach Kohanim all the practical skills required to serve in the Third Holy Temple," it said in a statement.

The institute advocates what many in the region — including a number of Orthodox Jews — see as a radical goal: replacing the Dome of the Rock with a new Jewish Holy Temple. Muslim fears that Israel will change the status quo that has kept the site in control of a Jordanian authority, known as the Wakf, has led to repeated clashes over the years and inspired a recent wave of terrorist attacks aimed at Israelis.

The institute has reconstructed nearly all of the sacred vessels needed to perform the services in a rebuilt Temple, including the High Priest's breastplate featuring the 12 precious stones of the tribes of Israel, the half-ton golden menorah and the musical instruments of the Levitical choir.

The curriculum at the Nezer HaKodesh Institute for Kohanic Studies will include courses on the Temple service, theory and practice and the role and application of modern technology in the Third Temple, according to the Institute.

All this focus and activity around the temple, and in preparing the Levitical priesthood for service, will come at a price. Because the Jews have rejected Jesus Christ as their Messiah, they continue to look for His first coming rather than His return. This rejection has caused God to decree that unbelieving Israel must finally learn that Jesus is indeed Lord, God, and Savior. The cost will be great with 2/3 of Israel perishing (Zechariah 13:8). But God is merciful. Zechariah 12:10 describes His mercy:

"And I will pour out on the house of David and the inhabitants of Jerusalem a spirit of grace and pleas for mercy, so that, when they look on me, on him whom they have pierced, they shall mourn for him, as one mourns for an only child, and weep bitterly over him, as one weeps over a firstborn."

And so, all Israel will be saved.

February 21: Numbers 5:15 – Trial by Ordeal

(Numbers 5-6; Mark 4:1-20)

Certain passages of the Bible make us shake our heads in confusion before we move on in our reading, because we don't understand what's going on at a deeper level. In our westernized Christianity, we don't have the appropriate context to discern the true intent; rather than digging deeper, we add these things to our growing pile of Biblical mysteries and remain uninformed. As Dr. Michael Heiser says, to better understand Scripture, it takes work. Yet, if we put in the effort to learn one new idea every day, by the end of a year, think how much more we'd know!

The problem we face is that we look at the Bible from what we know today. But is that useful? Can you imagine someone 2,000 or more years from now reading about the "woke" movement or the "cancel" culture that's so prevalent around us and trying to comprehend it from their 41st century perspective? Whatever society would look like in those future days, people would surely have no clue about these concepts.

What the people in that time so far removed would need to do is to have the 21st century person's understanding in their heads. This would give them a basis to correctly interpret something dealing with these ideas that seek to elevate certain people because of what they supposedly know (woke) or eliminate others because they don't adhere to certain norms in society (cancel).

Likewise, the only way for us to really know what is happening behind the scenes in Scripture is to walk around with the ancient Israelite understanding in *our* heads. To that end, Yahweh continually attempted to change the hearts of His people to worship Him alone by trusting Him above every other god in the pagan societies of the nations surrounding Israel. God's desire was for the Israelites to have *believing loyalty* toward Him. This meant that they weren't double-minded, following Yahweh plus some other god with a Plan B – just in case – mindset. All their clichéd eggs were in His basket alone. Believing loyalty says, "I trust You God above every other god, and there is none besides You." This is the kind of faith that David had as a man after God's own heart. That was as true in Old Testament times as it is in the New Testament through our faith and trust in Jesus.

And so we come to the passage for today. In the ESV Bible, the heading in Numbers 5 beginning with verse 11 is *A Test for Adultery*. The text tells us that if a spirit of jealousy came upon a man over his wife's possible unfaithfulness

(Numbers 5:14), he was to bring her to the priest, who would then perform a strange ritual. Numbers 5:15 tells us:

> . . . then the man shall bring his wife to the priest and bring the offering required of her, a tenth of an ephah of barley flour. He shall pour no oil on it and put no frankincense on it, for it is a grain offering of jealousy, a grain offering of remembrance, **bringing iniquity to remembrance**.

The priest would perform what is commonly known as Trial by Ordeal. To our Western eyes, it might look suspiciously like divination. He put dust from the floor of the tabernacle into water and placed a curse of bitterness upon it. The woman repeated an oath and drank the water. If she'd been unfaithful, the curse entered her body and caused terrible things to happen, i.e. the iniquity was remembered. If the accusation was false, and she'd been faithful to her husband by not defiling herself, she would be free and able to conceive children.

If not divination, what was really going on here?

God wanted the Israelites to completely rely on Him in every facet of their lives, even in their marital relations. They were to place their trust in Him to ensure that He would root out unfaithfulness among them or confirm their fidelity (because that's what He wanted for Himself!). By showing them that in the day-to-day aspects of how they lived, He would oversee even these matters, God would be proven trustworthy in even greater things. Yahweh wanted to convict His people to place all their confidence in Him.

Isn't that what God truly wants for us today? Isn't that what it means for us to make Jesus, not only our Savior, but also our Lord? Doesn't the concept of *Lord* mean master or ruler? Shouldn't this apply to everything we think, say, or do; that it reflects back to our relationship with Christ so that we demonstrate we are His children? He should be our Master and rule completely in our hearts like the loving Father He is.

Thus, even in thorny marital issues, in matters such as jealousy and fidelity, we need to turn to Him for answers. Because He loves us so much, He will help us through the difficulties of life.

February 22: Mark 4:26-29 – How Grows the Kingdom?

(Numbers 17; Mark 4:21-41)

Many have attempted over the years to thwart the growth of God's Kingdom. Incited by Satan and his minions, men have done all in their power to keep the Gospel from going forth and "infecting" others. The topic reminds me of numerous examples where – on the surface – it appears as though the God haters were successful, but God has His ways, and His plans and purposes for the redemption of mankind will not be stopped.

The first issue we need to address in this subject is why evil men try to keep God's Word from spreading. Of course, the answer is simple. Those who do all in their power to keep Jesus Christ from being known are in thrall to Satan. God has given to all men the ability to know Him. He has shown who He is through the wonders of this world, from the creation order and beauty of nature, to the almost inexhaustible complexity of life that science has revealed. As Paul said in Romans 1:20:

For his invisible attributes, namely, his eternal power and divine nature, have been clearly perceived, ever since the creation of the world, in the things that have been made. So they are without excuse.

This being the case, what is their excuse? They have chosen to reject the evidence and so opened themselves to spiritual deception. If someone won't believe what God has painstakingly given him to enable his belief in a transcendent being above all others, then he will seek other answers and be subject to the lies that Satan so readily conceives. When a person hears and believes the falsehoods of the enemy, he turns further from God and appropriates the hatred of the beings in the spiritual realm, who are themselves attempting to avoid His judgment and everlasting punishment.

From the beginning, Satan and his followers have formulated different ways to prevent the fulfillment of God's Word. If they could only show God up as a liar, they figured they could gain the upper hand. But, He has continually devised His own schemes to counter those of His opponents. This is where Mark 4:26-29 comes into play:

And he said, "The kingdom of God is as if a man should scatter seed on the ground. He sleeps and rises night and day, and the seed sprouts and grows; he knows not how. The earth produces by itself, first the blade, then the ear, then the full grain in the ear. But when the grain is ripe, at once he puts in the sickle, because the harvest has come."

To the constant frustration of Satan and his human sycophants, the growth of God's Kingdom is a mystery. How is the seed scattered far and wide? How does it grow in seemingly arid conditions? How does it produce such an abundant harvest?

Consider nations that are hostile to God, whose gods are Communism, Islam, or Hinduism. From the outside, it seems as though these ideologies would prevail. With the government, friends, even family members against those who turn to Jesus, it seems hopeless that Christianity could spread and flourish. When all those around the followers in Christ are intent on snuffing out their faith through persecution of unimaginable wickedness, how in the world can the kingdom of God grow?

But, it does. The roots of a plant grow underground – often wide and deep – before any greenery sprouts. We only have to think of the underground church in China. Some years ago it was estimated there were only about 100,000 believers in all that huge country. More recently, the numbers are believed to be upwards of 100,000,000 Christ-followers.

For all their efforts to stamp out Christianity, the communist authorities must be beside themselves. Communism and Christianity are incompatible. A person cannot follow both in any way, shape, or form. Communism is an anti-God ideology with the State as sovereign and above all; it alone must be worshiped. That's about as far from true Christianity as one can get.

To repeat the overused expression: God has a wonderful plan for your life. Yes, He does, but it's so much more than "your best life now" in this world. God has determined that human beings have value; so much worth, in fact, that He wishes to transform us so as to put us to work on eternal matters. He will continue this process begun in our fleshly bodies as He Raptures His true church and causes our metamorphosis into having glorified, spiritual bodies. As 1 Corinthians 2:9 says:

But, as it is written, "What no eye has seen, nor ear heard, nor the heart of man imagined, what God has prepared for those who love him"—

God's Kingdom will prevail. I, for one, can't wait!

February 23: Numbers 9:16 – Supernatural

(Numbers 8-10; Mark 5:1-20)

The Bible is a book filled with wonders, all of which point to God. Why is it that given all we're shown He can do, that we still try to limit Him? How is it that we can accept some supernatural aspects of God and His kingdom, yet are loathe to believe others? What is it about the paradigms of God's ways that we readily welcome certain ones in our Christian faith, but can't swallow others that go against our fleshly sensibilities?

As true, Bible-believing Christians, there are several non-negotiable doctrines the majority of people, regardless of denomination, take for granted. Among them are the virgin birth, the resurrection of Jesus, and the indwelling of the Holy Spirit upon our salvation. These are miracles. They are supernatural aspects of God that make no sense in the natural – in fact, are an obstacle to belief for some – but because we know that God is a being far above and beyond us, we who are His receive with open arms.

But, let's be honest. Does a woman getting pregnant by a Spirit rather than a man make any sense at all? Someone rising from the dead – seriously? A transcendent God living inside people? What's with all these far out ideas? Christianity is a wacko religion – right? Well, not so much. Through the Bible – the inerrant, infallible Word of God (another obstacle to the supernatural-averse) – the Lord tells us these past events happened and that being born-again is a real phenomenon. More than that, it's experiential; many of us know the Holy Spirit lives within us because we also experience His presence.

This is all well and good. As Christians, we've got this supernatural, miracle working God thing all figured out. We can attend church, know these things, and go home in our little, comfortable, ideological cocoons.

Then we come to verses in the Bible that challenge us. During the Exodus, God did many miraculous things to convince the Israelites He was real and greater than the gods they'd known in Egypt. One of the most incredible was the evidence of His constant presence among the people, as summarized by Numbers 9:16:

So it was always: the cloud covered it by day and the appearance of fire by night.

During the entire forty years the Israelites wandered in the wilderness, God was there. He never left them. Upon His direction, they constructed the tabernacle, i.e. the ark of the testimony, as the reminder of God's covenant with them. On the days they traveled, a supernatural cloud hovered above them and led them in the direction God wanted them to go. When they camped for the night or for an extended period, the cloud turned into a fiery plume directly over the ark.

Can you imagine? I don't know how dramatic the cloud by day was, but certainly the nighttime flame of fire – always there – always catching the eye wherever anyone was in the darkness of the camp – had to make an impression on people. "Yes, Yahweh is here. He never leaves us nor forsakes us." (Of course, despite these visible reminders, the Israelites were a stiff-necked people, who still many times somehow thought God had abandoned them.)

The question becomes: How many of these supernatural occurrences will we in our comfortable Christianity accept? One of the big ones that significant numbers of Christians have problems with is the account of the sons of God (*bene Elohim*) in Genesis 6:1-4 coming down from their heavenly abode and having sexual relations with human women, who then birthed a race of hybrid beings known as Nephilim. As the pushback goes: Not possible; angels can't procreate. Didn't Jesus say that in Matthew 22:30? This account must really be referring to the sons of Seth. It was an all human interaction.

Actually no. Briefly: Jesus said that angels while in heaven don't marry; He said nothing about what happens when they leave heaven and the capabilities they have on earth. Additionally, the text in Genesis says what it says. What was Moses, the ancient Israelite, thinking when he wrote this? What was in his head that he knew about God's kingdom? What was the context? Wouldn't Moses have tried to communicate something commonly known among others of the day so they'd understand it? The thought of Seth in this account certainly never entered Moses' mind.

One other issue of many that's contentious from a humanistic versus supernatural perspective is the pre-Tribulation Rapture. For some reason, those who don't believe this is God's intent apparently think that Jesus didn't pay the full price for our redemption when He hung on the cross. Just like Catholics, they think we whom Jesus saved still need to prove something in our flesh to earn our salvation. For the Roman Catholic Church, salvation only comes through a Jesus "and" faith, e.g. Jesus and attending Mass, Jesus and consuming the Eucharist, etc. For the anti-pre-Tribbers it's almost like a badge of honor that they have to enter the Tribulation. "I'm prepping and I'm ready. Got my guns; got my food supplies. When I see Antichrist, I'm going to kick his sorry rear end from here to Kingdom come. Plus, I need to be present to make sure people get saved."

Aside from the overwhelming textual evidence of the pre-Trib Rapture, an attitude similar to the above certainly smacks of pride. It also evidences a serious lack of understanding as to how horrible times will be during the Tribulation. Prepping won't get people through. Antichrist will be far more powerful than these people imagine. God doesn't need their help in saving people; He's got it covered.

So, what's the problem? Perhaps it's a lack of trust in God – that He loves His Bride, the church, so much He wouldn't think of allowing us to suffer in the same way unbelievers must who have chosen to reject His free offer of salvation. Or, maybe it's that a supernatural event that suddenly disappears millions of people from the earth is too much for them to swallow. A virgin birth, the resurrection, the indwelling of the Holy Spirit are fine; but the catching away of believers into the clouds? No way.

God's wonders and what He does are unfathomable to our human ways of perceiving. Yet, if we let God be God, and let the Bible speak for itself, we can more likely come to the point of believing Paul. To repeat from the other day what he wrote in 2 Corinthians 2:9:

"What no eye has seen, nor ear heard,
*   nor the heart of man imagined,*
what God has prepared for those who love him"—

God loves us. Let's rejoice in that. And, let's give Him more credit for the supernatural than we seem inclined to believe. It may even increase our faith!

February 24: Numbers 11:4 – Rabble Rousers

(Numbers 11-13; Mark 5:21-43)

The effects of discontent can carry over well past an initial display of someone's grievance. They can have disastrous consequences that go beyond one person's bad thinking about something. There's a contagious aspect about dissatisfaction; an infestation of sorts that creates a festering wound.

The Israelites had a problem. They'd known nothing of Yahweh for 400 years other than tales of Him around their campfires at night. He was a distant mythical entity, impossible even to visualize; unlike the gods of Egypt which all had idols to them of gold and silver. When I AM showed up and spurred Moses to lead these people to the land of promise that Yahweh had pledged to their ancestors, it was difficult for them to grasp. To make matters worse, there were some numbers among them who weren't Israelites (e.g. Exodus 12:38: *A mixed multitude went with them...*). Thus, when things got seemingly hard, people were in their midst who had even less knowledge of Yahweh and what He intended than the Israelites themselves.

And so, we come to Numbers 11:4 which initiates a string of events that reflect poorly on the people and trigger a strong response from God:

Now the rabble that was among them had a strong craving. And the people of Israel also wept again and said, "Oh that we had meat to eat!

The Hebrew word for rabble – *asaphsuph* – means exactly what the Exodus reference above says: a mixed multitude. These were camp followers; in modern day language they were groupies. They were enamored by what they'd seen Yahweh do among His people and were hangers-on, looking for what He could do for them in their personal lives, but having no commitment to the Lord.

This was a problem. It's the old situation where someone begins inciting others. He stirs up one or two, and suddenly there are ten. More and more people feel the sting of discontent, and a faceless, nameless, outraged mob emerges.

The pressure built and came down on Moses. The people complained as if he had caused their problems. He lashed out, not at the rabble, but at God. He wasn't a happy camper because he felt the Lord had allowed all this indignation to fall on him, and what was he supposed to do about it? He was only following the commands of Yahweh. If it hadn't been for God, Moses would still have been tending sheep in Midian. So, basically Moses yells at God for putting him in this position.

That had repercussions. To the people's complaints about how much better a life they had in Egypt with unlimited food and leisure, God brought them more food – in the form of an inexhaustible supply of quail – than they could possibly eat. Before they could consume more than a couple mouthfuls, the Lord's anger burned, and He caused a plague to come upon them. Their cravings brought death. When the people who died were buried, the Israelites called the place of burial "graves of craving."

The discontent from that original group of rabble rousers didn't stop there. Pride rose up in Miriam and Aaron. They were prophets and servants of the Lord; didn't they merit greater recognition and favor? When God confronted them in the presence of Moses, He put a quick end to that by immensely humbling Miriam. He made it clear that the humility evidenced by Moses (Numbers 12:3) was what He wanted.

And still, the effects of this infection of distrust continued. Despite God's promises of what He would do for His Chosen People, the spies who went into Israel came back with a bad report. They'd seen the bounty of the land, but fear of its inhabitants turned to rebellion. These naysayers had their way, and all but a faithful few wanted to cross the Jordan and face the giants. The outcome was inevitable. God took that as the slap in the face that it was and consigned them to forty years of wandering until that entire generation died in the wilderness.

Such responses and their consequences have been with us always and will carry forward into the Tribulation. The rebellion of the Jewish people and skepticism of God's Word has resulted in a secular society in Israel whose hearts the Lord must turn to accomplish His purposes. That same lack of faith has caused great apostasy in the church, since many no longer view the Bible as inerrant and infallible. Those who have chosen to reject the free gift of salvation through God's Son Jesus Christ will pay a very high price.

They are part of the latter day rabble; the crowd of malcontents who believe their feelings trump God's Word. Just as Yahweh brought tragic outcomes to those in the past who went their own way, so He will do in days to come.

The rabble with its mob mentality, always causes trouble. The crowd stirred up by the Pharisees demanded Jesus' crucifixion, which brought God's wrath upon the nation of Israel to this day, despite His mercy in so many aspects of their lives.

This is one reason Paul reminds Christ-followers that this world is not our home. We don't have to be concerned with the issues about which the rioters complain. We're to keep our eyes on Jesus and the eternal home that He promised. When we do, all these things will seem strangely distant, and we can live in peace regardless of all the chaos that swirls around us.

February 25: Mark 6:22 – Herodias' Daughter

(Numbers 14-15; Mark 6:1-32)

It's one thing for someone to reject Jesus, but another thing altogether when that person causes another to sin. Due to the choices one makes, in a sense, it's easy to see how progressive sin brings him (or her) to a very bad place. During the Exodus, Yahweh dealt with this downward slide of iniquity quite forcefully because of the seriousness of the transgression.

God made it clear that unintentional sin happened. Because people are human, mistakes result. When a person realizes what he's done, he can make atonement for that error. We see this in Numbers 15:27-28:

*"If one person **sins unintentionally**, he shall offer a female goat a year old for a sin offering. And the priest shall make atonement before the Lord for the person who **makes a mistake**, when he sins unintentionally, to make atonement for him, and he **shall be forgiven**."*

God is extremely lenient in this kind of inadvertent situation. The game changes when sin is committed intentionally. Consider Numbers 15:30-31:

*"But the person who **does anything with a high hand**, whether he is native or a sojourner, **reviles the Lord**, and that person shall be cut off from among his people. Because he has **despised the word of the Lord** and has **broken his commandment**, that person shall be **utterly cut off**; his iniquity shall be on him."*

These verses describe the committing of deliberate sin done through pride and arrogance. It makes for a completely different situation and response from God. He considers this diving-into-sin attitude as one that reviles Him; it's a despising of who He is, and a breaking of His commandments. The Hebrew word *karath* means to be cut off or cut down. Strong's Concordance #3772 has a lengthy entry regarding this word, but ultimately it means to be destroyed or consumed; in a sense, to be chewed up. It's not a good thing. It appears this ultimately means to be killed, although why Moses didn't use the specific Hebrew word for killed isn't clear. The one thing it certainly implies, at the least, is a separating of the guilty party from his people, probably in a permanent way.

Moving forward in time to the account of King Herod and his dealing with John the Baptist, we see a form of this sinful action – and more. Herod feared John and was fascinated by him, but he had sinned by marrying his brother's wife, Herodias, against John's speaking against him doing so. For John's condemnation, Herodias hated the prophet and schemed to kill him. When Herod gave a birthday bash for himself, Herodias struck.

No doubt from the child's birth, Herodias had tainted and twisted the mind of her daughter. Herodias had taught the girl pagan sexual practices, along with how to scheme and manipulate the minds and sensibilities of men so as to get her way. At the party, Herodias sent in her daughter to the revelers, and Mark 6:22 relates:

For when Herodias's daughter came in and danced, she pleased Herod and his guests. And the king said to the girl, "Ask me for whatever you wish, and I will give it to you."

The girl asks her mother what she should request. Without a second thought, Herodias demands the head of John. The young vixen relays the request, and because Herod had made a foolish vow, in order to save face, he complies. The wayward child then brings John's head to her mother on a platter.

Look at this from the perspective of the passage in Numbers above. Herodias literally plunged into sin. Why? Because her pride had been wounded from John's rebuke and arrogance rose in her. She would show him!

That's bad enough, but she goes a step further. She has molded her daughter from youth to see men as objects to be manipulated and used. The mother has destroyed any moral sensibilities the girl had, and so she willingly does what Herodias wants.

The child had been an innocent. Herodias caused her own guilt to fall upon her daughter. Later, not in response necessarily to this incident, Jesus declared in Matthew 18:6:

"But whoever causes one of these little ones who believe in me to sin, it would be better for him to have a great millstone fastened around his neck and to be drowned in the depth of the sea."

Jesus' indictment for stirring up sin in a child is dire. Here He's pronouncing a guilty sentence of great import. The sea is always a place of chaos in the Bible, where anti-God forces dwell. To metaphorically have a millstone fastened around one's neck and be cast into the sea would imply severe punishment – one that would cause the person to sink to the lowest depths – perhaps to a place similar to Tartarus, the lowest region of hell.

What do we learn from all this?

Deliberate sin has severe consequences. God's grace is one thing, and it covers a multitude of sins. However, God does not view intentional sin with favor. It goes against His Word, breaking His Law. Think of those who adhere to a hyper-grace theology. According to God's Word, it seems that's a dangerous road to walk.

Worse yet are those who corrupt the minds and hearts of children. The wrath of God surely is upon them, and He will judge them most harshly. We've seen a dramatic rise in child sex trafficking as we near the Tribulation period. It's part and parcel of the darkness of the human heart that God will reckon with in the final days. He states as much in Revelation 21:8 in His condemnation of lawless unbelievers He will bring to account:

"But as for the cowardly, the faithless, the detestable, as for murderers, the sexually immoral, sorcerers, idolaters, and all liars, their portion will be in the lake that burns with fire and sulfur, which is the second death."

God is love, but His wrath burns brightly against those who deliberately trespass against His commandments. We can rejoice He has showered His mercy and grace upon those of us who believe. For those who don't – for those who reject His miraculous, free gift of salvation – there is only a future of fearsome judgment.

February 26: Numbers 16:11 – Presumption

(Numbers 16-17; Mark 6:33-56)

Korah's rebellion during the Exodus reveals several issues that are worth considering. The situation arises following two events. Moses had sent the twelve spies into Israel, and ten of them came back with a bad report. Their rebellion against God's Word, through their lack of trust that resulted in the people refusing to cross into the land, didn't go over well with Him. The people had risen up against Moses for simply doing what the Lord commanded. Despite them acting against Moses, he interceded for them, but God killed by plague the ten chiefs who'd come back from Israel grumbling (Numbers 14:37). On the heels of that, the people attempted to go up on their own into Israel after God said the time for their incursion was over – He would cause them to wander in the wilderness to teach them a lesson. Regardless of God's Word, the people acted once more in their own will as Numbers 14:44 recounts:

But they presumed to go up to the heights of the hill country, although neither the ark of the covenant of the Lord nor Moses departed out of the camp.

For this act of presumption, God allowed the Amalekites and Canaanites to handily defeat the Israelites.

Then comes the man who disobeyed the law for working on the Sabbath. He was caught gathering sticks for firewood, and the Lord ordered him stoned to death (Numbers 15:36).

This was too much for the Levite Korah, a couple of other high-ranking men, plus another 250 chiefs of the entire congregation. They challenged the authority of Moses and Aaron, essentially asking the following questions:

- Why was Moses making the rules?
- Why did they have to do what he said?
- Why did he order the man to be stoned to death simply for picking up sticks on an arbitrary day he called the Sabbath?
- Why couldn't they now go into the promised land instead of him telling him they had to wander in the wilderness?
- What was it about Moses that he was the one who should tell them how to live?

Their act of presumption is captured in Numbers 15:10-11:

"... and that he has brought you near him, and all your brothers the sons of Levi with you? And would you seek the priesthood also? Therefore it is against the Lord that you and all your company have gathered together. What is Aaron that you grumble against him?"

At this grumbling act of defiance, what does Moses do? Earlier, in a verse that some people snicker at because it seems presumptuous to them, we're told in Numbers 12:3:

Now the man Moses was very meek, more than all people who were on the face of the earth.

But in these situations where the people come against Moses, and thus, are really coming against God, what do Moses and Aaron do? Look at Numbers 16:22 in part:

And they fell on their faces...

Time and again Moses interceded for these stiff-necked people. They grumbled, came against Moses, and in so doing challenged God. But Moses, in his meekness – his humility – offered himself up for them. The people never seemed to learn, but Moses fell face down before the Lord asking for Him to relent and not kill them all. Their short memories constantly put them in jeopardy of their lives, and they never seemed to realize it. Moses did, and as their God-anointed leader, he caused God to refrain from His intent.

Moses' intercession was for the people; it wasn't for the leaders of the rebellion. As a result, Korah and those who had conspired against Moses all perished. The next day another uprising occurs. Once more a portion of Numbers 16:45 shows us about Moses and Aaron:

And they fell on their faces...

This time it didn't stop God from sending a plague that consumed a huge number of the people, but because Moses pleaded for them before God, He stopped when *only* 14,700 of them died (Numbers 16:49). The implication is that it could have been many more.

In the weeding out of the righteous, where Moses and Aaron are shown to be approved by God, the 250 chiefs had been told to light censers so that God would act and reveal His approval. Upon their doing this, God sent fire to destroy these men for their presumption, but here is an interesting fact we learn from Numbers 16:37-38 as Moses speaks:

*"Tell Eleazar the son of Aaron the priest to take up **the censers** out of the blaze. Then scatter the fire far and wide, **for they have become holy**. As for the censers of these men who have sinned at the cost of their lives, let them be made into hammered plates as a covering for the altar, for they offered them before the Lord, **and they became holy**. Thus they shall be a sign to the people of Israel."*

The act of these men lighting these censers and offering the incense to God caused the vessels to become holy. From that, God instructed Moses to make them part of the altar, as the altar itself was holy. The censers had been consecrated to the Lord, much as the Israelite firstborn had been, and then the Levites in their places. Something offered to the Lord became holy and had to be treated as such.

The rebellion of Korah and the associated aspects of the incident fascinate us to this day. It's a dramatic incident. The presumption of Korah and the many men with him is staggering given all these people had witnessed. Throughout all the Exodus adventures to that point, Moses was obviously appointed by God to lead the people, yet somehow the thinking arose that he was simply acting on his own volition.

Moses' humble and sacrificial demeanor is put on display numerous times throughout these passages. He was truly a man of God who didn't value his own life above those of the ones God had sent him to lead.

As to the holiness of something that is offered as sacred to the Lord, surely that has value for us to consider in our Christian walk. What is it that we offer to God when we commit to following Jesus Christ? Is it not our very bodies – the life that He has so freely given us? Isn't this the concept behind our saying that Jesus shouldn't only be our Savior; that He should also be our Lord? As our Lord, that makes Him our Master. The idea encompassed in that term is that He owns us. We are holy and consecrated in this relationship. Shouldn't that change us? Shouldn't we then live out this most unique connection we have with Him as though it's the most important thing we'll ever do?

February 27: Numbers 18:5 – Wrath No More

(Numbers 18-20; Mark 7:1-13)

Yahweh had separated the Levites as a unique tribe among the twelve in Israel to serve Him. Because they had stood against the depravity that the children of Israel engaged in during the incident of the golden calf, God ordained them for service (Exodus 32:29). The Lord made many pronouncements about what this meant and how it was to work. Primarily the Levites guarded and maintained everything that related to Yahweh. They cared for the tabernacle, the ark of the covenant, and all the implements necessary for worship. Their duties were extensive. In Numbers 18:5 we see one more requirement that God placed upon them:

"And you shall keep guard over the sanctuary and over the altar, that there may never again be wrath on the people of Israel."

The trust that Yahweh imputed to the Levites was sacred. Among their consecrated duties was the necessity to protect everything that pertained to God. If they did their job properly, it had incredible power. It would prevent God's wrath from falling upon the people of Israel. In return for this tremendous responsibility with its dire implications, God made it clear that His favor would be upon the Levites. Consider Numbers 18:12,14 in this regard:

"All the best of the oil and all the best of the wine and of the grain, the firstfruits of what they give to the Lord, I give to you... Every devoted thing in Israel shall be yours."

For their faithful service to Him with this sacred trust, God would provide immense blessings to the Levites.

Unfortunately, as we'll see in our progression of reading through God's Word, the Levites went terribly off the rails. One such instance is recorded in Judges 17, which details how a Levite became a priest in the household of an Ephraimite named Micah to facilitate the worship of his household gods. The story progresses in Judges 18 to where this Levite accompanies the men of the tribe of Dan to gladly be their priest in service to their idols. In another incident in Judges 19, a Levite allows his concubine to be ravaged by evil men in Benjamin, when he willingly gives the woman up to them to protect himself. Then he cuts her lifeless body to pieces, sends parts of her throughout Israel, and stirs up the people to come against the wickedness of the Benjaminites, which almost wipes out this chosen tribe of God (Judges 20).

These blasphemous incidents among the consecrated Levites – along with the continual apostasy of the children of Israel- brought God's wrath, judgment, and punishment upon the people. Instead of maintaining their purpose and following the will of God, the Levites became like those in the culture around them. They became like the world. It didn't end well.

Moving to the time of Jesus, we see the evolution of this story. The Israelites, during the time of silence after the prophet Malachi, realized they needed to turn back to Yahweh. This resulted in the rise of the religious, law-adhering Pharisees. These were not necessarily Levites, as witnessed by the fact that the Apostle Paul was originally a Pharisee from the tribe of Benjamin. They had become so rigid in following the Law and tradition that Jesus spoke forcefully against them for the hardening of their hearts. Mark 7:8 gives us a view into Jesus' attitude toward them:

"You leave the commandment of God and hold to the tradition of men."

Because of their wayward leadership, Israel missed the coming of Jesus as their Messiah. Israel once more earned God's wrath that will come to a head during the Tribulation.

Now, consider briefly that sacred trust which God invested in the Levites to prevent His wrath upon the people. Pastors and leaders of churches today have that same duty for their flocks. Sadly, just as with the Levites, vast numbers of churches have fallen into apostasy and become no different from the secular culture around them. The fault lies squarely upon those whom God called to lead these congregations.

Religious leaders have forgotten God and actually made a mockery of His Word. The consequences of rejecting Him are as disastrous today as they were in the days of ancient Israel. God has removed His hand of protection upon the churches and upon America. The fire of His wrath is falling. There are many wolves in sheep's clothing in the churches, and the nation has rejected God at the highest levels of government.

This will not end well.

For those of us who still honor and revere God, who have made Jesus our Savior and Lord, our job in these darkening days is to continue shining the light of Christ and to persevere. Jesus is coming back soon for us. We need to hold on and occupy until that glorious day.

February 28: Numbers 22:6 – Balaam's Attempted Divination

(Numbers 21-22; Mark 7:14-37)

From the very beginning when God interacted with Abram (Abraham), He pronounced a decree with everlasting consequences. The Abrahamic Covenant in Genesis 12:3 specifies an amazing law that is in effect to this day:

"I will bless those who bless you, and him who dishonors you I will curse, and in you all the families of the earth shall be blessed."

This is such a powerful commandment that every person or nation that acts in any way – or that even plots – against Israel, God will curse them in some way. Conversely, those which do favorably for Israel receive God's blessings.

Bill Koenig, a Christian White House correspondent, has chronicled this phenomenon in his book, *Eye to Eye: Facing the Consequences of Dividing Israel* (https://www.amazon.com/dp/B01FYCULB6/). Looking at America over the years and at how various presidential administrations have approached the Mideast situation in regards to Israel, Koenig has shown a direct correlation between positive and negative actions our nation has taken toward God's Promised Land and His Chosen People. Inevitably, when we have taken steps to divide Israel, or so much as plot how to effect a two-state solution with the so-called Palestinians, God has taken that as a personal affront and executed His wrath. Often, severe weather catastrophes come upon different parts of our country; many times with storms arising suddenly with our having no foreknowledge.

On the other hand, through the years, as America has acted favorably toward Israel, God has immensely blessed our nation. Unfortunately, because we've tended to simultaneously act in Israel's interests while also doing something that will harm her, our blessings and curses have been intermingled.

During the Exodus, as God led the children of Israel steadily to the north on the east side of the Jordan River, they encountered hostile nations. One such was Edom. Look at what God declares later in Isaiah 34:5 for how Jacob's brother (Esau founded Edom) treated Israel:

"For my sword has drunk its fill in the heavens; behold, it descends for judgment upon Edom, upon the people I have devoted to destruction."

When Israel reached the border of Moab, King Balak grew fearful and summoned the prophet Balaam to curse her. Balaam is an interesting character. As a legitimate prophet, he heard from Yahweh, but he was not a Hebrew. Balaam was a pagan prophet who practiced divination (Numbers 22:7), and who likely sought counsel from gods other than Yahweh as well. He wasn't an obedient follower of God. We learn later that his advice caused the Moabites to seduce the Israelites (Numbers 31:16).

In this account, King Balak makes a statement concerning Balaam. He says in Numbers 22:6:

*"Come now, curse this people for me, since they are too mighty for me. Perhaps I shall be able to defeat them and drive them from the land, **for I know that he whom you bless is blessed, and he whom you curse is cursed**."*

Balak attributes to the prophet Balaam the ability to curse and bless as though he is acting according to the Abrahamic Covenant. In a sense Balak is usurping this command of God to use for his personal reasons. And, as we subsequently see, Balaam apparently believes he has this power in regards to Israel. But God will not allow a pagan prophet to appropriate His authority against the nation of Israel which He has called forth and shepherded. This law of blessings and curses cannot be used for any purpose other than what it was intended. When Balaam attempts to speak curses, God makes only blessings come from his mouth (Numbers 23:11). It confounds both the king and Balaam.

God specifically spoke this mandate in Genesis 12:3 to reflect His glory and power. He made it a universal edict so that His protection upon Israel would be known. Whether from the lips of Balaam or from an American president, when God's Word is despised, He will not remain idle. Yahweh is God Most High, and He will not be mocked.

February 29: Numbers 25:1-3 – Yoked to Baal

(Numbers 23-25; Mark 8:1-21)

The Israelites had a constant problem. Despite the presence of Yahweh in many forms, and in their witnessing His awesome majesty, the children of Israel simply couldn't help themselves. They seemed to have an irresistible urge to follow any god but the One who actually delivered them from slavery.

While in Moabite territory, the Israelites once more fell into disobedience. It's not clear how much they were aware of King Balak's attempts through the prophet Balaam to curse them. Perhaps they didn't care. The men of Israel had long ago been infested with the desires and lusts of the pagan gods of Egypt. They acted out in the flesh what they had acquired in their hearts. We saw this occur when Moses ascended Mount Sinai to receive the Ten Commandments in the incident of the golden calf (Exodus 32). Here again we see a similar embracing of sinful cravings in Numbers 25:1-3:

While Israel lived in Shittim, the people began to whore with the daughters of Moab. These invited the people to the sacrifices of their gods, and the people ate and bowed down to their gods. So Israel yoked himself to Baal of Peor. And the anger of the Lord was kindled against Israel.

The men of Israel lusted after the beautiful pagan women of Moab. As inevitably happened, the women corrupted the men in two ways:

1. They lured them into sinful sexual relations contrary to God's Word
2. Through seducing them to engage in these immoral acts, the women confused the minds and hearts of the men to follow after their god, a direct violation of the 1st of the Ten Commandments

By yielding to their flesh, the Israelites yoked themselves to Baal. Any pagan god named Baal, or Ba'al, was one whom people worshiped as owner, master, or lord (Strong's Concordance #1167). Thus, the men of Israel were declaring that Baal owned them and not Yahweh. As is typical in these incidents, God didn't take this well. For every man involved, we see in Numbers 25:4:

And the Lord said to Moses, "Take all the chiefs of the people and hang them in the sun before the Lord, that the fierce anger of the Lord may turn away from Israel."

After Israel's judges had done this, while the people were still grieving both their disobedience to Yahweh and the loss of their brothers, one man defied the Lord and His authority. In plain sight of the people, Zimri took his Midianite consort, Cozbi, to his tent – the implication being that he was going to continue having sexual relations with her.

That act apparently triggered an immediate response from God in letting loose an affliction upon the Israelites. It was only the swift action of the priest Phinehas in killing Zimri and Cozbi that halted the plague, but only after 24,000 people had instantly died.

God made it clear that Phinehas had saved the day when He told Moses in Numbers 25:11:

"Phinehas the son of Eleazar, son of Aaron the priest, has turned back my wrath from the people of Israel, in that he was jealous with my jealousy among them, so that I did not consume the people of Israel in my jealousy."

God's jealousy was for His people. He knew that when they acted against His commands, bad things would happen as a result, both naturally and through His judgments upon them. We also see that when one man stands against the forces of darkness, what a difference that can make. In fact, Phinehas' resolve made such an impression on God, that He showered him with His goodness, as seen in Numbers 25:12-13:

"Therefore say, 'Behold, I give to him my covenant of peace, and it shall be to him and to his descendants after him the covenant of a perpetual priesthood, because he was jealous for his God and made atonement for the people of Israel.'"

Phinehas wasn't yoked to Baal. He was yoked to Yahweh. God was his Lord and his King – his Master. For that faithfulness – what we call believing loyalty – God poured out blessings that will last in perpetuity.

Should not each one of us have the zeal for God that Phinehas did? Should we not also be jealous for His Name – the Name above all Names – in the same way as this ancient Israelite priest? Can you imagine how each of our lives would change for the better if we also exhibited the believing loyalty that pleases God to the very bottom of His inexhaustible and loving heart?

Awaken

Lessons from Scripture

March

Reading Through the Bible in a Year

Old Testament: Numbers 26 – Judges 5
New Testament: Mark 8:22 – Luke 7:50

Reading Schedule for March

March 1 – March 31			
Mar 1	Num 26-27, Mark 8:22-38	**Mar 17**	Deut 29-30, Mark 16
Mar 2	Num 28-29, Mark 9:1-29	**Mar 18**	Deut 31-32, Luke 1:1-23
Mar 3	Num 30-31, Mark 9:30-50	**Mar 19**	Deut 33-34, Luke 1:24-56
Mar 4	Num 32-33, Mark 10:1-31	**Mar 20**	Josh 1-3, Luke 1:57-80
Mar 5	Num 34-36, Mark 10:32-52	**Mar 21**	Josh 4-6, Luke 2:1-24
Mar 6	Deut 1-2, Mark 11:1-19	**Mar 22**	Josh 7-8, Luke 2:25-52
Mar 7	Deut 3-4, Mark 11:20-33	**Mar 23**	Josh 9-10, Luke 3
Mar 8	Deut 5-7, Mark 12:1-27	**Mar 24**	Josh 11-13, Luke 4:1-32
Mar 9	Deut 8-10, Mark 12:28-44	**Mar 25**	Josh 14-15, Luke 4:33-44
Mar 10	Deut 11-13, Mark 13:1-13	**Mar 26**	Josh 16-18, Luke 5:1-16
Mar 11	Deut 14-16, Mark 13:14-37	**Mar 27**	Josh 19-20, Luke 5:17-39
Mar 12	Deut 17-19, Mark 14:1-25	**Mar 28**	Josh 21-22, Luke 6:1-26
Mar 13	Deut 20-22, Mark 14:26-50	**Mar 29**	Josh 23-24, Luke 6:27-49
Mar 14	Deut 23-25, Mark 14:51-72	**Mar 30**	Judg 1-2, Luke 7:1-30
Mar 15	Deut 26-27, Mark 15:1-26	**Mar 31**	Judg 3-5, Luke 7:31-50
Mar 16	Deut 28, Mark 15:27-47		

March 1: Numbers 27:4 – Feminists

(Numbers 26-27; Mark 8:22-38)

There are many misinformed and foolish people who say the Bible is misogynistic. They characterize God as a woman-hating male supreme being that wants to put women down and keep them in their place (barefoot, pregnant, and in the kitchen?). In their culturally deluded thinking, they believe that what they imagine is the situation today was the same at the time of ancient Israel. That couldn't be further from the truth.

The culture depicted in Scripture was a product of the times. The pagan nations surrounding Israel had immense influence. We see this in many ways throughout the Bible. For instance, the Abrahamic Covenant that Yahweh made with Israel was patterned after a Mesopotamian Suzerain Vassal Treaty. Such a covenant had a greater party and a lesser party who came to terms. In this case the greater party was Yahweh - the Suzerain - and the lesser party was Israel - the Vassal. The suzerain would provide certain benefits such as protection and land rights, while the vassal would be the debtor and owe its master loyalty and financial tribute. Yahweh and Israel had such a relationship.

That kind of covenant is foreign to us; we are more familiar with agreements in which both parties are more or less equals, such as in a contract to purchase a house.

In order to understand much of what happens in the Bible, we simply cannot look at it through the lens of what we know today. Our culture is not what the culture was in the Ancient Near East (ANE). With that in mind, how women were seen and generally treated in Scripture was how things were back then.

However, just like with the issue of slavery, which is another sticking point with people who don't understand this concept of now-then cultural differences, simply because this was the way things were didn't mean that God was satisfied with or promoted them. Yahweh worked within the system and changed it from the inside out. (Come to think of it, that's how God works in our hearts and lives to transform us!) Slavery was a fact of the cultural milieu. God gradually showed there was a better way. In time, His people promoted His love to demonstrate the value of human worth. That came from God's people and from within the church. It was the church of Jesus Christ that brought about the end of slavery.

ANE society had a lesser view of women. They were often valued at half the price of a man, or worse. The people of Israel didn't know any better until God started changing the terms of the game. Yes, the Bible depicts a male dominated society, but consider what happened when the Israelites were about to finally cross the Jordan River to take possession of the land that God had promised them.

God declared that each tribe would have its portion of land based on the size of the tribe (Numbers 26:54). They took a census, and the men leading each tribe were listed along with its number of people. Then an anomaly occurred.

The four daughters of Zelophehad came to Moses with a request. Their father hadn't had any sons to whom the land could be apportioned. They would be left out and the name of their father forgotten if something wasn't done. They said in Numbers 27:4:

"Why should the name of our father be taken away from his clan because he had no son? Give to us a possession among our father's brothers."

Would an unjust, misogynistic deity pay any attention to such an appeal? Of course not. Moses brought their case before Yahweh who agreed with them. He said in Numbers 27:7:

"The daughters of Zelophehad are right. You shall give them possession of an inheritance among their father's brothers and transfer the inheritance of their father to them."

In fact, seeing the justness of this situation, God went further and made the outcome of their case a statute. In the next verse, Numbers 27:8, God says:

"And you shall speak to the people of Israel, saying, 'If a man dies and has no son, then you shall transfer his inheritance to his daughter."

From this incident, we understand that God has nothing against women. They are His children, daughters of the Most High, and are as much heirs to the throne of Heaven as are men who are His sons.

God values all humanity. He made us for a purpose - men and women. He made us different so as to accomplish His purposes, but the message of these first feminists is that God values each and every one of us and showers each of us with His lovingkindness.

March 2: Mark 9:2 - Satan On Notice

(Numbers 28-29; Mark 9:1-29)

As is often the case in Scripture, more is going on behind the scenes in many passages we read than first meets the eye. This is particularly true of the episode known as The Transfiguration. The account begins in Mark 9:2 which says:

And after six days Jesus took with him Peter and James and John, and led them up a high mountain by themselves. And he was transfigured before them.

First let's notice that Jesus and His disciples climbed a high mountain. Which mountain? One chapter back in Mark 8:27, the text gives us a clue:

And Jesus went on with his disciples to the villages of Caesarea Philippi. And on the way he asked his disciples, "Who do people say that I am?"

Caesarea Philippi is in the far northeastern part of Israel. It is in the territory of Dan where a temple to the Greek god Banias (a.k.a. Panias or Pan) was carved out of the rock. This rock, in fact is the place where Jesus in Matthew 16:17-19 made a prophetic pronouncement about the church:

And Jesus answered him, "Blessed are you, Simon Bar-Jonah! For flesh and blood has not revealed this to you, but my Father who is in heaven. And I tell you, you are Peter, and on this rock I will build my church, and the gates of hell shall not prevail against it. I will give you the keys of the kingdom of heaven, and whatever you bind on earth shall be bound in heaven, and whatever you loose on earth shall be loosed in heaven."

There is no other mountain in Israel that can legitimately be called high except the one that dominates all of Israel in the north. That is Mount Hermon. It was Mount Hermon that Jesus, Peter, James, and John ascended, and at whose foot Jesus said that hell itself could not overcome the church.

These are dramatic and powerful scenes. The question must be asked: Was there something special about Mount Hermon that might have caused Jesus to initiate these things there?

Recall from Genesis 6:1-2 that the sons of God (*bene Elohim*) came down to earth from their heavenly abode. They trespassed the divine boundaries that God had ordained for them and procreated with human women. The ancient Jewish understanding of this incident is that these rebellious spiritual beings descended from Mount Hermon.

This area of Israel has always been known as one with extreme demonic activity (e.g. the giant Rephaim King Og of Bashan). Now we see why. Disobedient spiritual entities came to earth here. A temple to a major pagan god was built in this location. As a bonus, we also have the tribe of Dan, which had serious disobedience issues with Yahweh that later causes their tribal name to be omitted in significant prophetic texts (e.g. Revelation 7 - Dan does not provide any Tribulation witnesses).

So, what is going on with Jesus and this demonic area?

Jesus came to this world to redeem mankind. He had serious opposition to this task from Satan and the various spiritual forces of evil that Paul notes in Ephesians 6:12. Much earlier, Yahweh had declared in Genesis 3:15 that the Seed of the woman would take on Satan (the nachash - the serpent) who had caused Adam and Eve to sin.

When Jesus was transfigured on Mount Hermon, this demonstrated to the entire spiritual realm that Jesus was the One who would bring them down. He reinforced this in declaring that the gates of hell would not prevail against the church, which was His chosen instrument to facilitate mankind's redemption. These incidents put Satan and his minions on notice that their time was short.

As an exclamation point to the threat that Jesus brought to his enemies, when He and the disciples came down off the mountain, He cast out the spirit from the young boy. It was not only a physical act, but a symbolic one. Jesus would cast out all the rebellious, unclean spirits that had infested the world. The King had come, and nothing could stand in the way of accomplishing His purposes.

Is it any wonder that Satan incited the religious authorities to crucify Jesus? Yet, it was a setup. God had deceived the deceitful one. Jesus had to be crucified in order for man's sins to be imputed to Him. The crucifixion was exactly what had to occur. Satan didn't know this, and he fell into God's trap. Yahweh accomplished exactly what He needed to through Jesus' death and resurrection. He made a way for man to be reconciled to Him. Do you think Satan would have caused Jesus to be killed like this if he'd known it was what must take place to fulfill the prophetic Word?

We can rejoice that our God is sovereign and mighty, far above all powers and principalities. Jesus is already victorious in this ages-old war. In Him, we too are triumphant. When the enemy attacks us, we have only to remember who we are in Christ. We're already victors!

March 3: Numbers 31:49 - Not a Man Missing

(Numbers 30-31; Mark 30-50)

The sorry incident of the prophet Balaam attempting to curse the Israelites had many consequences. King Balak of Moab had teamed up with his allies the Midianites to hire Balaam to facilitate the destruction of God's people. That method didn't work, so Balaam suggested another way to achieve the same result. He counseled that the women of these nations should seduce the Israelite men to accomplish their purposes (Numbers 31:16).

This approach worked so well that the Israelites openly sinned in defiance of God's commands (e.g. Numbers 25:6), and overall because of the plague the Lord brought on them for their disobedience, 24,000 of them died before Phinehas courageously stepped into the fray to intercede.

Midianites and Moabites are somewhat interchangeable in this account, although they are distinct people groups. Their association with each other must have been quite close because the narrative speaks of them often in the same breath. To punish the Midianites for their part in this drama, God instructed Moses to send 12,000 men against Midian. In the course of battle, Balaam was killed (Numbers 31:8).

Often, when God wants certain people groups totally annihilated, He'll command the Israelites to devote their enemies to destruction. He doesn't do this here. However, following the battle, Moses is upset with his commanders because they didn't deal appropriately with the women who caused the Israelite men to sin (Numbers 31:15-16). He tells them to kill these women so that they can no longer be a temptation to anyone.

In the accounting that follows, we see that the Israelites took large numbers of livestock in their victory. We don't get a count of the Midianite women who Moses said must die, but 32,000 virgins from their tribe remained. If there were that many young women who hadn't lain with a man, how many might there have been who'd had sexual relations? The text doesn't tell us, but from the overall numbers of livestock and virgins the Israelites took from the five Midianite kings, there were probably a lot! Beyond that, given those numbers, how many Midianite men were put to the sword? Again, we don't know, but it's probably a good estimate that there were several hundred thousand.

Why does this matter?

Consider the statement the officers of the Israelite army made to Moses in Numbers 31:49:

"Your servants have counted the men of war who are under our command, and there is not a man missing from us."

How could this be? The Israelites had taken part in what was certainly a fierce battle. The amount of plunder - livestock and women - surely wasn't taken without significant resistance. How in the world could there be no - zero! - casualties among the Israelites?

The answer lies in Leviticus 26, which is later echoed in Deuteronomy 28. Yahweh had laid out for His people the blessings and curses He would bring based upon their obedience or disobedience. The battle with Midian was still early in the process, so God needed to show Israel what His Word meant and why she could rely on Him. Leviticus 26:8 details what more than likely happened in the battle with the Midianites:

Five of you shall chase a hundred, and a hundred of you shall chase ten thousand, and your enemies shall fall before you by the sword.

If five Israelite soldiers chased and killed one hundred of their enemies, or one hundred Israelites took down 10,000 men, how do those numbers shake out? We know that 12,000 Israelites went to battle. If my math is correct, there could have been as many as 240,000 to 1,200,000 of the enemy destroyed based on these percentages.

We don't have confirmation of those high numbers, but we do know what is possible from the Word of the Lord. Even if only half this quantity of enemy troops came against Israel, for 12,000 men to rout and kill them, this was an astounding display of God's might and supernatural protection of His people.

Let's consider the numbers from another perspective. When Gideon confronted these same Midianites some years later, we're told his 32,000 men were outnumbered four to one; the Midianites had at least 132,000 soldiers (Judges 7) God whittles Gideon's men down so that he ends up with only 300; the rest go home. Thus, the percentage of Gideon's men to the enemy came down to one Israelite versus 426 Midianites. To put it another way, if Gideon had the 12,000 men that Moses had from the twelve tribes, he could have dispatched over 5,000,000 enemy troops! Gideon's victory was such a piece of cake, it's a wonder God didn't reduce his number of men down to thirty or so!

The point of all this math is that human numbers actually mean very little to the Lord. He has the ability to eliminate huge numbers of His enemies with a single Word. Can you imagine how great Israel might have been in the past if she had obediently followed Yahweh?

Of course, we'll see a similar display of God's power at the very end of the Tribulation when the armies of the world gather on the plains of Armageddon to destroy Jerusalem and presumably God Himself. Jesus comes in His glory with the Raptured saints - His Bride whom He'd snatched from the earth to fulfill His vows - to do battle against this great assembly. But, it's not much of a battle. One Word from Jesus and all are destroyed.

Aren't you glad you're on God's side?

March 4: Numbers 33:55 - Trouble in the Land

(Numbers 32-33; Mark 10:1-31)

Because of what the Israelites had learned in Egypt over their 400 years of captivity, Yahweh had a deconditioning project to accomplish with them. They had been in the midst of a pantheon of pagan gods and gotten used to deities whose image they could see. The verbal history of their people had probably taken on something like mythic proportions, i.e. that of a God who was Spirit and who didn't have any graven images to represent Him. He was something far removed from their everyday experience. This was a long-term problem with the Hebrew people. They constantly wanted to turn to idols and to worship what they deemed as more real that this unseen God who spoke to Moses.

Undeterred, Yahweh showed them through His miraculous acts and provision that He was greater than all the Egyptian gods they'd known. Yet, they had extremely short memories and were particularly obstinate about wanting what they likely conceived of as "the real thing," i.e. a god represented by a visible idol. To help them in their mental turnabout, Yahweh gave them the Ten Commandments and carried out the consequences of their breaking His Law with severe judgments. He wanted to pour out His love upon His children, but because of their hard hearts had to resort to a carrot and stick approach. That showed up in Leviticus 26 with the declaration of God's blessings for obedience and punishments for disobedience.

Upon the advent of the Israelites crossing the Jordan River to enter the land Yahweh had promised them, He spoke through Moses to relay the following message in Numbers 33:52:

"*. . . then you shall drive out all the inhabitants of the land from before you and destroy all their figured stones and destroy all their metal images and demolish all their high places.*"

This was a three-pronged command. The Israelites were to:

1. Drive out the inhabitants of the land
2. Destroy all idols of pagan gods
3. Demolish the worship areas to these gods that were typically erected in high places

The inhabitant of Canaan were a combination of human and Rephaim, i.e. descendants of Nephilim. They had to be eliminated so that the Israelites wouldn't cross-breed with them and risk contaminating their blood with non-human DNA. There was no true God but Yahweh; He wouldn't allow any double-mindedness among His people. He could not have them drawn to the remembrance of pagan gods by exposure to idols. Similarly, Yahweh had instructed His children that He resided in the Most Holy of Holies; there alone could He be worshiped. The high places were altars to other gods and had to go.

Yahweh warned the Israelites of the dangers of not adhering to His Word, making it very clear in Numbers 33:55-56 what would happen if they didn't:

"But if you do not drive out the inhabitants of the land from before you, then those of them whom you let remain shall be as barbs in your eyes and thorns in your sides, and they shall trouble you in the land where you dwell. And I will do to you as I thought to do to them."

By allowing the land's inhabitants to remain, they would constantly trouble the Israelites. They would prevent God's people from fully realizing their inheritance. Worse, by His people not removing the land's inhabitants as commanded, God would bring the punishments due to the pagans upon His own children. The Israelites would never know the peace and prosperity that God intended for them.

How does this concept apply to Christians today?

The inhabitants of our land are the many besetting sins that plague us. The flesh is always weak and prone to temptation. This includes such things as the pursuit of wealth, power, even friends or family as they become our highest goal. Our gods are the many baubles we enjoy by living in a land of ease and comfort. These baubles might be playthings we turn to in our leisure or people whom we admire to the extent that we idolize them. These are the barbs and thorns that trouble us in this land because they keep our focus on anything but God.

Are we any different from the ancient Israelites in this matter? Not at all. We tend to go where our eyes and hearts lead us. What we do may seem good, but if Jesus isn't at the center of our lives, just like with the Israelites, we face trouble in the land.

And what is that trouble? If we follow pagan ways in disobedience to God - even as Christians - the punishment due to those who despise God will come round to us. How can they not? If not obedient, we are in rebellion. A people in rebellion will never know the true blessings of the Lord.

We have to drive out those pesky inhabitants of the land; we have to eliminate the sins that cause us to stray. God has made the way for us to accomplish this. He sent His Holy Spirit who dwells within every believer. When we listen to Him and do as He commands, our conscience will guide us. We will walk in righteousness. And, we will please God.

Gary W. Ritter

March 5: Numbers 35:33 - Blood Pollutes the Land

(Numbers 34-36; Mark 10:32-52)

Some of the final instructions to the Israelites before they crossed the Jordan River into the land of Canaan gave them important principles that we in modern times should have heeded, but did not. They display the character and intent of God, which ultimately His people ignored, and which we likewise have disdained in the sophistication of our *civilized* age.

God's bottom-line command in the directives He gave are found in Numbers 35:33:

"You shall not pollute the land in which you live, for blood pollutes the land, and no atonement can be made for the land for the blood that is shed in it, except by the blood of the one who shed it."

Read that again. *Blood pollutes the land. No atonement can be made for the land...except by the blood of the one who shed it.*

This statement was made in the context of God's decrees regarding the killing of another person. Yahweh described two instances of this sin:

1. The killing of someone without intent (Numbers 35:11)
2. The deliberate murder of someone (Numbers 35:16)

Basically, these two conditions speak of unintentional manslaughter and deliberate homicide. The text also relates what the punishment shall be for these crimes and who is to carry out the sentence.

Someone who committed manslaughter could flee to a city of refuge where he could remain safely until his trial. The city of refuge was his safe haven; but even if judged not guilty, if he strayed beyond this city's boundaries, he was subject to being killed by the one tasked with avenging the death of the person whose life he inadvertently took. The sentence remained in effect until the high priest died. Only then could he go in peace back to his actual home.

The one who deliberately murdered another could similarly go to the city of refuge. At his trial, at least two witnesses were required to accuse him. The testimony of a single witness wasn't sufficient. If found guilty, the killer was to be put to death immediately.

The tracking down of someone who killed another under either condition fell to a person known as the avenger of blood (Numbers 35:19). He was the executioner, usually the nearest male relative of the deceased. When a person took that role, he had the solemn duty to carry it out. Why? Because of God's decree in Numbers 35:33 noted earlier.

Polluting the land with blood has been a problem from the very beginning. When Cain killed Abel in an act of deliberate homicide, the Lord knew and was grieved. He said the following in Genesis 4:10-11:

"What have you done? The voice of your brother's blood is crying to me from the ground. And now you are cursed from the ground, which has opened its mouth to receive your brother's blood from your hand."

The act of murder - the shedding of blood upon the land - brings forth a curse. The blood must be avenged in order for atonement to be made.

As Israel fell further from Yahweh in her years of disobedience, have no doubt that this command went ignored. Worse, it was the shedding of Jesus' blood that brought about the curse of the final destruction of Israel that led to the diaspora of the Jewish people. Consider what the people cried out when Pilate gave them the choice of freeing Barabbas or Jesus in Matthew 27:25:

And all the people answered, "His blood be on us and on our children!"

Did they have any idea how serious this vow was? The Pharisees and other leaders had incited the mob. The blood of Jesus was upon them all. Within one hundred years, Israel was no more. Jesus' blood, and that of many others, had polluted the land. There was no human avenger of blood for Jesus, so God Himself took on that role.

What about us today? Has the blood of innocents been shed? Has it been avenged? Think, of course, of the 60 million unborn children callously murdered in the womb. Does their blood cry out? Consider the perversion of our justice system where murderers spend their lives in prison. Is the blood they shed avenged?

Our nation has forgotten God in many ways. This is only one such instance. We have not only allowed murder to go unpunished, we have encouraged it through the passing of laws that actually facilitate it. We even contribute huge sums of taxpayer money to an organization that has literally poured a river of blood onto the land. Does the land not cry out to God against

Planned Parenthood and all those who support it? Do we really think God will let this atrocity stand?

He will not. The Tribulation for the unbelieving world is coming. God will indeed execute judgment upon all who have not confessed Jesus as Lord. He will pour out blood upon the guilty as part of their punishment (e.g. Revelation 8:8 - the 2nd Trumpet Judgment). When Jesus returns at the final death throes of these most horrible seven years, avenged blood will flow freely (e.g. Revelation 14:20 - the final harvest).

We have mocked God all these years, but He will uphold His holy Name against all who have profaned it. We grieve now at the injustice, but God's Word will prevail. We can rest assured that all innocent blood will be accounted for. God is sovereignly in charge. His will, unquestionably, will be done.

March 6: Deuteronomy 2:34 - No Survivors

(Deuteronomy 1-2; Mark 11:1-19)

The book of Deuteronomy is the second telling of the Law. Often, what it provides is more detail from the narrative of the previous books that comprise the 5-volume Torah (Genesis, Exodus, Leviticus, Numbers, Deuteronomy). We get a good dose of that in the first two chapters and learn some very interesting details about the prior inhabitants of the lands surrounding Canaan that God had sent the Israelites to conquer and inhabit.

In their wilderness wanderings during the Exodus, the children of Israel spent their many years east of the Jordan River. The possessors of those lands south to north included Edom (Esau), Moab (Lot), Ammon (Lot), and the Amorite kingdoms of Heshbon and Bashan.

When God first directed the Israelites to cross the Jordan into the hill country of Canaan, ten of the men sent on that spying expedition came back with a bad report. Numbers 13:28-29 tells us what the majority of the spies said:

"However, the people who dwell in the land are strong, and the cities are fortified and very large. And besides, we saw the descendants of Anak there. The Amalekites dwell in the land of the Negeb. The Hittites, the Jebusites, and the Amorites dwell in the hill country. And the Canaanites dwell by the sea, and along the Jordan."

They had seen the sons of the Anakim inhabiting the land, and they completely freaked out. Why?

The sons of Anak included these different tribes noted above. They were considered Rephaim, descendants in some fashion of the Nephilim. We know from Genesis 6:1-4 that the Nephilim were the offspring of the union of the sons of God (*bene Elohim*) with human women. They were the mighty men of old, giants in the land, and the reason for every nation on earth having mythologies about various gods with their enormous prowess and sexual appetites. The Israelite spies encountered the Amorites, failed to remember Yahweh was with them and, in their human frailty, convinced the people the Amorites were too powerful for them to conquer as Numbers 13:33 notes:

"And there we saw the Nephilim (the sons of Anak, who come from the Nephilim), and we seemed to ourselves like grasshoppers, and so we seemed to them."

Where at this time were these giants in the southern lands of Edom, Moab, and Ammon? Scripture doesn't record the conquests, but these descendants of Abraham had previously encountered the giant clans and, with the Lord's help, defeated them. Look at these verses that describe this:

Deuteronomy 2:9-11
"And the Lord said to me, 'Do not harass Moab or contend with them in battle, for I will not give you any of their land for a possession, because I have given Ar to the people of Lot for a possession.' (The Emim formerly lived there, a people great and many, and tall as the Anakim. Like the Anakim they are also counted as Rephaim, but the Moabites call them Emim.)"

Deuteronomy 2:12
"(The Horites also lived in Seir formerly, but the people of Esau dispossessed them and destroyed them from before them and settled in their place, as Israel did to the land of their possession, which the Lord gave to them.)"

Deuteronomy 2:19-22
"And when you approach the territory of the people of Ammon, do not harass them or contend with them, for I will not give you any of the land of the people of Ammon as a possession, because I have given it to the sons of Lot for a possession.' (It is also counted as a land of Rephaim. Rephaim formerly lived there—but the Ammonites call them Zamzummim— a people great and many, and tall as the Anakim; but the Lord destroyed them before the Ammonites, and they dispossessed them and settled in their place, as he did for the people of Esau, who live in Seir, when he destroyed the Horites before them and they dispossessed them and settled in their place even to this day.)"

Deuteronomy 2:23
"(As for the Avvim, who lived in villages as far as Gaza, the Caphtorim, who came from Caphtor, destroyed them and settled in their place.)"

Edom, Moab, and Ammon had all previously fought and destroyed the many sons of Anak, i.e. the giant Rephaim which so frightened the ten spies and the rest of the children of Israel. God had been in the midst of these tribes (Israel's "brothers," i.e. relatives, of Israel by descent from Esau and Lot).

But, giants remained on the east side of the Jordan. In order to prepare the new generation of Israelites for the battles ahead in Canaan, God had them march north to encounter the remaining Amorite tribes in Heshbon - led by King Sihon; and in Bashan - led by King Og.

All of the first generation of Israelites had died in the wilderness, so God was starting out with a fresh slate of leaders. Yahweh told Moses and the people in Numbers 2:24:

"Rise up, set out on your journey and go over the Valley of the Arnon. Behold, I have given into your hand Sihon the Amorite, king of Heshbon, and his land. Begin to take possession, and contend with him in battle."

Israel obediently followed Yahweh's commands this time. King Sihon couldn't stand against God's people, and Moses reported in Deuteronomy 2:34:

"And we captured all his cities at that time and devoted to destruction every city, men, women, and children. We left no survivors."

King Og would be next as Deuteronomy 3 records. However, look at the language of this last verse. The Israelites devoted their enemies to destruction; they left no survivors. This is critical to our understanding of God and His purposes. Why?

The Rephaim, i.e. all these tribes mentioned in this narrative, were descended from the Nephilim. Satan, along with his cohort - the sons of God - determined to cause God's Word to fail. If His Word wouldn't come to pass, they knew that their ambitions to replace Him as God Most High could be realized. By their procreating with human women, these rebellious spiritual entities corrupted humanity's DNA. The Nephilim as their descendants were no longer fully human. Jesus came to redeem mankind. These creatures couldn't be redeemed. If all the earth were populated with these beings, God would be a liar, as Jesus (the Seed of the woman in Genesis 3:15) would have none to save. This is why God determined in Genesis 6:5:

The Lord saw that the wickedness of man was great in the earth, and that every intention of the thoughts of his heart was only evil continually.

It was because of this overwhelming depravity that God brought the flood to destroy all corrupted creatures on the earth, finding only Noah and his sons as having pure human blood.

The Israelite conquest of the east side of the Jordan was critical for them to have the confidence to take the land of Canaan - also populated with giant clans - for themselves as the people of God. By successfully defeating the Amorites on the east of the Jordan with God's might, they learned they could likewise accomplish what He had for them to do west of the river.

Yahweh was always with His children, but they had short memories. Trusting Him was something they could never fully do for any length of time.

But...

A day is coming when all surviving Israelites will turn to God in that trust He has longed for since the very beginning. The remnant of Israel at the end of the Tribulation will trust Jesus as their Messiah, Savior, and Lord. It will be a difficult lesson learned as 2/3 of the people of Israel will perish. However, of that remaining 1/3 all Israel will be saved. At that time, they will truly be God's people who follow Him with heart, soul, mind and strength. God's purpose for His children Israel will be achieved. What a glorious day that will be!

March 7: Deuteronomy 4:15 - Watch Yourselves

(Deuteronomy 3-4; Mark 11:20-33)

When Moses repeated the Word of the Lord to the children of Israel prior to his death and their crossing the Jordan River into Canaan with Joshua at the helm, he gave them severe warnings along with a reminder of who their God was.

The Israelites were to heed God's Word for their own safety and protection. He first told them in Deuteronomy 4:2:

"You shall not add to the word that I command you, nor take from it, that you may keep the commandments of the Lord your God that I command you."

One huge reason for this was how other nations and tribes would view Israel. By their diligently doing what Yahweh commanded, they would receive an important byproduct that He outlined in Deuteronomy 4:6-7:

"Keep them and do them, for that will be your wisdom and your understanding in the sight of the peoples, who, when they hear all these statutes, will say, 'Surely this great nation is a wise and understanding people.' For what great nation is there that has a god so near to it as the Lord our God is to us, whenever we call upon him?"

This is exactly what God intended from the very beginning: Israel would be a blessing to all nations (Genesis 12:3). By observing God's favor upon His people, others would also seek Him and be likewise blessed.

In order to impress upon His people who He was - the Great I AM - Yahweh gave them a significant demonstration. Deuteronomy 4:12-13 expands upon the narrative from Exodus. Moses reminds the Israelites:

"Then the Lord spoke to you out of the midst of the fire. You heard the sound of words, but saw no form; there was only a voice. And he declared to you his covenant, which he commanded you to perform, that is, the Ten Commandments, and he wrote them on two tablets of stone."

The Exodus text omitted these details. Here we learn that Yahweh didn't just appear to Moses and speak to him. He also spoke verbally to the Israelites and gave them the Ten Commandments from His own mouth.

Moses goes on to extol Yahweh above every other god. He warns the Israelites in Deuteronomy 4:15:

"Therefore watch yourselves very carefully. Since you saw no form on the day that the Lord spoke to you at Horeb out of the midst of the fire."

Why?

There are indeed other so-called gods who the peoples of the earth worship, but there is only One true God. And, what is it about Him? Deuteronomy 4:24 makes it clear:

"For the Lord your God is a consuming fire, a jealous God."

Yahweh is the only God whose Word is true and righteous. He is jealous for His children, not jealous of them. God knew the disastrous consequences the Israelites would bring on themselves by letting their hearts be led astray by other gods. More than that, if they followed these imposters against Yahweh's command, He personally would punish them. Moses succinctly laid this out in Deuteronomy 4:26-27:

"I call heaven and earth to witness against you today, that you will soon utterly perish from the land that you are going over the Jordan to possess. You will not live long in it, but will be utterly destroyed. And the Lord will scatter you among the peoples, and you will be left few in number among the nations where the Lord will drive you."

The Israelites were warned. Unfortunately, they would forget and ignore Moses' admonition. The outcome would be bad news and good news. Deuteronomy 4:30 spells it out:

*"**When** you are in tribulation, and all these things come upon you in the latter days, you will return to the Lord your God and obey his voice.*

This wasn't in doubt. Israel would and **will** go through the fire. And they did; all the way through the holocaust. But, it won't stop there. Because of their disobedience, Israel must continue to suffer. The Tribulation is coming, and 2/3 of Israel will perish (Zechariah 13:8).

But, here's the really Good News for God's children Israel, which Deuteronomy 4:31 explains:

"For the Lord your God is a merciful God. He will not leave you or destroy you or forget the covenant with your fathers that he swore to them."

The day is approaching when all Israel will be saved!

March 8: Deuteronomy 7:14 - Blessed Above All Peoples

(Deuteronomy 5-7; Mark 12:1-27)

The Lord wanted to bless His children Israel. He told them time and again all that He wanted to do for them. When they responded positively to His giving them the Ten Commandments, listen to the yearning of Yahweh's heart in Deuteronomy 5:29:

"Oh that they had such a heart as this always, to fear me and to keep all my commandments, that it might go well with them and with their descendants forever!"

To that end, God tried to help them by giving them guidance, such as what He said in Deuteronomy 6:20:

"When your son asks you in time to come, 'What is the meaning of the testimonies and the statutes and the rules that the Lord our God has commanded you?'"

The Israelites must have wondered why God wanted to be so good to them. In Deuteronomy 7:6 and verses following He expounded on this:

"For you are a people holy to the Lord your God. The Lord your God has chosen you to be a people for his treasured possession, out of all the peoples who are on the face of the earth."

Maybe what God said was too good to be true. In the passage Deuteronomy 7:12-24 He tells them of the many ways He would shower His children with His love:

v13 - He will bless the fruit of their womb, i.e. they will be fruitful and multiply (just like He wanted for Adam and Eve and Noah's family)

v13 - He will bless the fruit of their ground, i.e. everything they touch in the earth will produce in abundance

v14 - He will bless them above all peoples on the earth, i.e. none will be more blessed than Israel

v15 - He will take away all their sickness and disease, i.e. unlike other nations, He will keep them from affliction v16 - He will enable them to prevail in battle above all other nations

v18 - He will help them to remember what He has done for them in the past

v20 - He will go before them in battle so that others flee as though attacked by a swarm of hornets

v24 - He will make a way to destroy all opposition so that none can stand before them

In return for all these blessings, what did Israel have to do?

Yahweh required them to have believing loyalty in Him. They were to reject all other gods and put their faith in Him alone.

How simple was that? Deuteronomy 7:26 makes it clear:

"And you shall not bring an abominable thing into your house and become devoted to destruction like it. You shall utterly detest and abhor it, for it is devoted to destruction."

All that God detested, Israel was to detest. When He told them to utterly destroy certain people and their idols, He had a reason. They were to obey unquestionably.

So simple, yet so difficult. Their wicked, sinful hearts were continually led astray.

And all these blessings?

They had a taste of them during David's and Solomon's reigns. Before and beyond those years? Lost opportunities.

Yet, the promises of God will be fulfilled when Jesus returns and all Israel is saved (i.e. the 1/3 remnant per Zechariah 13:8). God's beloved will finally realize all these blessings.

Why?

Because they will sing "Hosannah in the Highest!" to their Messiah Jesus Christ, and He will finally reign in their hearts.

March 9: Deuteronomy 9:3 - A Consuming Fire

(Deuteronomy 8-10); Mark 12:28-44)

God created us with an ego, but that sure can get out of hand! The Oxford English dictionary says about ego that it's "a person's sense of self-esteem or self-importance." Certainly the self-esteem part of the definition is critical simply so we can function on a daily basis. We have to feel a sense of self-worth; otherwise, how we value ourselves would be minimal. Many people consider themselves useless because they have no self-esteem.

On the other hand, once self-esteem creeps into the area of self-importance, that's when we begin seeing ourselves as greater than we are. An exaggerated sense of self-importance leads to pride and arrogance. We think who we are and what we accomplish is beyond what they actually are.

Yahweh knew the Israelites had this problem; they were human - we all tend toward pride as a condition of being alive. It may be one reason the Bible emphasizes that Moses was so humble (Numbers 12:3).

As Moses continued to remind the children of Israel of who they were in God prior to their crossing the Jordan River, he warned them about the danger of forgetting humility. Yahweh was giving them an abundant land. He would be going before them to cause their enemies to flee. It was He who had sustained them in the wilderness. Yet He knew the danger of pride in that it causes one to believe he is the reason for all that he has. Moses in Deuteronomy 8:14,17 said that if the Israelites thought this way...

"Then your heart be lifted up, and you forget the Lord your God, who brought you out of the land of Egypt, out of the house of slavery...Beware lest you say in your heart, 'My power and the might of my hand have gotten me this wealth.'"

They had already encountered the sons of Anak - the Anakim and the Amorites. They were Rephaim; a remnant of the Nephilim of old. As such, they were great and mighty warriors, huge and fearsome. Moses minced no words. *"Who can stand before the sons of Anak?"* (Deuteronomy 9:2)

The Israelites couldn't stand by themselves, but God was with them. Moses gives them this comfort and encouragement in Deuteronomy 9:3:

"Know therefore today that he who goes over before you as a consuming fire is the Lord your God. He will destroy them and subdue them before you. So you

shall drive them out and make them perish quickly, as the Lord has promised you."

But, here's the thing: God wouldn't do this because of how wonderful, humble, faithful, and righteous the Israelites were. No. Moses tells them in Deuteronomy 9:4:

"Do not say in your heart, after the Lord your God has thrust them out before you, 'It is because of my righteousness that the Lord has brought me in to possess this land,' whereas it is because of the wickedness of these nations that the Lord is driving them out before you."

The people in the land of Canaan were wicked. They were a stench in God's nostrils. It was because of how sinful and depraved they were that Yahweh was thrusting them from the land. Moses wanted the Israelites to know exactly how God considered them. In Deuteronomy 9:6, he says:

"Know, therefore, that the Lord your God is not giving you this good land to possess because of your righteousness, for you are a stubborn people."

It's all because of God and who He is. The sense of self-importance the Israelites were prone to in their pride was nothing. God as a consuming fire was the reason for all that His children had throughout those forty years of wandering in the wilderness, and all they would have in the Promised Land. Moses hoped and prayed they'd remember this. But, of course, they wouldn't.

How different are we? Does our exceedingly humble nature cause us to fall flat before the Lord when someone impinges upon our sensibilities? When our ego is hurt for some minor reason, do we offer ourselves as a living sacrifice before God like Moses did? Do we say to the Lord, "Slay me, but do good to that other person?" If you're like me in any way, that attitude is difficult, to say the least.

Progressive/liberal Christians today want to do away with the Old Testament. They want us in our modern Christianity to "unhitch" from that antiquated book. Some of them even believe that Yahweh in the OT is a different God from the One we encounter in the New Testament.

For true, born-again believers who actually read their Bibles, this is nonsense. God - Jesus Christ - is the same yesterday, today, and forever. It is

He who created us. It is He who provides everything necessary for our lives. It is He who saves us.

As Moses reminded the Israelites, let us remind ourselves. We ourselves are not the source of who we are and what we have. All things come from our loving God. Let's give Him praise and glory for the goodness in our lives.

March 10: Deuteronomy 12:23 - Don't Eat the Blood

(Deuteronomy 11-13; Mark 13:1-13)

We read of certain prohibitions the Lord commanded Israel and may wonder what's behind them. One such that we come across today in our reading is Deuteronomy 12:23 in which Yahweh declares through Moses:

"Only be sure that you do not eat the blood, for the blood is the life, and you shall not eat the life with the flesh."

Now, you may think: "I like a good rare steak. What is God saying here? Does this mean I can't enjoy meat cooked in this way?" (Of course, there are others who choke on the thought of eating rare meat; well done is their preferred and only option. But I digress!)

Let's read a little further in the text and see what we come up with. Consider the several verses comprising Deuteronomy 12:29-31 under the ESV heading *Warning Against Idolatry*:

"When the Lord your God cuts off before you the nations whom you go in to dispossess, and you dispossess them and dwell in their land, take care that you be not ensnared to follow them, after they have been destroyed before you, and that you do not inquire about their gods, saying, 'How did these nations serve their gods?—that I also may do the same.' You shall not worship the Lord your God in that way, for every abominable thing that the Lord hates they have done for their gods, for they even burn their sons and their daughters in the fire to their gods."

Context is everything. There is one Christian apologist who says: "Never read a Bible verse." Greg Koukl isn't telling us not to read our Bibles; rather, he's saying that we should never read a single verse without understanding those surrounding it, i.e. the context of the verse. Dr. Michael Heiser makes the same point. Never pull out one verse from Scripture and think you understand all it means. Especially don't make doctrine out of an isolated verse. Understand what's going on in the passage around it.

So, we see following the injunction not to eat blood, that there is a relationship in doing that to idolatry, specifically the worship of other gods.

The Israelites had a propensity for defeating their foes because of God's mighty hand, then wondering about their gods to the extent that they became ensnared by them. God's children would inquire about these pagan entities and begin to follow them. Imagine how contrary this is to logic of any kind. You defeat an enemy, specifically knowing that God has done the heavy lifting to provide that victory, then you begin to worship the gods of these nations that you've just defeated. These gods had no power. They could do nothing against the God of heaven. In fact, He made them look foolish in many instances. Yet, you abandon the One who brought you to the dance for someone else who apparently whispers in your ear that he really-really is so much better than your date. So you follow him home to the other side of the tracks. You see his poverty and how worthless he is, but he's enchanted you. As a result, you go like a dumb oxen to the slaughter. It's only after you've been mistreated and lost all your self-respect that you finally come limping home to your One true love.

Yahweh had good reasons for His warnings. The practices of the pagan gods were abominable to Him. They practiced child sacrifice. In their pagan ceremonies, they drank (ate) the blood of animals - perhaps even of humans - they had killed.

Contrast this with the value God places on life - particularly human life. As our first verse above says, *the blood is the life*. God created all. He made life in such a way that when blood flows in the veins of any creature, it lives. When blood is shed, it must be accounted for. Blood sacrifices that Yahweh demanded of His people were always to be done with reverence to Him as the One who made all creatures. These sacrifices were offered to Him for the atonement of various sins. Never once did He command human sacrifice as a way of appeasing His wrath.

Pagan deities inevitably demanded the shedding of blood and the eating of it. Their purpose was to counter God's ways; to do the opposite of what His righteousness demanded. Anything that Yahweh wanted, the pagan gods required a 180 degree turn from that. Think about this in light of what we know of satanic masses. What do they do? They display an upside down cross, sacrifice animals (or humans!), and drink their blood. All in the interest of poking a stick in God's eye and for their own self-glorification.

Is it any wonder that the text goes on to read that a person who entices someone else to serve other gods should be literally despised and put to death (Deuteronomy 13:6-8)? God knew that human flesh is corruptible. People are weak. They are easily led down the primrose path because it looks so alluring. Unfortunately, in their deception, they lose their way and often perish. Yahweh wanted to prevent this destruction coming upon His children. He wants to keep us today from the same dangers.

It's why we're shown in Scripture that Jesus is the only way, truth, and life. He alone saves us from ruin. This is why we must resolve to follow only Him *and* to believe that His Word is the only one that delivers us into God's Kingdom. Jesus is the only means for someone to enter heaven. All other paths lead to eternal darkness.

By the way, concerning that steak: Intent is everything. If we eat it as an offering to other gods, that's the problem. If we eat it because that's our preferred method, and it has nothing to do with pagan worship, I don't think that's an issue. The same holds true for tattoos. They aren't my thing, but are they against God's will? Again, intent is everything. Tattoos used to be the means for someone to declare his allegiance to a pagan god. If someone today gets a tattoo, and there is no intent to worship another god in this act, I don't think God has a problem with that. In these various acts, it all hinges on one's relationship to God and/or whether the doing of them takes someone in a direction contrary to following Him.

God loves us. He desires that none shall perish. All these other gods? Their desire is for us to perish with them. Why follow such losers? Jesus has won the victory over death and the grave. Shall we not cast aside the pretenders and go with the victor?

March 11: Mark 13:19 - In Those Days

(Deuteronomy 14-16; Mark 13:14-37)

The disciples must have been astounded at what Jesus told them during what we know as the Olivet Discourse. They had exclaimed about the grandeur of the temple, and He told them it would be completely destroyed. They asked when that would happen and what the sign indicating the temple's destruction would be, and He told them about the end of the Church Age. Talk about a non-sequitur! The future that Jesus bombarded them with must have had their minds reeling.

There were many disturbing things that Jesus told the disciples. Given their initial focus on the temple, what must they have thought when He spoke of its desecration? In Mark 13:14, Jesus said:

"But when you see the abomination of desolation standing where he ought not to be (let the reader understand), then let those who are in Judea flee to the mountains."

Of course, the parenthetical admonition was Mark's as the author. But how shocked the disciples must have been at Jesus saying this about the temple. They must have immediately reflected on the event perpetrated by the Greek king Antiochus Epiphanes some 200 years prior in 167 BC. His army had come into Jerusalem and captured the city. He thrust aside the altar of Yahweh and erected a statue of the Greek god Zeus in its place. On that altar, he sacrificed a pig, an unclean animal, to show his disdain for the Lord God of Israel.

Can you imagine what the disciples were thinking? "What? Our sacred temple will be desecrated once again? How can this be? How can Yahweh allow such a thing?"

Then it gets worse. Jesus tells them that not only will this beautiful temple be destroyed, but the people of Jerusalem will of necessity flee from the city. Now, the way Jesus foretold this wasn't chronological. The disciples couldn't apprehend the sequence of events. We know from history that the Second Temple during Jesus' time was the one that would not have a single stone remaining on top of another. This temple was razed in 70 AD when the Romans destroyed it completely. The reason no stone remained, as Jesus described, was due to the fire that burned everything to the ground and melted all the gold furnishings. To get at this rich bounty, the Roman soldiers literally tore the stones apart in their goldlust.

Jesus then jumped 2,000 plus years into the future to discuss the next temple desecration during the 7-year Tribulation. By saying the Second Temple would be destroyed, then telling the disciples the temple would be desecrated, He was clearly saying that a Third Temple would be built in order for these things to happen.

At the time of this horrendous event, the warning Jesus gave is of grave importance to the Jews in Israel today and for believers who come to Christ during that Tribulation period. Jesus says in Mark 13:19-20:

"For in those days there will be such tribulation as has not been from the beginning of the creation that God created until now, and never will be. And if the Lord had not cut short the days, no human being would be saved. But for the sake of the elect, whom he chose, he shortened the days."

Jesus warns of the terrible final 3 1/2 years of the Tribulation. It will be so bad that He admonishes the Israelites to flee immediately once the temple event occurs. Don't turn back to get anything, He warns. You won't have time. For those who have become His followers during the Tribulation, He tells them that as they see this day approaching to pray for it to happen during a propitious time. Winter can be difficult in Israel with rains and flooding streams making travel a challenge. If it's Sabbath (sundown Friday through sundown Saturday) all transportation in Israel is shut down. No buses, trains, or taxis will be running. Those without a vehicle will be forced to ride with those who have cars or flee on foot. They will be heading toward Petra in Jordan, which is about 125 miles away. If a woman is pregnant, her difficulties will be amplified during this time of flight.

Jesus describes this last half of the Tribulation as the worst time ever in the history of the world. The stresses and challenges for mankind will be enormous - in fact, beyond man's ability to cope. The one piece of good news that Jesus brings is that the Tribulation has an expiration date. If God allowed the events during this period to continue, all humanity would be destroyed. But, God has mercy upon those who come to know Him through His storm of judgment. He will cut short the event and limit it to only seven years. Beyond that and nothing on this earth would be left.

This day is indeed approaching. It bodes great darkness for those on the earth who haven't previously confessed Jesus as Savior and Lord, and been snatched away by Him as a protection for His Bride.

That's the exceedingly Good News in this story. Christ will not allow His beloved to be beaten and destroyed prior to their wedding. He loves His true church too much - those who love Him and desire with all their heart, soul, mind, and strength to honor and revere Him. All we can say is, Thank You, Lord, for Your mercy!

March 12: Deuteronomy 18:20 - The Prophet Who Presumes

(Deuteronomy 17-19; Mark 14:1-25)

Recent years have seen the rise of a whole class of so-called prophets and apostles. Their lineage comes from what has previously been known as Dominionism or Kingdom Now theology. These New Apostoloic Reformation (NAR) adherents are generally considered to be part of the hyper-charismatic movement. They believe in the gifts of the Holy Spirit, but to an extreme extent. One of their main doctrines is the belief that they are a new generation of those called by God to shepherd the church. They consider themselves anointed and effectively on a par with the apostles of Jesus' day to declare the words they speak are from God Himself. As a result, they will proclaim, "Thus saith the Lord."

Truth be told, their prophetic declarations have been a mixed bag. It appears they get some pronouncements correct, whereas they also make many prophecies that do not come to pass. When in error, they say they simply didn't hear correctly from the Lord and experience no rebuke. Their community appears to be quite accepting of incorrect prophecies. Those who follow this group of NAR apostles and prophets - which is quite large on a worldwide scale and infiltrated to many churches in America and elsewhere - don't seem to have an issue with receiving false words in the Name of God. They'll highlight the predictions that have apparently come to pass and ignore those which didn't.

As with all things we encounter in this world, it's important to hold them up to the standard from the Word of God. Do they pass the test of God's approval as shown in Scripture, or do they fail?

Deuteronomy 18:20-22 gives us this standard by which to judge prophets:

"But the prophet who presumes to speak a word in my name that I have not commanded him to speak, or who speaks in the name of other gods, that same prophet shall die.' And if you say in your heart, 'How may we know the word that the Lord has not spoken?'— when a prophet speaks in the name of the Lord, if the word does not come to pass or come true, that is a word that the Lord has not spoken; the prophet has spoken it presumptuously. You need not be afraid of him."

Several injunctions in this passage jump out as we consider this issue:

1. The prophet who presumes to speak in God's Name
2. The prophet who speaks in the name of other gods
3. The prophet who speaks in the Name of the Lord whose word does not come to pass
4. God declares this prophet presumptuous
5. God says don't fear such a prophet
6. God declares the false prophet shall die

That's a high standard for prophets. According to the Bible, any prophet who speaks as though his words come from God, and his foretelling doesn't materialize, God declares that he is presumptuous - a false prophet - and deserves the death penalty!

How is it that these men and women running around with the self-proclaimed titles of apostles or prophets suffer no consequences? Why do they continue to be lauded as successors of the apostles who walked with Jesus? How is it they have no fear of giving wrong prophecies in God's Name?

The so-called pandemic of the Wuhan virus has brought many prophetic words from these NAR seers. They've made declarations that were supposed to stop the infestation in its tracks, pronounced insights into various behind-the-scenes machinations, and prophesied extraordinary healings. Most of these things never happened.

In contrast, an interesting phenomenon also arose in this time of chaos and confusion; those who had dream visions, but never proclaimed they were prophets. The most prominent of these was Pastor Dana Coverstone of a small church in Kentucky. He posted the dreams he began having for his congregation, and they went viral with hundreds of thousands of people watching and hearing.

At the time of this writing, Pastor Dana has probably had twenty or so dreams. In his conveying of what he's seen in these visions, he has fervently believed they are from God. The one thing Pastor Dana has continually declared is that he is not a prophet. He indicates he is being obedient to God in relaying the dreams, but he has stressed that people can make up their own minds as to the veracity of them. In this author's opinion, the dreams have been highly symbolic, yet extremely accurate in their portrayal of that which is occurring in the political realm and in the church.

What does God's Word have to say about dreamers? We get the best description of this in Joel 2:28-29, which is then echoed by Peter in Acts 2:17-18. From Joel:

"And it shall come to pass afterward,
that I will pour out my Spirit on all flesh;
your sons and your daughters shall prophesy,
your old men shall dream dreams,
and your young men shall see visions.
Even on the male and female servants
in those days I will pour out my Spirit."

"Afterward" in Joel becomes *"in the last days"* in Peter's rendition. A couple questions arise:

1. In what time period is this prophesied to occur?
2. Who are the sons and daughters?

As to question #1, it seems as though it could pertain both to the time leading up to the Tribulation, as well as during that most horrible of seven years. If it applies to these latter days before the Rapture and the subsequent Tribulation, what we're seeing from Pastor Dana (and actually many others who are reporting dreams from God) is a fulfillment of this prophecy.

Regarding question #2, the sons and daughters are ordinary people; certainly not those who claim an imprimatur from God and having any special type of anointing.

The important thing to also notice is that this is something God said would happen and has His approval. There is no negative connotation with people having prophetic dreams, and no penalty associated with their foretelling.

So, what are we to think about these two very different situations of prophecy? As noted earlier, we must hold everything up to the light of God's Word. We should be Bereans as noted in Acts 17:11:

Now these Jews were more noble than those in Thessalonica; they received the word with all eagerness, examining the Scriptures daily to see if these things were so.

Just as critical, we should be as the men of Issachar from 1 Chronicles 12:32:

Of Issachar, men who had understanding of the times...

Knowing where we are on God's prophetic time clock is critical. Prophetic words and dream visions can help us to understand this - as long as they are truly from the Lord.

As Pastor Dana stresses, we should pray about what we hear and make sure Jesus is at the forefront of everything prophetic.

Why? Because that's what God's Word instructs us in Revelation 19:10:

"Worship God." For the testimony of Jesus is the spirit of prophecy.

March 13: Deuteronomy 22:21 - An Outrageous Thing

(Deuteronomy 20-22; Mark 14:26-50)

Consider how the morals in America - as well as in the world - have changed through the years. Do you think they've improved? Are they pleasing to God? Sadly, no.

When Yahweh chose Israel to be His special heritage (Deuteronomy 32:9), it was to raise up a nation wholly devoted to Him, so that it could then be a blessing to the world (Genesis 12:3). God wanted to pour out His favor upon all mankind because of His great love for His creation.

Free will - a gift to man - was also our downfall. It is free will that enables us to choose - to be independent agents from God. Because of the free will He gave us, we are moral creatures separate from Him, not robots that act only in accord with what He desires.

God gave each man a conscience, i.e. an imprint of His character and virtues. Being made in the image of God, we start out with the knowledge of right and wrong, good and evil. However, the nature of our heart is wicked, deceitful above all things (Jeremiah 17:9). Our sin nature quickly challenges the goodness that God implants in each of us. Through our free will choices and the sin that pulls us away from the good that is God, our conscience doesn't last long in that pristine imaging of God in which it began. Every act contrary to God's nature hardens us a little more and separates us from who He is and what we could be.

Through the nation of Israel, God intended to show the sinful world there was a better way than that which man (and the world) decided was best. God made humanity, male and female (Genesis 1:27), and effectively declared that only when a woman left her father's house in a marital union was she to have sexual relations with a man (Genesis 2:24). They were to be monogamous in their relationship.

That didn't last long. We see in Genesis 4:19 that by the seventh generation from Adam and Eve, Lamech took two wives. Did that contribute to his moral character, or lack thereof? Several verses later in Genesis 4:23, Lamech declares that he has killed a man, following in the footsteps of his great, great, great grandfather Cain. We also know that during this period the sons of God descended from their heavenly abode to take human women for themselves (Genesis 6:1-4), and that this caused contamination of the human bloodline and depravity to enter the world. Sin plus depravity equals abomination in God's eyes.

In trying to teach His children Israel His ways rather than those of the world around them, Yahweh laid out certain laws regarding sexual immorality. In expounding on these laws, God let it be known that a young woman - a virgin - was to remain that way while in her father's house until she should be married. This was so important to retain morality in the land that He declared in Deuteronomy 22:20-21:

"But if the thing is true, that evidence of virginity was not found in the young woman, then they shall bring out the young woman to the door of her father's house, and the men of her city shall stone her to death with stones, because she has done an outrageous thing in Israel by whoring in her father's house. So you shall purge the evil from your midst."

A number of times throughout the book of Deuteronomy, God emphasizes that Israel should *"purge the evil from your midst."* In the sight of God, the loss of a woman's virginity, i.e. her innocence, was such an outrageous thing that it had to be met with the death of the young woman. Wow. Why was that? Because of the continuing corruption of morals that sex outside of marriage brought into the thinking of a family, a village, and the nation.

The Apostle Paul in Romans 1:24-25 explained what happens to man's thinking in this context:

Therefore God gave them up in the lusts of their hearts to impurity, to the dishonoring of their bodies among themselves, because they exchanged the truth about God for a lie and worshiped and served the creature rather than the Creator, who is blessed forever! Amen.

Lust brings impurity, which leads to the dishonoring of one's body, which causes someone to believe a lie, which inspires that person to worship creation rather than the Creator God. Sexual immorality is the road one travels to apostasy.

Is it any wonder that in our world today - in this once great nation of America - we have fallen so far from God and the truth of His Son, Jesus Christ? Even though it had been present from close to the very beginning, once we embraced the notion that sex outside of marriage (or multiple intimate relationships) was the good and proper way for us to have male-female relations, everything went downhill from there.

The 1950s was a decade portrayed as promoting the nuclear family. Remember shotgun weddings? A young woman sexually engaging with a young man brought shame to the family. That all changed in the 1960s - the decade of free love.

Look at where we are now.

God has His good and righteous reasons for every command He gives us. This nation doesn't have much time left before it dissolves and merges into the rest of the world, as the global mindset brings us down to the lowest common denominator of worldly morals. However, true Christians continue to have the choice of honoring God.

The only way we can be salt and light in the midst of the rot and decay of the culture around us is to be obedient to God in all ways. Anyone who considers him- or her- self a Christ-follower and is in an immoral relationship, i.e. a sexual relationship outside of marriage, must make that right before God. There is a price to pay for immorality.

If we don't stand with and for God in all He stands for; we stand against Him.

March 14: Mark 14:71 - I Don't Know This Man

(Deuteronomy 23-25; Mark 14:51-72)

Do you know Jesus? Peter, one of His closest disciples declared that he didn't. Mark 14:71 reveals about Peter:

But he began to invoke a curse on himself and to swear, "I do not know this man of whom you speak."

How could that be? Peter had walked with Jesus for three years. From the very first when Jesus called him, he responded without hesitation. Can you imagine the miracles he saw? Jesus healed the blind and the deaf. He cast out numerous demons. In Peter's presence Jesus raised the dead. Peter witnessed Jesus walk on water in the midst of a storm. More than that, at Jesus' command, Peter himself had walked on the turbulent waves. On the heights of Mount Hermon, with his very eyes, Peter saw Jesus as He really was in all His glory, not to mention two of the most famous of all Israel's prophets speaking to Him. At a point of true revelation, Peter declared that Jesus was God.

Yet, in humanity's darkest hour before Jesus was to be unjustly crucified, when confronted by the accusations of a little servant girl, Peter denied that he even knew Jesus. What kind of man was this? Where was his courage? Where was the faith he had acquired during his amazing time with this God-man? What was Peter's problem?

It's the one we all have. We're human. Our flesh is weak. To top it off, although Peter believed that God Himself was in their midst, neither he nor the other disciples had God living inside them. None of them had yet received through faith the free gift of the Holy Spirit. They didn't have the *Wonderful Counselor, Mighty God, Everlasting Father, Prince of Peace* (Isaiah 9:6) living within. *Emmanuel* had been with them but wasn't in them. That wouldn't happen until later when Jesus breathed on the disciples and said, *"Receive the Holy Spirit."* (John 20:22)

What does Jeremiah 17:9 say?

The heart is deceitful above all things, and desperately sick; who can understand it?

It all goes to show that without our Lord animating us and giving us life through His indwelling presence, we're toast. If Peter, this robust, presumably fearless fisherman, denied Jesus, what can any of us do?

Jesus said in Matthew 10;33:

"Whoever denies me before men, I also will deny before my Father who is in heaven."

1 John 2;23 follows that up with:

No one who denies the Son has the Father.

Is Peter then lost? How can any of us stand? Paul in Romans 1:16 made the definitive statement about this:

For I am not ashamed of the gospel, for it is the power of God for salvation to everyone who believes, to the Jew first and also to the Greek.

The truth of the matter is that first we must receive the Holy Spirit. Without Him, true faith of any kind is impossible. With Him, all things are possible (Matthew 19:26).

Peter wept and repented. He had grievously sinned, and he knew it. Yet. he was still helpless as a mere man.

God knows our weaknesses. He understands that even with the Holy Spirit there are times our faith and courage fail us. There are numerous stories of such failures among believers who are persecuted and caused to suffer. In that trial, the pain of their flesh overwhelmed them. The stories are also plentiful of these same men and women repenting and recanting, then being tortured once more but standing firm in Christ.

God is infinitely merciful. Wrapping our heads around that fact is something we all struggle with. God loves us with an everlasting love. He wants none to perish, but all to have eternal life with Him. He alone makes our faith possible. Only His holy presence living inside us gives us the ability to stand - to not be ashamed. Yet, we still may fail. In the midst of that, God continues to woo us to Himself. If we have fallen. He will pick us up. He redeemed Peter. He will redeem us.

Lord. give us the strength to stand for You. We know that trials and tribulations will come. Pick us up. Place us back on our feet. Keep us on the firm footing that we have only in Jesus. We ask this in His holy Name.

March 15: Deuteronomy 27:2-3 - Stones on Mount Ebal

(Deuteronomy 26-27; Mark 15:1-26)

When Yahweh delivered His children Israel from Egypt, He showed them clearly how He was different from every other god. For four hundred years they had been immersed in a culture that worshiped the creation. God declared there is One who made all of creation, and they were to lift only His Name on high. Not only did He tell them, He gave them signs and wonders that no other god could do. In order for Israel to "get it," Yahweh had to provide the evidence of clear separation from all other gods. God's children had been surrounded by people who lived in ways and practiced many things that were anathema to Yahweh and His way. He used that surrounding culture to distinguish Himself from all Israel had known and gave them commandments, precepts, statutes, rules, and laws by which to live.

The Ten Commandments were the basics of the moral law that demonstrated the virtues and characteristics of this all-consuming God who was new to the Israelites' understanding. Many of the items on this list were common sense and integral to the conscience God has given each human being, but the commandments in stone solidified what man already innately knew. As the people of Israel were about to cross the Jordan, Moses reiterated the Law to those he had led for so long. But, God wanted them to again have a clear demonstration of how He intended for them to live.

Yahweh instructed Moses, who conveyed to the elders, a physical, literal witness of the Law. Deuteronomy 27:2-3 gives us His command:

"And on the day you cross over the Jordan to the land that the Lord your God is giving you, you shall set up large stones and plaster them with plaster. And you shall write on them all the words of this law, when you cross over to enter the land that the Lord your God is giving you, a land flowing with milk and honey, as the Lord, the God of your fathers, has promised you."

Upon Mount Ebal, God had Moses set up large stones and plaster them over. The Ten Commandments were then inscribed on the plaster for all to see. Following that, Moses separated the tribes so that six of the elders of the twelve tribes stood on Mount Ebal and the other six stood on Mount Gerizim. Those on Mount Ebal then called out the curses of the Law.

The picture God painted for the people was that disobeying the Law brought His curses upon them. The Law brings only a curse. By following the

Law, one wouldn't come under its curse, but who could live up to its demands? That was the problem. In their flesh, the Israelites would inevitably fail and realize the curse of the Law. They might be able to avoid building a graven image or refrain from stealing, but who could live every day and not commit an infraction of some kind against such a holy God with His stringent requirements for righteousness?

But, God had a better plan that he would institute at the right time. The Apostle Paul stated in Galatians 3:24:

Therefore the law was our tutor to bring us to Christ, that we might be justified by faith.

We learn by the law. We see that it is strict with no grace - no leniency. It declares, it judges, and it punishes. How wretched we are if we must live under the Law!

This is why Christ came. The Law was an impossible taskmaster. Jesus showed there's a better way - the mercy of God. It's His mercy that enables us to be forgiven for our trespasses under the Law and to live by faith. The grace of God cleanses us from the filth of our sin that accumulates in our human condition living apart from Him.

It is through Jesus' life, death, and resurrection that we are given a reprieve from the Law when we believe. Not all choose to accept the free gift of salvation that God offers us through His Son. We who have chosen to receive this can only praise the Lord for His mercy that He convicted us of our great need and have turned to Him.

Thankfully, the stones on Mount Ebal no longer call out their curses to us. We hear a different voice - that of the love of our Savior.

March 16: Deuteronomy 28:15 - All These Curses

(Deuteronomy 28; Mark 15:27-47)

Let's do a thought experiment. Suppose at the founding of America, God spoke to the men who led us so capably, who devised our Constitution, and who created our Republic. Imagine that these men heard directly from God, who laid out some basic principles for our nation to follow. Picture God saying to our founders the following from Deuteronomy 28:1:

"And if you faithfully obey the voice of the Lord your God, being careful to do all his commandments that I command you today, the Lord your God will set you high above all the nations of the earth."

Wouldn't that be amazing? Here is the God of all creation promising to make our nation greater than any other throughout the entire world. But God doesn't stop there. He explicitly and extensively lays out what He means. Literally everything the people of this land set their hands to, He will bless. He will bring increase in every aspect of what they do. This includes, all commerce, agriculture, economic prowess, and military superiority. No other nation on the face of the earth could come against us and succeed. Surely the inhabitants of our nation would jump at the prospect. All each person would have to do would be to diligently follow God and do what He commanded. That would bring such goodwill from the Lord that literally everyone would abound in God's favor.

Would the people hearing of these potential blessings agree to follow God in this way? What if they were given even more incentive? What if God in making all these promises also said there was a downside when they didn't honor and revere Him? What if instead they decided to go their own way and do whatever they wanted? Carrot and stick. What if God declared the negatives of such an arrangement as in Deuteronomy 28:15:

"But if you will not obey the voice of the Lord your God or be careful to do all his commandments and his statutes that I command you today, then all these curses shall come upon you and overtake you."

Not stopping there, in letting the people understand the import of His Words, what if God gave a thoroughly dispiriting list of all the horrible consequences that would befall America and its people should they turn away from Him? The curses would include such a lengthy list that hearing all these bad things would be enough to depress anyone. Among them would be failure in all commercial endeavors; plague and pestilence affecting their agricultural efforts; financial ruin; poor health; lack of any capability to defend the borders, leading to complete and overwhelming loss of national sovereignty; and one other awful result. Because of the absence of any ability to do anything useful or worthy, and through the siege of our cities, many people would resort to cannibalism. Mothers and fathers would eat their young and horde the flesh of their children, keeping others from partaking, even their spouses.

With that kind of failure looming with its terrible aftermath, wouldn't the good people of America come together in agreement that following God and His commandments was a prudent and wonderful thing to do?

You'd think.

But just like the people of Israel when given these two options by Yahweh who had delivered them from slavery in Egypt, who had given them His promises of blessings, and proof in many ways that He loved and cared for them, America would likewise turn away.

Why? Because of sin, depravity, and self-gratification, i.e. the desire for people to do what they wish without anyone looking over their shoulders and saying their actions are wrong.

No, America, if given these choices at our founding, would have acted in exactly the same manner as Israel did. Israel rejected God. They wanted to be like the nations around them and absorb their cultures and their gods. This attitude triggered the many curses Yahweh declared, and Israel went down.

Our nation wasn't founded as a theocracy with its rulers consulting God and its people answering to Him. At least not directly. But all peoples everywhere must answer to a sovereign God. They must respond to Him through the Spirit and truth He brings. When they reject Him, they reject His promises of blessings and trigger His curses. The penalties may not be as specifically detailed as they were to Israel, but God has given His Word, which lays out exactly what He requires of mankind. When men turn from Him, they can expect only the worst to happen.

However, if the people don't know God and haven't read His Word, their ignorance is no excuse. God showers a nation and its people with mercy and grace, but He also draws a red line. If that's crossed with no turning back, just like with Israel, a nation will fall.

Although America isn't Israel, we likewise have turned far from God. The blessings from following Him are long gone. Sadly, because of our hatred for Him as a nation, we can only expect a disastrous end.

If only we had listened and obeyed!

March 17: Deuteronomy 29:18 - Poisonous & Bitter Fruit

(Deuteronomy 29-30; Mark 16)

God so wanted His children Israel to love and follow only Him. Unfortunately, it wasn't an easy sell. Spending 400 years in the midst of a pagan culture that worshiped many gods tainted them. It wasn't like what we're told today in Hebrews 11:1 concerning our belief in Jesus Christ and all He has for us:

Now faith is the assurance of things hoped for, the conviction of things not seen.

First, Yahweh had to get their attention, which He did as noted in Deuteronomy 29:2-3:

And Moses summoned all Israel and said to them: "You have seen all that the Lord did before your eyes in the land of Egypt, to Pharaoh and to all his servants and to all his land, the great trials that your eyes saw, the signs, and those great wonders."

God did amazing things before the very eyes of His people so that they would see how different He was from the gods they'd known for centuries in Egypt. Interestingly, even as Yahweh showed Israel all these signs and wonders, He withheld something vital , which Deuteronomy 29:4 tells us:

"But to this day the Lord has not given you a heart to understand or eyes to see or ears to hear."

In Old Testament times and even to the present, has God ever given Israel such a heart? We know that in the final days of the Tribulation, when all Israel is saved, that their hearts will finally turn to Him (Zechariah 13:8-9), but prior? Perhaps this is true only for the few who call on Jesus today and know Him as Messiah.

Moses made God's desire plainly known in Deuteronomy 29:12-13, as he had conveyed many other times to His people:

"...so that you may enter into the sworn covenant of the Lord your God, which the Lord your God is making with you today, that he may establish you today as his people, and that he may be your God, as he promised you, and as he swore to your fathers, to Abraham, to Isaac, and to Jacob."

God wanted His children to settle in the Promised Land; to be fruitful and multiply in the many blessings He had planned for them. Yet, knowing their sinful hearts, God warned them time and again of the pitfalls of looking elsewhere besides to Him. Deuteronomy 29:18 spells it out:

"Beware lest there be among you a man or woman or clan or tribe whose heart is turning away today from the Lord our God to go and serve the gods of those nations. Beware lest there be among you a root bearing poisonous and bitter fruit."

The danger always was, and continues to this day, for anyone - Jew or Gentile, one of the Chosen People or a true Christian – is that pagan gods form a snare. The gods of the other nations were real. We've discussed this extensively that they are the fallen, rebellious sons of God (*bene Elohim*) who set themselves up in the place of Yahweh. Just like the serpent's whispered exhortation to Adam and Eve that they believed, so it likely was with these many spiritual beings: *"You shall be as gods"* (Genesis 3:5). Mankind believed the lie; God's spiritual sons believed it as well.

Whether for human or divine, that deceit was and is a root that bears poisonous and bitter fruit. As Christians, we know someone by their fruit, even as Jesus warned in Matthew 7:17-20:

"So, every healthy tree bears good fruit, but the diseased tree bears bad fruit. A healthy tree cannot bear bad fruit, nor can a diseased tree bear good fruit. Every tree that does not bear good fruit is cut down and thrown into the fire. Thus you will recognize them by their fruits."

Anyone who follows false gods, or sets himself up as one, is rotten at the root. The fruit such a person bears is worthless. The worship of false gods leads to the fire, i.e. eternal damnation.

Because the people foolishly chose the gods of their neighbors rather than Yahweh, Israel suffered the consequences, of which she was warned as shown in Deuteronomy 29:23:

"... the whole land burned out with brimstone and salt, nothing sown and nothing growing, where no plant can sprout, an overthrow like that of Sodom and Gomorrah, Admah, and Zeboiim, which the Lord overthrew in his anger and wrath—"

God effectively threw the land of Israel itself into the fire because of the poison and bitterness of the root that had grown in the people's hearts. (Note: for a vivid description of this, read Mark Twain's book *The Innocents Abroad*.) It was a tough lesson.

However, God chose Israel as His special inheritance (Deuteronomy 32:9), to love her and to be a blessing to the world (Genesis 12:3). Despite knowing that His children would betray Him, God declared that He would bring them back into the land after scattering them and bless it as He originally intended.

Israel today remains largely secular. The people haven't yet turned their hearts to the God of their fathers. But, they will. God has a plan and a purpose; He also has His timing.

That day is approaching. How glorious it will be for those Jews who turn to Jesus as Savior and Lord, and how wonderful for all the world!

March 18: Deuteronomy 32:17 - Gods They Had Never Known

(Deuteronomy 31-32; Luke 1:1-23)

Context when reading the Bible is everything. Consider *The Song of Moses* in Deuteronomy 32. Yahweh instructed Moses to recite the words of this song to all Israel (Deuteronomy 31:30). They were Words of warning to God's children because He knew their hearts and how unfaithful they would be. He wanted to remind them from where they had come, the dangers of other gods, and the consequences of following them. The context is that by pursuing other gods, Israel would bring upon herself Yahweh's wrath. He gives the promise of abundant blessing, but the primary intent of the song is to show how when Israel would ignore God and worship foreign gods instead, disaster would result.

Deuteronomy 32:8-9 are verses that I've cited often as the *Deuteronomy 32 Worldview*:

> *When the Most High gave to the nations their inheritance,*
> *when he divided mankind,*
> *he fixed the borders of the peoples*
> *according to the number of **the sons of God**.*
> *But the Lord's portion is his people,*
> *Jacob his allotted heritage.*

In previously mentioning these verses, I've stressed the importance of reading them in the only translation that gets it right - the English Standard Version (ESV). (The ESV in these verses uses the Dead Sea Scrolls, which provide the gold standard for translation.) The reference of the passage is to the Tower of Babel incident in Genesis 11. Mankind disobeys God to scatter throughout the earth. He comes down and does the scattering for them, in the process confusing their language. At this time Yahweh places His divine sons - the sons of God (*bene Elohim*) over all these newly created nations. The job of these holy ambassadors is to point people to God while He shepherds the new nation of Israel as His special inheritance.

The reason I say this must be read in the ESV is because most other Bible translations, instead of saying "*the sons of God*," say "*children of Israel*" or "*sons of Israel*." Why is this wrong? Consider the context.

God is declaring that His children Israel have strayed far from Him. He wanted them to remember the days of old, referring specifically to what occurred in Babel. God reminds them that He alone was the God who cared for them; it's always been that way. But this is a prophetic song. Yahweh states that Israel will grow fat and lax in following Him.

Why? Because they looked to other gods. In fact, Deuteronomy 32:17 is effectively a proof text for Deuteronomy 32:8:

> *They sacrificed to **demons** that were no gods,*
>   *to gods they had never known,*
> *to **new gods that had come recently**,*
>   *whom your fathers had never dreaded.*

The Hebrew word for demons is *shedim*. It means the rebellious sons of God, having a geographical context; the word primarily coming from Mesopotamian origins. The gods that had come recently were *elohim*, which, depending on context, means either gods or God.

Where did these foreign gods come from? Surrounding nations. How did they get there? They were originally faithful princes in the heavenly realm, i.e. sons of God, who turned away from Him in disobedience, just like Satan did. We get a glimpse of one of these mighty rulers over the nations in Daniel 10:13, when the angel Gabriel attempts to deliver a message to the prophet:

> *"The prince of the kingdom of Persia withstood me twenty-one days, but Michael, one of the chief princes, came to help me, for I was left there with the kings of Persia."*

Who is the Prince of Persia? Surely no human ruler could cause such delay for a powerful angel like Gabriel. He is one of the *shedim*, one of the *bene Elohim*, who rules over the nation of Persia (now Iran).

Moses' song continues by stating that these spiritual entities will turn the hearts of God's children and make Him jealous for them. They are gods that are no gods (Deuteronomy 32:21). In other words, they are pretenders to their thrones. Their very presence causes the Lord's intense anger. God's wrath upon them is so great that in Psalm 82 we see that Yahweh gathers all the heavenly host into a Divine Council meeting and declares judgment upon His faithless sons. In Psalm 82:6-7 God pronounces their fate:

> *I said, "You are gods,*

sons of the Most High, all of you;
nevertheless, like men you shall die,
  and fall like any prince."

Angels, cherubim, seraphim, sons of God - these are holy, spiritual beings. They are immortal, i.e. they never die - right?

The transgression of these heavenly entities is so great, i.e. they've turned the hearts of so many against Yahweh - particularly the hearts of His children Israel - that He sentences them to death like any mere mortal.

There is a much larger story in the Song of Moses. Gods that Israel had never known lured her into apostasy. This is the context, i.e. that other gods exist and operate contrary to God's will.

It's the age-old story of Israel, and it's our story as well. Satan and his minions desire to lead humanity to the same fiery place of punishment where they will dwell for eternity. The demonic powers in high places (Ephesians 6:12) will do everything they can to thwart God's purposes in the earth, i.e. to redeem mankind so that in our glorified state we will inhibit eternity alongside what is now the heavenly host.

The more we understand the cosmic war in which we're engaged, the better we can resist the enemy in the power of Jesus Christ. Let's study our Bibles well and engage Scripture with greater understanding by reading in context.

March 19: Deuteronomy 34:5-6 - The Holy Stapler

(Deuteronomy 33-34; Luke 1:24-56)

In reading Scripture, primarily the Old Testament, we see there are places where the author of a named book simply couldn't have been the one who wrote certain passages. There had to have been another person - an editor - who wrote parts of the work itself, or at least assembled the writings. That concept tends to rub many of us the wrong way because of the inspiration of the Bible that we attribute to God and His chosen authors.

However, we plainly see this concept in operation in the closing chapter of Deuteronomy with the account of Moses' death. To choose a couple verses, consider Deuteronomy 34:5-6 which says:

So Moses the servant of the Lord died there in the land of Moab, according to the word of the Lord, and he buried him in the valley in the land of Moab opposite Beth-peor; but no one knows the place of his burial to this day.

Unless Moses wrote this from the grave, it's obvious he didn't put these words on the holy scroll. And, if he didn't write them, are they inspired?

Dr. Michael Heiser, author of *The Unseen Realm*, has a favorite phrase that many seem to attribute to describe the process by which a number of these OT books were written.; he calls it using the Holy Stapler.

It's probably a little easier to see with the writings of other prophets besides Moses. Let's consider Ezekiel, as I paraphrase how Dr. Heiser describes the undertaking:

Each day that Ezekiel gets up he makes many prophetic declarations; he often does some very strange things in the course of that day. Now, he himself may write down some of the Words the Lord gives him, but he also has followers. These men hang with Ezekiel day in and day out because they're hungry to know the Word and the will of Yahweh. This group of men came to be known as the School of the Prophets. We see them show up in the accounts of Elijah and Elisha.

As Ezekiel spoke, it would not have been unusual for these men to capture the many things he said for posterity. They never knew what Ezekiel would proclaim on a given day, or what prophetic concept he might act out, such as lying on one side or another for weeks to illustrate what Yahweh wanted conveyed, or going around naked to depict something else. However, these students of the anointed prophet were always ready with pen and parchment to capture what he said and did.

Once the prophet died, someone in the group would likely say, "Hey, we need to put all that we know about Ezekiel together in a book for future generations. Everybody go home and gather up all your writings." They would do this and bring back all the proverbial slips of paper and notebooks in which they'd written Ezekiel's words.

The question then becomes: Did they simply assemble all these items into a nice neat pile, aligning all the edges just right, bring out the Holy Stapler, and go *kah-thunk*? "Okay, there's the book of Ezekiel - all done."

Not likely. They probably would have surveyed their group to find who was a good writer and/or someone with editing skills. That person would have taken all these many bits and pieces of Ezekiel's doings and sayings, put them into an agreed upon order, added some context, and created the book. The concept of the Holy Stapler, where everything is just assembled willy-nilly, doesn't really make sense. There had to be an editor.

If that's the case, going back to what we see in the final passage in Deuteronomy, another writer and/or an editor had to have at least put these words about the events surrounding his death into the book. Another clue throughout Deuteronomy may be where Moses is referred to in the third person. Perhaps Moses did that through the humility that's attributed to him in Numbers 12:3:

Now the man Moses was very meek, more than all people who were on the face of the earth.

Or, maybe someone else noted that about him. In his humility, would Moses have actually stated that about himself?

This takes us back to inerrancy. If the process of writing many of the OT books included one of assembly and editing, can we consider the result inerrant?

Of course we can! God chose the main characters of these books. He prepared them for what He intended in order to accomplish His purposes. All they'd learned through reading and experience in life brought them to the place that God providentially wanted them to be. If that's true for Moses in the Old

Testament or Paul in the New Testament, wouldn't that also be the case for anyone else tasked with completing the given book of the Bible? Wouldn't God's hand also be on each of those men?

I think we can safely say that would certainly be true. We have the Holy Scriptures. They came about through the inspiration of God working on whomever He chose to make His Word and will known.

We don't have books created by the Holy Stapler; we have the Word of God superintended by the Holy Spirit to produce exactly what He intended.

March 20: Luke 1:45 - She Who Believed

(Joshua 1-3; Luke 57-80)

There are some number of us who lament the fact that few in the church today take an interest in Bible prophecy. We see that as a lack of teaching and preaching from the pulpit, and the subsequent disinterest in the congregation, because they're not inspired to search deeper into the Word of God in order to understand the times. Most people appear to be content with the sermon the pastor preaches, perhaps think on that for a few hours, then after that neglect what God determined should be their daily approach to life.

As Joshua was about to lead the Israelites over the Jordan to take the Promised Land, Yahweh implored the people to do the following, as stated in Joshua 1:7-8. His purpose was to prepare His people so that He could continue to guide them in all their ways:

"Only be strong and very courageous, being careful to do according to all the law that Moses my servant commanded you. Do not turn from it to the right hand or to the left, that you may have good success wherever you go. This Book of the Law shall not depart from your mouth, but you shall meditate on it day and night, so that you may be careful to do according to all that is written in it. For then you will make your way prosperous, and then you will have good success."

All that Moses commanded the Israelites was contained in the Book of the Law. They were to read and study the Words of God every day, throughout the day. Its Words - God's Words - were to be constantly present in their minds and hearts and on their lips. This was one of those implied conditional statements that Yahweh inevitably told His children. The effective "if" was that *if* they kept God's Word always before them *and* were obedient to all it said, *then* He would bring them prosperity and success in all they did.

It was a simple condition for living well. In fact, God had previously stated that when they had a king ruling over them, upon his taking the throne, *he* was to write out the Law and keep it with him, reading it daily, so that he would be righteous in the sight of the Lord and rule justly.

As time passes and the Israelites achieve victory over the inhabitants of the land and they settle into it, as ease and comfort overtake them, they quickly forget the One who brought them to the dance. The book of Judges follows that of Joshua, and that sad chronicle depicts this problem acutely.

How different is it for the church today? As noted above, not much. The majority of those who sit in the pews don't read their Bibles regularly or deeply. Pastors by and large haven't encouraged that practice. Another part of the problem is that in this void, Bible prophecy and its understanding have also suffered. Seminaries and Bible colleges somewhere along the way ceased to teach all of the Bible; in that process much of God's Word was spiritualized. Yes, we must be careful not to take Scripture too literally where the Biblical writers didn't intend that; such an approach can result in foolish misunderstandings. But, to relegate the 30% of the Bible that is prophecy to a spiritual purpose only, or just to past events, neglects what God intended to accomplish. This has caused much ignorance and apathy regarding Bible prophecy.

In the New Testament we're given a singular result of someone who diligently believed and applied God's Word to her life. Mary, the soon-to-be mother of Jesus was hailed by the angel Gabriel when he came to her. In Luke 1:28 look at what he said:

"Greetings, O favored one; the Lord is with you."

Goodness, that's a strong and positive message from God. To be given these words was troubling to Mary. Who was she to gain such favor? She was nothing but a young girl who had been faithful to the Lord; but why did that make her special?

I think that the verse before her Magnificat, where she bursts out in prophetic praise, is significant in this regard. In Luke 1:45, Mary herself provides the answer:

"And blessed is she who believed that there would be a fulfillment of what was spoken to her from the Lord."

We know that Mary had to be found faithful in her life for the Lord to notice her and bring this blessing. Faithfulness would have meant doing what God said His children should do. What was that? Exactly that which was noted earlier: Mary meditated on the Law and was careful to follow it. It was this that brought God's favor, even as He had declared.

Mary believed what God had spoken in the past and spoke now through Gabriel. She believed in the fulfillment of God's Word. To put it another way, she believed and accepted the prophetic Word of God. As far as she was concerned, Bible prophecy was real and alive; Mary actually encountered its fulfillment.

If people today - pastors and pew sitters - don't take such a view as Mary did, and neither are they reading the Word - especially all the Word - how can God pour out His favor? Many in the church seek revival, i.e. a move of God in their midst, but will He do that if they haven't prepared? The first chapter of Luke brings us the story of John the Baptist, who God brought into the world to prepare the way of the Lord. Without John first proclaiming God's Word, and it subsequently softening the hearts of the people to bring them to repentance, would they have been ready for Jesus to come? In the same manner, how can the church be ready for a move of God if they haven't consecrated their hearts and repented?

God wants His people to be ready for all He has. He continually warns us to watch and to be alert. The people perish for lack of knowledge (Hosea 4:6). How many will perish who haven't come to truly know Jesus as Lord and Savior, perhaps because they never were taught Bible prophecy that confirms God is real, and all that He says will come to pass?

March 21: Joshua 5:15 - Take Off Your Sandals

(Joshua 4-6; Luke 2:1-24)

To be in the presence of the Lord is an awesome thing. Coming before the Holy One of Israel must have been a heart-stopping experience. In many places in the Bible, we see mere mortals fall down in wonder when an angel appeared; consider how much more breathtaking it was when God Himself stood before them.

Angels - messengers or servants of the Lord - always deflect the homage that someone wants to heap upon them. They inevitably say, "Don't bow down before me. Worship God." We can know when it's actually Yahweh in these situations because He accepts the honor and reverence. When in God's presence, the ground on which a person stands becomes holy. All glory and praise is due to the Lord God Almighty.

The first instance we see of this occurs in Exodus 3:5:

Then he said, "Do not come near; take your sandals off your feet, for the place on which you are standing is holy ground."

Moses has been in the wilderness tending sheep for forty years with the Lord preparing him for this day. He turns aside when he sees a bush burning but not being consumed. In the flames arising from that bush, Moses sees a figure. It is the angel of the Lord (Exodus 3:2). According to the text with what this being says, the ground itself has transformed into something holy.

The question becomes: Is the angel of the Lord Yahweh Himself? Isn't God a Spirit?

Second temple Jewish literature speaks about the Two Yahwehs, or the Two Powers in Heaven. From their study of the Scriptures, it became evident to the Jews at that time that though Yahweh was One, there were two instances of Him. There was the Yahweh who could not be seen, and there was the Yahweh who appeared often in human form. Amazingly, many passages depicted these two Yahwehs appearing at the same time.

In this scene, the angel of the Lord manifests visibly, demands that Moses remove his sandals, and declares that He is God in Exodus 3:6:

And he said, "I am the God of your father, the God of Abraham, the God of Isaac, and the God of Jacob." And Moses hid his face, for he was afraid to look at God.

It's hard to argue that the angel of the Lord isn't God when He says specifically that He is.

When Joshua led the Israelites over the dried-up Jordan River to the plains of Jericho, he encountered another such manifestation. Rather than the text saying He was the angel of the Lord, it tells us in Joshua 5:14 that this being was *"the commander of the army of the Lord."*

Was this entity Yahweh, one of the Two Powers in Heaven? Look at what He told His servant in Joshua 5:15:

And the commander of the Lord's army said to Joshua, "Take off your sandals from your feet, for the place where you are standing is holy." And Joshua did so.

He instructed Joshua to remove his sandals for the ground had become holy. Holy ground only becomes that way in the presence of the Lord. The commander of the heavenly host was Yahweh in physical form, and Joshua knew that He was God.

When we see these verses, we know now that this second Yahweh is the pre-incarnate Jesus. He is the One who stood before Moses at the Tent of Meeting, and he is the One who gave up all His heavenly trappings to come to the earth and be born of a virgin.

The ground where God stands is holy. Those who come into His presence cannot help but fall down in awe to worship the very dirt at His feet. Have you ever been worshiping God and His Spirit is so heavy that you can do nothing but fall to the ground?

Besides the knowledge that those who are resurrected finally gain, at the end of the Millennium as they stand before the Lord in judgment, it is because God's presence is so overwhelming that every tongue confesses and every knee bows (Philippians 2:9-11).

Our Lord is a holy God. There is none like Him. When we come before Him in praise and worship, in prayer, or in reading His Word, we are on holy ground. Let us bow down and give Him the glory which is His alone.

March 22: Joshua 7:11 - Secret Sin

(Joshua 7-8; Luke 2:25-52)

Quite often in Scripture, the events that occurred in the Old Testament are a living example of what can take place in the church body, or even within our families. They show us human failure and the repercussions of that. God is holy - plus, He sees all! He will not allow sin to contaminate His house and His people.

When the Israelites overcame Jericho by the hand of the Lord, He commanded that everyone and everything in that city be devoted to destruction. This meant that all people and things were to be destroyed and dedicated to Him. He also said that the choice possessions made of precious metals were to be placed in the temple (tabernacle at the time) treasury (Joshua 6:18-19). Unfortunately, there was a man whose flesh got the best of him, and he paid the price.

The man, Achan, took some of the items from the victory over Jericho as his own in direct disobedience to God's Word. That which belonged to God went into Achan's own tent. When Israel subsequently went up against the Amorite city of Ai, God allowed them to be soundly defeated because of this.

It's interesting how this plays outs. Joshua sends spies, and they report that because the enemy is so few, there's no need to send many men against them. Their assessment is flawed, and Ai thoroughly whips them.

Because of Achan and his offense against the Word of Yahweh, that sin causes blindness. In this case, it's the blindness of deception. The spies cannot see what is really there since sin has misled them into unwarranted arrogance. They think Israel cannot be defeated. Their pride in the taking of Jericho has completely blinded them.

In his distress, Joshua comes before the Lord, who instructs him what to do. Yahweh tells his servant they have a serious problem, as Joshua 7:11 outlines:

"Israel has sinned; they have transgressed my covenant that I commanded them; they have taken some of the devoted things; they have stolen and lied and put them among their own belongings."

Achan's sin was committed in secret. Yet from God's perspective with Israel, it was infectious. One man's trespass affected the entire nation of Israel. This caused God's people to literally become what they were supposed to eliminate. Consider how God puts this in Joshua 7:12:

"Therefore the people of Israel cannot stand before their enemies. They turn their backs before their enemies, because they have become devoted for destruction. I will be with you no more, unless you destroy the devoted things from among you."

He says the Israelites themselves have become devoted to destruction as a result of their not completely devoting to destruction all those things that He has commanded. That single individual brought his sin upon the entire body; all Israelites suffered from his iniquity.

The only way to correct the problem was to completely eradicate all traces of this sin. In this case, God commanded that Achan, his entire family, and all his possessions must be removed; they all had to be burned by fire. I can't even imagine the growing knot in Achan's stomach as God narrowed down who had committed the sin: by tribe, by clan, by household, and finally by Achan. The approaching dread the man felt had to be awful.

Upon discovery, Achan confessed to those things he had stolen. His words in Joshua 7:21 are telling:

"Then I coveted them and took them."

Achan coveted. He lusted after something that was not his to have. He had directly trespassed against the Tenth Commandment as well as the First. He had put these things into his heart in place of Yahweh.

Before Israel could bring God's punishment upon Achan, He directed His children to consecrate themselves (Joshua 7:13). To do His will, they needed to first be purified of sin themselves. God told Israel to stone Achan and everyone in his household. He required them to burn all that they owned. The infestation of sin had to be completely rooted out. Only then was Israel relieved of the burden of Achan's iniquity.

This has direct application to the church today. Often, sin begins in secret with just one person. However, sin is not content to remain isolated. It has a voracious appetite. The sin of one easily spreads to another. The members of a person's own house may look the other way when sin appears because of embarrassment, or any of a number of other reasons. Perhaps a friend in the church learns of the sin in this family. He keeps it confidential, but then someone else hears, perhaps because of gossip. The infestation spreads. Maybe another person becomes tempted upon hearing of the pleasures of the initial sin. Who knows? Eventually, if not appropriately dealt with, an entire church can be consumed. From there, it can be an entire denomination that falls.

Extreme, you say? How then have we ended up with homosexual pastors in the pulpits sanctioned by the governing authorities in various denominations? I doubt if I need to spell it out further for you. Sin is a plague that can ultimately impact everyone. Because these churches and denominations accepted the initial sin of an individual rather than appropriate God's righteous wrath against that first person, whole bodies have fallen into apostasy. God gave instructions on how to approach someone who sins. When that procedure was ignored, the consequences were drastic.

For those who study Bible prophecy, all this is expected. We know that in these latter times, apostasy within the Body of Christ would cause many to fall away. They have, and more will follow. For those of us who remain faithful, our job is to continue that way, first and foremost. We are also to reach out as we can to rescue those in sin. Perhaps our meager effort will keep someone from the eternal flames.

God has shown us the true and righteous way to live. We're to be obedient to that and not let sin creep in where it doesn't belong.

March 23: Luke 3:8 - Fruits of Repentance

(Joshua 9-10; Luke 3)

Without repentance, there is no salvation. Paul in 2 Corinthians 7:10 tells us:

For godly grief produces a repentance that leads to salvation without regret, whereas worldly grief produces death.

Accompanying repentance, one who experiences this 180-degree turning, or change of mind (Greek: *metanoia*), should first have Godly grief. Why? Because this kind of grief is an understanding and acknowledgment of one's sins. We must have that awareness as the underlying condition in order to repent. It is then only through that repentance that salvation is even possible. True repentance is the key to a legitimate born-again experience, which leads to a true relationship with Christ.

There are many today who don't believe in sin. They consider men as basically good. If they take the "Good Person Test" and are asked if they think they'll go to heaven, they often say, "I hope so." Why? "Because I'm a good person." The idea of sin has never really entered their minds or been properly taught to them.

Worse are those with New Age thinking that is based on karma and reincarnation. People in this camp don't believe that sin separates them from God because they *are* God(!); it's simply that their awareness must be awakened to that fact. Thus, they must evolve through many lifetimes so as to reach that ultimate stage of consciousness.

This is in direct contrast to what John the Baptist preached as the forerunner of Jesus Christ. He wasted no words in declaring that people were all sinful and subject to God's coming wrath. He told them there was only one way out in Luke 3:8:

"Bear fruits in keeping with repentance. And do not begin to say to yourselves, 'We have Abraham as our father.' For I tell you, God is able from these stones to raise up children for Abraham."

John was speaking to the children of Israel, but his words are as relevant for us today. For the Israelites, they thought that simply because they were descendants of Abraham, this was enough for their salvation and to come into the presence of God. John corrected them of that false notion. Similarly, with the common thinking of being good or being on the wheel of karma that we have no need of repentance because there's another way to heaven, John's words declare the truth of the matter.

However, what John said had a condition associated with it. First, to be repentant, someone had to experience Godly grief. Secondly, for true repentance in a person's life, they had to show the fruits of that repentance. If these conditional aspects weren't present, neither was repentance as far as John was concerned. As we saw above, Paul took this a step further in that repentance was a necessary condition for salvation itself.

The people asked John for examples of the fruits of repentance. He was happy to oblige. Among those examples are sharing what we have with others, not cheating someone, and not extorting from someone or lying about them. Essentially, John was giving an abbreviated version of the Ten Commandments, which Jesus then boiled down to two: Love God; love your neighbor as yourself. True repentance leads to these actions.

All too often today is the practice of leading someone in a prayer of salvation. The thinking is that once someone repeats that prayer, they're saved. Boom! Mission accomplished; notch on the belt; move on to the next sinner.

Perhaps we might want to pause and examine that practice. Many years ago, Ray Comfort, the noted evangelist with Way of the Master, pastored a church. Many people came forward for altar calls to be saved. The problem Ray noted was that they would tell him they had repeated this exercise for salvation numerous times, having responded to altar calls over many years when they were seven, twelve, sixteen, etc. Discerning a problem, Ray examined their confession of faith and realized that none of these had ever experienced true repentance. Thus, they weren't actually saved, and as a result, felt they needed to repeat the process. Upon learning this key fact, Ray was able to minister in such a way that repentance of one's sins became the cornerstone of real faith. His teaching of this called *Hell's Best Kept Secret* has helped many people to gain legitimate salvation and to enable others to help many with their struggles so that they might be truly born-again.

John the Baptist was on to something. God gave him the necessary tools to prepare the way for the Lord. We would do well to adopt John's approach just as Ray Comfort did. Let's make sure that when we witness, we stress the problem with sin and the absolute necessity of Godly repentance from that. Even when someone confesses faith in this manner, perhaps we should subsequently observe their lives. Do they exhibit the fruits of repentance? If not, it may be that their confession wasn't heartfelt and true.

We cannot judge the faith or salvation of other people, but we can certainly watch how they live. If we discern a potential problem, doesn't Scripture encourage us to warn them and thus pull them from the fire?

March 24: Luke 4:30 - Through Their Midst

(Joshua 11-13; Luke 4:1-32)

When Jesus began His ministry, He wasted no time riling up the religious community. In the power of the Holy Spirit following the 40 days of temptation in the wilderness, Jesus soon went into the synagogue on the Sabbath.

A report had gone throughout Galilee that He was apparently a holy man. Have you ever heard of men of God today who have fasted for 40 days? The Holy Spirit is strong in them. As it was with Moses after his time on the mountain receiving the Ten Commandments, these people have - if not an actual glow - then certainly a metaphorical glow. Their speech rings with the truth of God; sometimes they have insightful words of wisdom and knowledge; often they have a healing touch. If this is true of ordinary men, consider what it must have been like with Jesus!

This presumed holy man enters the synagogue and unrolls the scroll of Isaiah to read. The indication He gives is that the words He reads pertain to Him. Everyone is dumbfounded. Aside from John the Baptist, God has been silent for 400 years. Is this man the fulfillment of whom John spoke would come? Has Yahweh finally returned to raise up Israel once more as His Chosen People, even as He promised through the prophets? Could this man be the Prince to Come? Would He be the One to deliver Israel from captivity? All these kinds of thoughts are likely going through the minds of those present.

Then, someone points out that Jesus is the son of Joseph the carpenter. Remember Jesus? He was that snot-nosed kid who was always so smart-alecky; after all, He knew the answers to all the questions people had about God. He even pretended to be on a par with the learned rabbis when He went up to Jerusalem. Remember how He caused His parents such worry? Who is He to teach the Words of Isaiah and to even claim that He is God's chosen man to fulfill the prophecy? Absurd!

The men in the synagogue are now in heated discussion. Some say that any man who spends 40 days in the desert must be holy; others argue that no prophet has ever come from Galilee. This man is surely an imposter.

Jesus then speaks Words that cut to the quick. He rebukes them in their flawed thinking that a prophet couldn't arise in their midst. Besides, if He can't do miracles here like what He did in Capernaum, He must be a fraud. Really?

Then, Jesus thoroughly irritates them. He speaks of how God moved among pagans in the days of the prophets. Elijah did a miracle of provision with the widow of Zarephath; Elisha healed Naaman the Syrian of his leprosy. Were there no needs in Israel at the time? Of course there were. But God chose to make Himself known to unbelievers rather than His own children. The clear implication that Jesus makes is the accusation that Israel wasn't worthy of Yahweh doing these things for them. These pagans had faith; but Israel didn't.

How could that be? Wasn't Israel the offspring of Abraham? If so, then no others were worthy of Yahweh's touch (maybe a little pride working through all this?). How dare Jesus point this out! Their indignation rocketed off the charts.

Jesus so offended them that they were determined to kill Him. He had obviously blasphemed by implying that God was working through Him. They would avenge Yahweh and rid themselves of this heretic!

So, these men of God (remember, this all started in the synagogue) took Jesus to the cliff outside of town, intending to throw Him over it and eliminate Him from among them. Luke 4:30 tells us what happened next:

But passing through their midst, he went away.

How did this happen? Let's not miss the import of this short sentence. Jesus was surrounded by hostile men. They wanted nothing more than to rid themselves of His presence. Surely, they had hustled Him up that hill holding firmly to Him the entire time. At the moment they attempt to cast Him over the cliff, their grip loosens; somehow they no longer have hold of Him. He turns and walks through this crowd of angry men. They can do nothing. Do they see Him passing by or are they blinded? The text doesn't tell us. All we know is that Jesus has supernaturally escaped.

When He'd gone, what might have been the response from these men? Were they astounded? Did they remain full of rage? Had they witnessed this miracle or had their eyes been veiled? Did some believe? Were there a few who became accusers in the ongoing effort to silence Jesus?

Jesus came to seek and save those who were lost. These men were among those. Although, there were many who recognized that Jesus was the God who had come to deliver Israel, as a whole His children failed to see because their hearts were hard. This resulted in Israel remaining barren for another 1,900 years until God once more decided the time was right to redeem His people.

Sadly, as Jesus lamented over the lost opportunity to the people of His day, great catastrophe would befall them because, as Luke 19:44 records His Words:

"... you did not know the time of your visitation."

March 25: Luke 4:41 - They Knew That He Was the Christ

(Joshua 14-14; Luke 4:33-44)

The Gospels show us that Jesus cast out demons everywhere He went. For the people of Israel, this was astounding - no one had ever done this in such a manner. Luke 4:36 reports:

"And they were all amazed and said to one another, "What is this word? For with authority and power he commands the unclean spirits, and they come out!"

Just as Yahweh needed to get the attention of the Israelites when He re-introduced Himself to them in the time of Moses, in the same manner He had to re-acquaint His children with their Father. This was one of the purposes that Jesus had in His earthly incarnation. After all, just as the Israelites had been in captivity in Egypt for 400 years with no direct knowledge of Yahweh, so it was when Jesus appeared. God had been silent 400 years; they had heard of Him, but they didn't know Him.

However, consider the demonic spirits that Jesus cast out of so many with the power and authority of God. At a Word from Jesus, they had no means to resist. Luke 4:41 tells us:

*And demons also came out of many, crying, "You are the Son of God!" But he rebuked them and would not allow them to speak, because **they knew that he was the Christ**.*

The people in Israel didn't know He was the Christ; to them He might have been a prophet, but beyond that His identity was a mystery. It wasn't until Peter identified Him in Matthew 16:16 as the Christ that anyone had any clue to this fact. But, the demons knew.

Why and how?

The first thing we must do is identify the demons. What were they? Where did they come from? God certainly didn't make them.

The only logical answer goes back all the way to Genesis 6:1-4, when the sons of God (*bene Elohim*) trespassed their heavenly boundary and came to earth. The text reveals that they married, i.e. had sexual relations and procreated with, human women. And in that day Nephilim were on the earth. The presumption is that from the union of the rebellious, spiritual sons of God that took human form, the Nephilim were birthed. The account also reveals that violence was the order of the day. These mighty hybrid beings had an innate violent nature. Half divine and half human, they were an abomination in the eyes of God. His disobedient sons wanted to be gods and supplant their Father. Just as Satan whispered to Adam and Eve: *You will be like God*" (Genesis 3:5), so did these spiritual entities have the same desire. They wanted to create offspring and to have their children populate the earth in place of Yahweh's children.

God couldn't let that happen. When He saw the wickedness that had corrupted the entire earth, He was grieved and had to act. The reason for the flood was to eradicate the depravity that consumed the planet (Genesis 6:11-12).

In the course of the flood, God cast His rebellious sons into the lowest pit of hell known as Tartarus (Jude 6). Except for Noah, his family, and the animals he saved, all other creatures in the world died. But the Nephilim are an interesting case, because they were hybrid beings. Their human bodies died, but their angelic spirits survived. In the birthing of the Nephilim, they retained this divine aspect. When they died and lost their physical bodies, the spiritual nature remained. It is from this separation that demonic spirits – unclean spirits - were released. They are bodiless and restless. They know they are supposed to reside in a body, but do not. This is why they roam the earth seeking for a body to inhabit (Matthew 12:43).

These demonic spirits know who God is because He is the One who caused them to wander without a resting place. When the 2nd Person of the Trinity walked the earth, these beings knew all too well who He was. It's why Luke 4:41 describes their interaction with Jesus as it does: ***they knew that he was the Christ***.

As the son of God - as God Himself - Jesus demonstrated that He was Emmanuel - God with us. His power and authority are absolute. Satan and his demons continue to do everything they can to thwart the will and purposes of God. During the upcoming Tribulation, they will have a field day, thinking their reign of terror will persist despite God's Word to the contrary.

But, just as God destroyed the earth in a flood to eliminate the depravity that consumed it, so will He cause all disobedient flesh in our time to die. More than that, He will cast all rebellious, unclean spirits into the place created for them: the Lake of Fire. They can pretend to be like gods now, but their fantasy will not endure. Jesus Christ is the victor. He has the final Word.

March 26: Joshua 18:3 - Possession of the Land

(Joshua 16-18; Luke 5:1-16)

God promised His children they would take possession of the land of Canaan. All that He had told them that He would do since delivering them from slavery in Egypt, He made good on His Word. Time and again He demonstrated to the Israelites that they could trust Him. God allowed an entire generation to perish in the wilderness for lack of belief. The next generation started out well by following His commands at Jericho and, after the incident with Achan, by gaining victory over Ai. Joshua, with the anointing of Moses, continued to faithfully pursue all that the Lord had said in gaining the Promised Land.

However, after several of the tribes claimed their allotted portions, the remaining tribes seemed hesitant to follow through to claim their parcels. The people of the tribe of Joseph - who were quite numerous - complained that they didn't have enough room for everyone based on what they had so far. The half tribe of Manasseh was supposed to take land to the west of the Jordan River but failed to do so. Interestingly, Joshua 17:12 records:

Yet the people of Manasseh could not take possession of those cities, but the Canaanites persisted in dwelling in that land.

What was their problem? Was God's right arm not long enough? No, it seemed they were fearful of the Canaanites who dwelled in the hill country because of their iron chariots and military prowess. Joshua had to remind them that they as God's people had great power and would succeed. Despite that, there was a general reluctance on the part of the remaining tribes, necessitating Joshua to ask the question in Joshua 18:3:

"How long will you put off going in to take possession of the land, which the Lord, the God of your fathers, has given you?"

This remained a problem in that the Israelites failed in many instances to drive out the inhabitants in the land. Canaanites remained, although for a time Israel was able to dominate them and use them as forced labor. This changed in the subsequent years when God's people failed to follow Him, so that He allowed their enemies to grow strong as an object lesson (that they never fully learned).

What is the object lesson for us in this account? Let's substitute sin in our lives in place of the Canaanites that were a persistent thorn in the Israelites' sides.

It's a fairly simple message. When we turn from our life of sin to follow Jesus, the Holy Spirit comes to dwell within us. We are transformed and become new creatures in Christ Jesus. As such, we're to begin living for Him and like Him. However, just as God told the Israelites that He would not eliminate all their enemies at once because it would overwhelm them (Deuteronomy 7:22), so it is with some aspects of the sin in our lives. Our journey as followers of Jesus is one that must be taken a step at a time. We call the process progressive sanctification. Little by little we grow in the Lord, shedding the negative aspects of our past. This might mean that some of the sins from before our salvation cling to us. We are completely washed in the blood of Christ, fully forgiven and cleansed, but we haven't yet taken out all the trash from the past. In other words, like with the people of Manasseh, we still have some Canaanites dwelling in our midst.

Now, just as Israel tamed the Canaanites for a time putting them to forced labor, we may be able to live our lives in Christ with some prior sins lurking nearby. We subdue them but don't completely eliminate them. What this ended up meaning for Israel was that if they failed to completely follow the Lord, the Canaanites grew stronger and more numerous. This became a significant problem in the book of Judges.

This issue is one that many Christians face. Rather than living completely for Jesus, they do so half-heartedly and allow certain sins to remain. This can cause the problem going forward that when trouble strikes, those sins are ever-ready to rise up and contend for their portion of the land, i.e. the place in our life that they want to reclaim.

Joshua knew this would cause difficulties. It's why he asked the remaining tribes who hadn't yet done what God commanded how long it would be before they took full possession of all that He had provided.

In our Christian walk, Jesus asks us the same question: "How long will you put off going in to take possession of the land, which the Lord, the God of your fathers, has given you?"

How long will it be that we allow the sins of our past to live and to influence us? How long before we completely eliminate them from our lives?

When we follow Jesus in a half-hearted manner, we get a life that cannot receive all that God has for us. He wants to give us life and that more abundantly (John 10:10), but we have to eliminate all that will steal, kill, and destroy our life in Christ.

March 27: Luke 5:26 - They Glorified God

(Joshua 19-20; Luke 5:17-39)

When Jesus healed someone or cast out demons, He always had a purpose in doing so. Because the people of Israel were lost and had been without a shepherd for so many years, Jesus had to get them thinking once more who they were as a people and why they even existed. He had to transform their thinking about the gods of the surrounding cultures to God Most High. As important, He wanted to change the religiosity of the people from those who stressed Law and Law only, to seeing Yahweh as a loving God who desired to have a personal relationship with Him.

God had been silent in Israel for 400 years since the prophet Malachi. Israel had gone through much of what is known as the Second Temple period, i.e. the Intertestamental period, that began roughly about 400 BC and would end about 100 AD. During this time of God's silence, the Jews thought and wrote much about their understanding of God and His ways. From this they produced quite a lot of literature exploring these concepts. For instance, one of the works attributed to this period is the book of 1 Enoch that describes how the sons of God (*bene Elohim*), also known as the Watchers in Enoch and by Daniel (Daniel 4:13-17), came to earth, procreated with human women, and caused the massive amount of depravity that led to God destroying all creatures through the flood.

Jesus had a lot of work to do to get the heads of God's children turned back to Him in the right way. This had always been a problem. From the very first when Yahweh interacted with man in the Garden, he wanted to go his own way. The idea that Satan planted that man could be like God never left. It caused all humanity inevitably to turn from God. This led to the Tower of Babel incident where mankind disobeyed God's direct command to scatter. Since the people didn't do it on their own, God had to take it upon Himself to do the scattering. In the course of this, God effectively separated Himself from man - a sort of timeout - while He raised up Israel as His special heritage (Deuteronomy 32:9). God placed His divine sons (again, more *bene Elohim*) over the nations and mankind in this process (Deuteronomy 32:8 - ESV). In that position, God's sons were to point men back to God; instead, they rebelled and became the so-called gods over those nations contrary to what Yahweh intended.

This led to all sorts of problems, not the least of which was that the people of Israel found these foreign gods more attractive than Yahweh. One thing followed another, and through their wholesale turning from God in disobedience, He sent them into captivity in Babylon. Despite His mercy of permitting them to return to the land, they didn't learn the lesson, and God allowed them ultimately to go under Roman occupation, which set up the time and circumstances for Jesus to come. In that prior period the sect of the Pharisees determined that following the Law was the key to Yahweh's blessings. Naturally, they went too far and legalism set in. They had no heart for God, only for obeying His Law as they interpreted it.

So, along comes Jesus with the necessity of transforming the hearts of the people. It required Him to preach and teach; it necessitated Him confronting the Pharisees for their misunderstanding of what God wanted; and it called for Jesus to show the awesome love of God through the miracles, signs, and wonders that He did.

The reading today illustrates how this worked. It's the paralytic man's friends who have the confidence that Jesus will heal him. We're not told this man's level of faith. Perhaps he had given up on life in his poverty and presumed uselessness. But his friends believed. Isn't it amazing that he even had friends? This man could have been so depressed at his condition that he simply isolated from everyone other than in his times of begging.

Jesus knew all the circumstances surrounding this situation. He also knew what the response would be among those who saw what He intended to do. He forgave the man's sins. Had the man assumed that he was beyond forgiveness and that God hated him? Then, Jesus healed him. This miracle had two results as we see in Luke 5:25-26:

And immediately he rose up before them and picked up what he had been lying on and went home, glorifying God. And amazement seized them all, and they glorified God and were filled with awe, saying, "We have seen extraordinary things today."

The poor man, who had been paralyzed and without hope, ended up glorifying God. The people who witnessed this amazing healing also came away glorifying Him.

This seems to be one of the few instances that Jesus performed a miracle *not* on a Sabbath day, so the Pharisees didn't have that to complain about. But, they were present, and we know they took issue with Jesus. Who but God could forgive this man's sin (Luke 5:21)? One way or another, Jesus found a sore point with His critics, but always in the hope and with the desire of turning their hard hearts back to God as He wished for them to acknowledge Him.

Israel today remains separated from God because she didn't accept the fact that Jesus was the Messiah for whom they'd been waiting. To this day, they have not glorified God through His Son. That will change not too long from now. God will soon pour out His wrath upon this unbelieving world, including the nation of Israel. Through that horrible time, many will finally turn to the God of the Bible. A remnant of those remaining in Israel will be saved (Zechariah 13:8; Romans 11:26).

Soon, and very soon all the world will bow down and confess that God is mighty and glorious and deserves all praise and worship.

March 28: Luke 6:25 - Laughing Now

(Joshua 21-22; Luke 6:1-26)

The prophetic Word that Jesus speaks in the Beatitudes is both comforting and chilling. For those who hear what He said and love Him, there can be no greater promise. For those who don't hear, don't care to hear, and who either hate Him or are apathetic about God and the hope He brings, what Jesus foretells is a promise of disaster.

In His time on earth then, Jesus speaks a Word for NOW; a message of hope and one of hopelessness. Consider how He phrased the bookend statements that He made.

To those who love Him and hear His voice, who are the sheep in His pasture, He set forth a couple of circumstances that pertain to the human condition. In Luke 6:21 Jesus said:

"Blessed are you who are hungry now, for you shall be satisfied. Blessed are you who weep now, for you shall laugh."

Throughout history, people have endured physical and spiritual hunger. They have also undergone great, heartbreaking distress that can be a bane to the human soul. But Jesus says this need not be the case any longer. For those craving nourishment of the body or of the spirit; for those aching in grief from loss; there is an answer. A person who turns to Him finds life. In Christ alone he will be satisfied; in Him only will the sorrow dissipate. Such a message had never before been given; for us today we can receive it as a guarantee.

God's promises are always fulfilled. However, the one thing we never know is when. Through our prayers, belief, and confidence in Christ, He may deliver us in this life from these afflictions. But God is sovereign. His ways are not our ways. Regardless, these promises hold true. If not fulfilled in this lifetime, we can be assured that in the next, as blood-bought believers in Jesus Christ, He will bring them to pass. Thus, whether someone is hungry, is weeping, or has a body broken in illness, all these afflictions will disappear when Jesus returns. We will be like Him. He will give us glorified, perfect bodies. No more will we experience the sorrows of this world.

This is in contrast are those who don't know the Lord. Unless they turn from their evil ways, Jesus warns them that trouble awaits right around the corner. In Luke 6:25, here is what He says:

"Woe to you who are full now, for you shall be hungry. Woe to you who laugh now, for you shall mourn and weep."

As noted above, this is indeed a NOW Word. It often seems as if those who reject the Good News of Jesus Christ pay no penalty. Because God sends rain upon the just and the unjust (Matthew 5:45), many who fall into this unjust category appear to live the good life and experience no consequences for their wickedness. But Jesus says that everything will even out. Vengeance belongs to God (Romans 12:19). A day is coming when all who aren't covered by the blood of the Lamb will stand before God in judgment. Even before then, many will experience God's wrath in the soon-coming Tribulation. Some number of these people who have chosen to follow their own way, rather than that which Christ offers, will go hungry in that time; others will mourn and weep. However, even those who seemingly ride above the winds and waves during that horrible seven years will not escape. Their fate is assured, their eternity is one of torment.

Knowing this, shouldn't we whom Christ has redeemed have the heart for the lost that He has? What are we waiting for? We're nearer now to our redemption than when we first believed (Romans 13:11). Doesn't this also mean that those who aren't currently in Christ are closer to their doom?

Jesus gave all of us a command. We're to operate in His power and authority. Doing so, we're to make disciples and teach them about the love of God and all His ways (Matthew 28:18-20).

Time is running out. Shouldn't we get busy?

Gary W. Ritter

March 29: Joshua 24:15 - Choosing Poorly

(Joshua 23-24; Luke 6:27-49)

Both Moses and Joshua - righteous leaders of Israel - knew the dangers that would come upon God's children if they reverted to their old ways of following other gods. They warned the people with Yahweh's very Words numerous times, yet they were quite aware how deceitful the hearts of men were and their inclination to follow any other god.

Joshua reminded them in Joshua 24:3 what Yahweh did to bring them into the Promised Land:

"And you have seen all that the Lord your God has done to all these nations for your sake, for it is the Lord your God who has fought for you."

Don't be foolish, he says. Remember how you got here. And, he tells them in Joshua 23:7 how it's critical in their recollection and subsequent actions:

". . . that you may not mix with these nations remaining among you or make mention of the names of their gods or swear by them or serve them or bow down to them."

Doing so has a cost, which he outlines in Joshua 23:12-13:

"For if you turn back and cling to the remnant of these nations remaining among you and make marriages with them, so that you associate with them and they with you, know for certain that the Lord your God will no longer drive out these nations before you, but they shall be a snare and a trap for you, a whip on your sides and thorns in your eyes, until you perish from off this good ground that the Lord your God has given you."

The book of Judges will show us how they quickly forget these admonitions, even as Joshua 23:16 expresses exactly what would happen:

"if you transgress the covenant of the Lord your God, which he commanded you, and go and serve other gods and bow down to them. Then the anger of the Lord will be kindled against you, and you shall perish quickly from off the good land that he has given to you."

Let's take that lesson and apply it to the church in these latter days. Various Scriptures warn of what will happen, such as 1 Timothy 4:1:

Now the Spirit expressly says that in later times some will depart from the faith by devoting themselves to deceitful spirits and teachings of demons.

The list is long as to how this is playing out. Here are numerous examples without too much explanation. In no particular order, this is how churches are falling away today into apostasy:

- Approving of and marrying those "living together in sin" without proper repentance and separation
- Ecumenicalism: the joining of various churches with different beliefs, resulting in "faith" that approves of the lowest common denominator and even falsehoods contrary to the true Gospel; e.g. Evangelicals returning "home" to the Roman Catholic church with its many unbiblical doctrines
- Welcoming homosexuals into church without any expectation of change, i.e. come as you are, stay as you are
- Chrislam: Christianity in syncretistic joining with Islam with their widely divergent beliefs; e.g. Islam does not believe that God has a Son
- Placing lesbians in the pulpit, i.e. putting those in direct disobedience to God's commands in positions of leadership over vulnerable and naive flocks
- Embracing of the social justice gospel for salvation versus the true Gospel; this includes emphasis on "creation care" that holds to a climate change agenda with belief in a Gaia Mother Earth god
- Partnering with organizations such as Black Lives Matter that at their core follow a doctrine of demons
- Adopting the cancel culture and wokeness to be relevant rather than staying true to God's Word to seek truth and rest in it; a recent example is Wheaton College with its intent to dishonor the work and martyrdom of Jim Elliot among the savages (yes - savages!) of the Auca tribe, who were among the most violent people groups in the world before receiving the Gospel

I've probably missed some examples; feel free to add your own. The point is that the church has forgotten the lessons of Israel. It has mixed with other nations (Joshua 23:7) and forgotten how Christ died for our sins, i.e. how God fought for Israel even as He did for us (Joshua 23:4).

Rather than being in the world but not of the world, the church wants the world to love it, exactly the opposite of what we're told in 1 John 2:15:

Do not love the world or the things in the world. If anyone loves the world, the love of the Father is not in him.

With the church loving the world, what does John say results? Whether speaking of an individual or the collective body of the church, the Father is not in them. Again, this has a cost.

We are in the Laodicean-Philadelphia dispensation, as it were. Apostate churches abound. The wolves in the henhouse, have by and large, consumed the chickens. Conversely, a faithful remnant remains, one that's seemingly growing smaller by the day.

Just as God promised to uproot the nation of Israel from their land, He is doing so to the church. If a church isn't following God, it's preparing its people to enter the Tribulation. An uprooting is happening; it is growing. Before long, the true church will be removed in the Rapture when Christ comes for His own. The remaining apostate church will completely embrace what the world tells it is true. This church, along with all others on this planet will perish. Only those who find the truth of Jesus during the coming seven years of horrendous upheaval precipitated by God's hand will survive, some through death, others by persistent faith.

This world is doomed to extinction. However, we who love the Lord have the New Heavens and New Earth in our future. How glorious will that be? While we wait for Jesus to come for His true Bride, let's do all we can to bring some of the lost with us.

March 30: Judges 2:19 - They Turned Back

(Judges 1-2; Luke 7:1-30)

Many people consider the book of Judges the saddest in the entire Bible. It chronicles the persistent apostasy of Israel despite God's continuing mercy upon His children.

Yahweh had given the land of Canaan to the Israelites. He promised He would fight for them to drive out its wicked inhabitants. But, they had a responsibility; they were to take the land in partnership with God. He expected them to obey Him and follow in all His ways. In return, He would uphold His end of the bargain. Initially following Joshua's death, Judah inquired of the Lord, and He defeated their enemies. However, following that period, Judah and the various other tribes lost Yahweh's favor. Nine times in the first chapter of Judges we see that the tribes did not drive out the inhabitants of a particular area (e.g. Judges 1:21,27,28, etc.) Of these nine instances, the text tells us that God was with Judah, but they could not drive out those who lived in the hill country because of their iron chariots (Judges 1:19). We're not told specifically why, but it may be that those iron chariots loomed larger in Judah's eyes than the mighty right hand of Yahweh. Regardless, Israel failed in its half of the partnership, and the Canaanites and others continued dwelling among God's people.

This caused God - in the form of the angel of the Lord, i.e. the 2nd Person of the Trinity - to rebuke Israel for her disobedience. As an aside, why identify this angel with God Himself? Because He made that connection. When the angel spoke, He said that it was "I" who brought them out of Egypt and did all these other great things, but they did not obey "My" voice. This is God speaking in that physical angelic manifestation.

Interestingly, the people all wept that they had lost God's favor, but did they do anything about it? Nope. Judges 2:10 tells us what happened:

And all that generation also were gathered to their fathers. And there arose another generation after them who did not know the Lord or the work that he had done for Israel.

The generation that was rebuked and wept went its own way and never taught their children the commands of their God. This new generation did evil in God's sight by following other gods (Judges 2:11-12) and got what Yahweh had promised: defeat (Judges 2:15).

This began the cycle of Judges. God raised up various rulers to deliver Israel. In seeing God's work for them, they followed Him for a time while the judge was alive, then fell back into apostasy. They never owned their faith. In fact, in this process Judges 2:19 describes what happened:

But whenever the judge died, they turned back and were more corrupt than their fathers, going after other gods, serving them and bowing down to them. They did not drop any of their practices or their stubborn ways.

They became more corrupt and doubled down in their worship of pagan gods!

In the New Testament portion of our reading, we see a connection between the lack of true faith and the hard hearts of the people with those whom Jesus interacted. He was speaking of John the Baptist and explaining how John was the messenger spoken of in Malachi 3:1:

"Behold, I send my messenger, and he will prepare the way before me. And the Lord whom you seek will suddenly come to his temple; and the messenger of the covenant in whom you delight, behold, he is coming", says the Lord of hosts.

This messenger was the forerunner of Jesus Messiah, the One whom all Israel was awaiting to deliver them. However, consider the response of the religious elite in Luke 7:30:

. . . but the Pharisees and the lawyers rejected the purpose of God for themselves, not having been baptized by him [John].

What's the connection with Judges? *They did not drop any of their practices or their stubborn ways. - The Pharisees and the lawyers rejected the purpose of God for themselves.*

The Israelites of old followed the god Baal (Judges 2:11). The Pharisees followed the god of legalism. They didn't accept the baptism of John, which was one of repentance. Their god was their own righteousness in the Law.

Scripture details how people of all ages fall away from God when they ignore Him and His commands. It shows our desperate wickedness and great need for Him. The Bible clearly teaches us that when we stray from the Lord, we lose His favor and our blessings. He allows our enemies to live in the land and ultimately consume us.

The only hope the Israelites ever had was to love God in return for His amazing love for them and to be obedient to His Word. That also is our only hope today.

March 31: Judges 3:1-2 - To Test Israel

(Judges 3-5; Luke 7:31-50)

*Now these are the nations that the Lord left, **to test Israel** by them, that is, all in Israel who had not experienced all the wars in Canaan. It was only in order that the generations of the people of Israel **might know war**, to teach war to those who had not known it before. (Judges 3:1-2)*

Yahweh knew the heart of the people of Israel. He understood how wayward His children were and how inclined they were to follow other gods. He had made a pact with them. They were to obey everything that He commanded and follow Him unquestionably. In all that God had done to deliver and maintain the Israelites, this was not unreasonable. But, He had seen them turn from Him numerous times, even immediately following a supernatural event. Frankly, He knew they couldn't be trusted. So, He determined to test them.

Once they had taken the land of Canaan for their own possession - just as Yahweh said they would with Him going before them - the Israelites got comfortable and neglected to teach the next generation about all that He had done as their God (Judges 2:10).

When they'd fought their enemies to claim the land in the first place, they didn't drive out all their foes. These nations remained as slaves under the Israelites. In this condition, God allowed these peoples to grow strong, to rise up, to contend with Israel, and to overcome them. He brought testing upon His people, and He did it through the mechanism of oppression and war.

The question the Israelites had to answer to God's satisfaction was: Would they rely on Him in obedience, or follow the other gods of the pagan nations? Judges 3:7 succinctly spells it out:

And the people of Israel did what was evil in the sight of the Lord. They forgot the Lord their God and served the Baals and the Asheroth.

Obviously, no; they turned from Yahweh. The allure of foreign gods was too strong. Their eyes were dazzled by the bling; their itching ears were scratched. They failed the test.

In their failing, God allowed them to experience persecution and tribulation so they would eventually remember Him and cry out for the salvation only He could provide. But, they had to experience war so that God could teach them about Himself.

The object lesson wasn't just for Israel; it has been for mankind through the ages and for us today.

God knows the heart of His people in the church. Some are strong believers; others quite nominal. From the example of our brothers and sisters in the 10/40 Window across the world, we've seen how living in the midst of foreign gods either strengthens Christian faith or roots out those who don't truly believe. By experiencing persecution and suffering, i.e. tribulation, the true church has grown strong, even as it must endure while underground.

China is a prominent example. Before Mao's Great Leap Forward, it is estimated that there were perhaps 100,000 believers in China. The oppression and persecution accompanying this Marxist-Communist regime that developed drove the church underground. If a believer hasn't spent time in prison for his faith, others are actually wary of how true a believer he is. The resulting growth of Christianity in China has many estimates declaring that the church now comprises well over 100 million believers.

Another example is Iran. When Islam overthrew the Shah in 1979 and subjected the people to Sharia Law, the nation entered a very dark time. Since then, depression rates, alcoholism, drug use, and suicide in the population are among the highest in the world. Allah and his prophet Muhammad do not satisfy and fill the void in people's hearts. In this dark place, Christianity has shined a light that has given people immense hope. Because of the underground activities of a faithful few, Iran now has the fastest growing Christian population in the world.

I believe these examples of what has happened in other nations, and how God has worked through very dark conditions, is a template of sorts for us in America. The American church grew fat and lazy, spending its time and money on the trappings of religion, but not following the heart of God. In order to shake up the church, God has allowed the current political and social circumstances to rise so as to test those who call themselves Christians.

This is a time of winnowing. We are in the middle of an intense spiritual war. Those who truly believe are doubling down in their faith. Those who are on the fence must make a decision: follow the world or follow Jesus. In addition, God is giving non-believers a very real purpose to turn toward Him with all the fear and disruption that has come upon the world.

The wheat and the chaff are separating. Before long, God's process and purpose will be completed. He will have determined those who are truly the Bride of Christ and those who are not. Whatever His timing is for this, once it's completed, He will Rapture His true church.

Just as Yahweh rescued His people Israel during the time of Judges when they finally called out to Him, He will do the same for us after this coming period of tribulation (not The Tribulation) has run its course.

ABOUT THE AUTHOR

Gary W. Ritter is a Bible teacher, and lay pastor who previously served as Missions Director at his church. He is also a prolific fiction author. His *Whirlwind Series* is comprised of three books: **Sow the Wind, Reap the Whirlwind**, and **There Is A Time**. These books are contained in the collected volume of the *Whirlwind Omnibus*.

Gary has been given the *Christian Redemptive Fiction* award for two novels: **The Tattooed Cat** and **Alien Revelation**. He has also received this award in conjunction with his collaboration with Terry James on **The Minion Protocols**, part of Terry's *Second Coming Chronicles*.

From leading a class in his church with the initiative of reading the Bible through in a year, Gary produced daily study notes that became the basis for the **Awaken Bible Study Notes – Volumes 1-4**. As an aid to the understanding of Scripture, the four quarterly volumes emphasize Bible prophecy and the supernatural as God's Word is read from the viewpoint of the ancient Israelite writers. The **Awaken Bible Commentary and Reflections** volumes build on this initial effort by discussing lessons we can draw from God's Word for today.

One of Gary's recent efforts is **Tribulation Rising: Seal Judgments – The Coming Apocalypse** found on Amazon's Kindle Vella, a novella platform for serialized stories. He has also completed a sequel to Alien Revelation titled **Alien Zombie Plague**.

Gary's intent in all his writings is to bring a strong Christian witness to what people read. You can reach him at his website: www.GaryRitter.com. You can also find his older video Bible teachings on his Gary Ritter YouTube channel – look for the fish symbol. More recently, he has posted many Prophecy Updates on his Awaken Bible Prophecy channel on Rumble at: https://rumble.com/c/c-783217.

The Gospel of Jesus Christ

<u>Today is the day of Salvation:</u> Why would anyone put off the most important decision they could ever make in their lives concerning eternal life? If you die today are you going to heaven?

1 Corinthians 15:1-4 - The apostle Paul tells us what the gospel is: "Moreover, brethren, I declare to you the gospel which I preached to you, which also you received and in which you stand, by which also you are saved, if you hold fast that word which I preached to you—unless you believed in vain. For I delivered to you first of all that which I also received: that Christ died for our sins according to the Scriptures, and that He was buried, and that He rose again the third day according to the Scriptures.

Gospel means "good news." Your debt has been paid, the death penalty has been paid, you are free.

<u>Here's the Gospel of Jesus Christ</u>: *That Christ died for our sins according to the Scriptures, and that He was buried, and that He rose again the third day according to the Scriptures.*

Jesus brought in a little child as a living object lesson to show who enters the kingdom of heaven. Matthew 18:3 - *Jesus said: "Unless you become like this little child you will not enter the kingdom of heaven."* This is how to be saved, it is simply child-like, as simple as **ABC:**

A - <u>Admit that you are a sinner.</u> This is where that godly sorrow leads to genuine repentance for sinning against a righteous God and there is a change of heart, we change our mind and God changes our hearts and regenerates us from the inside out.
Romans 3:10 - As it is written: *"There is none righteous, no, not one."*

Romans 3:23 - *For all have sinned and fall short of the glory of God.* (We are all born sinners which is why we must be born spiritually in order to enter the Kingdom of Heaven).

Romans 6:23 - *For the wages of sin is death, but the gift of God is eternal life in Christ Jesus our Lord.* The bad news is that the wages of sin is death, in other words our sin means that we have been given a death sentence, we have the death penalty hanging over our heads, that's the bad news. But here's the good news: **The good news is that the gift of God is eternal life in Christ Jesus our Lord.**

Ephesians 2:8-9 - For it is by grace you have been saved, through faith —and this not from yourselves, it is the gift of God— not by works, so that no one can boast.

B - <u>**Believe in your heart that Jesus Christ died for your sins, was buried, and that God raised Jesus from the dead.**</u> This is trusting with all of your heart that Jesus Christ is who he said he was.

Romans 10:9-10 - That if you confess with your mouth, "Jesus is Lord," and believe in your heart that God raised Him from the dead, you will be saved. For it is with your heart that you believe and are justified, and it is with your mouth that you confess and are saved.

C - <u>Call upon the name of the Lord.</u> Every single person who ever lived since Adam will bend their knee and confess with their mouth that Jesus Christ is Lord, the Lord of lords and the King of kings.

Romans 14:11 - For it is written: *"As I live, says the Lord, Every knee shall bow to Me, And every tongue shall confess to God."*

<u>Don't wait until later — do this now.</u>

Romans 10:13 - For *"whoever calls on the name of the Lord shall be saved."*

"O God, I am a sinner. I'm sorry for my sin. I want to turn from my sin. I believe Jesus Christ is Your Son; I believe that He died on the cross for my sin and that He was buried and You raised Him to life. I have decided to place my faith in Jesus Christ as my Savior, trusting only in His shed blood as sufficient to save my soul and to take me to heaven. Thank You, Lord Jesus, for saving me. Amen."

Salvation

 Admit that you are a sinner.
Romans 3:10 "There is none righteous, no not one."
Romans 3:23 "For all have sinned and fall short of the glory of God."

 Believe that Jesus Christ died for your sins, and was raised on the third day.
John 3:16 "For God so loved the world that He gave His only begotten Son, that whosoever believes in Him shall not perish but have everlasting life."

 Call upon the name of the Lord.
Romans 10:13 "Whoever calls on the name of the Lord shall be saved."

jdfarag.org

Salvation

It is as simple as ABC

Printed in Great Britain
by Amazon

78298905R00149